Using Linguistic Lenses to Journey into Words

DR KATHARYN CULLEN

Using Linguistic Lenses to
Journey into Words

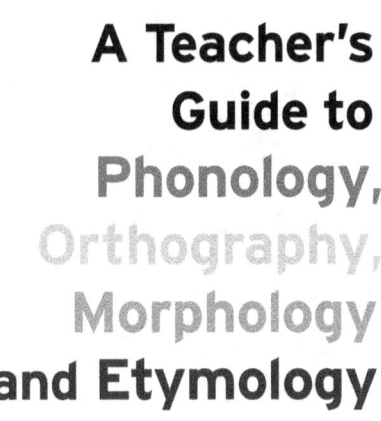

A Teacher's Guide to Phonology, Orthography, Morphology and Etymology

To the working parents, navigating the tightrope of school leadership while nurturing young children at home:

Who draft strategic school plans while juggling midnight feeds,
Who lead teams by day and bedtime stories by night,
Who chase deadlines and toddlers with equal determination,
You lead schools as if parenthood were a distant dream
And parent as though your career were but a fleeting thought.

You are the architects of tomorrow, building futures in classrooms and at kitchen tables alike.

Your relentless dedication and boundless love mould
not just your own children
But generations of learners to come.

You are seen in your struggle, valued in your sacrifice and extraordinary in your everyday triumphs.

To you, the wonder men and women of education and parenthood,
I dedicate this work.

Published in 2025 by Amba Press, Melbourne, Australia
www.ambapress.com.au

© Katharyn Cullen 2025

All rights reserved. No part of this book may be reproduced or transmitted in any form or by any means, electronic or mechanical, including photocopying, recording or by any information storage and retrieval system, without prior permission in writing from the publisher.

Cover design: Tess McCabe
Internal design: Amba Press
Editor: Will Allen

ISBN: 9781923215603 (pbk)
ISBN: 9781923215610 (ebk)

A catalogue record for this book is available from the National Library of Australia.

Contents

Introduction: Preparing for an Adventure		1
Chapter 1	The Lay of the Land	11
Chapter 2	The New Map—the Power of Four Lenses	21
Chapter 3	Your Guide to the Phonology Lens	29
Chapter 4	Your Guide to the Orthography Lens	83
Chapter 5	Your Guide to the Morphology Lens	139
Chapter 6	Your Guide to the Etymology Lens	191
Chapter 7	The Summit—Bringing It All Together	225
Chapter 8	The Briefing—Preparing for Your Linguistic Journey	249
Conclusion: Embracing Your Linguistic Journey		263
References		265
About the Author		269

INTRODUCTION
Preparing for an Adventure

> "The goal of systematic instruction has always been to show students how the system actually works. In order to understand spelling, we need to be aware of all the information encoded in written words."
> ~ *Sue Scibetta Hegland*

By the end of this chapter, you'll have these key insights:

1. **Trace the evolution of Linguistic Lenses:** Explore the journey from my classroom innovations to school-wide implementation as a leader.
2. **Foundations of Linguistic Lenses:** Understand the concept and importance of Linguistic Lenses in enhancing vocabulary and word study instruction.
3. **Practical application of Linguistic Lenses:** Learn how to use the Linguistic Lenses Guide, including its key components and practical applications.
4. **Adaptive literacy instruction:** Recognise the significance of flexible literacy instruction in addressing diverse student needs.
5. **Cross-curricular literacy champions:** Understand the role of all teachers as literacy champions across different subject areas.

Welcome, my fellow teachers, to *Using Linguistic Lenses to Journey into Words: A teacher's guide to phonology, orthography, morphology and etymology.* This is your comprehensive passport to a transformative approach to vocabulary and word study instruction, designed to revolutionise how you approach the teaching and learning of words in the upper primary and secondary school classroom.

From the Classroom to Leadership: A journey towards Linguistic Lenses

I have always had an unwavering belief in each child's potential. During my first four years of teaching, I taught Kindergarten, the first year of formal schooling in Australia (also known as Preparatory, Transition or Reception depending on which state or territory you live in), witnessing firsthand what teaching the truth of our English spelling system from the beginning could do for my learners. As a result, I have committed myself to enhancing teachers' understanding of phonology, orthography, morphology and etymology, because the research emphasises that children who are confidently aware of the linguistic structure of words learn to read, write and spell well.

Over the past eight years, I have developed a set of pedagogical tools called "Linguistic Lenses", which I have refined and put into practice in the classroom. The purpose of creating these Lenses was to support teachers in incorporating the language of linguistics into their classrooms, and I soon discovered that teachers were able to bridge the gap between theory and practice, thus enhancing their professional development. As a result of that mentorship, many teachers now have a range of instructional tools and strategies to support literacy instruction in their own classrooms and schools, boosting their confidence in teaching the perceived complexities of the English language. When asked what knowledge all teachers should have in their literacy toolbox, one colleague stated:

> *"Linguistic Lenses are top of the list. I think the tactile lenses are a powerful way to show students [the truth and logic of the English spelling system]. When you go through teacher training, you learn the theory, but you actually need the practical ways of understanding the knowledge and tools to teach morphology, etymology and phonology to understand English orthography. If I was having my time over again, I wish I'd had knowledge of the Lenses; I think that would have been of great benefit to me. For students beginning their teaching career, it would be extremely beneficial."*

Through practical demonstrations in classrooms across New South Wales, offering collaborative or one-on-one support sessions and presenting Linguistic Lenses at various state and national conferences, I have been dedicated to improving student outcomes, grounded in my belief in each student's potential.

At the beginning of 2019, I moved to South Australia to accept a position as a Literacy and Curriculum Specialist at an independent all-girls school. Six months into this new role, my career path took an unexpected turn when I was appointed to the role of Assistant Head of Junior School; then, from 2021 to 2024, I served as the Head of Junior School. However, I have always maintained that certain core responsibilities remain unchanged—that I must teach English across the Junior School and have the opportunity to collaborate with teachers to enhance literacy outcomes and accessibility for all.

Now it is time to share Linguistic Lenses with as many educators as possible. This book combines my own lessons, classroom and school leadership experiences, and case studies of students' work.

When I shared this approach at parent workshops and staff meetings across Australia, adults in the room regularly commented on how they had always struggled with spelling at school and to this day do not understand how to make sense of it—so much so that they feel embarrassment and shame. One teacher admitted:

> *"Early in my career I found spelling very difficult to teach because I didn't understand how language worked. I relied on spelling programs, word lists and textbooks to teach spelling. I was not able to explain 'spelling rules' accurately, and thus I avoided teaching spelling at times."*

My message for adults is the same as for students: spelling ability is not a measure of intelligence. We all learn differently; we all need to be shown another way to understand. Dr Peter Bowers, an esteemed educational researcher and the founder of the WordWorks Literacy Centre, shared a powerful insight during a structured word inquiry workshop I attended at the Nueva School for gifted learners in the United States. He emphasised that when a student struggles with reading the words on a page or spelling new vocabulary in their writing, it's essentially a plea to the adults around them for an alternative approach. In his words, "If a student is struggling, they are calling out to the adults around them, 'Show me another way'!"

Have you ever stood in front of your class, watching a student struggle, and wondered if there's a better way to reach them? As teachers, we've all been there. But what if the key to unlocking their potential isn't more of the same but a new approach which shows them the underlying logic of the English language?

What's our typical response to a student who's struggling with spelling? Often, we place them in programs focused primarily on building phonological skills. But here's the twist: many of these students are already grappling with phonological processing due to specific language-learning difficulties.

Dr Misty Adoniou, Associate Professor in Language Literacy and TESOL at the University of Canberra, calls this a "catch 22" situation (Adoniou, 2017). These students can't succeed in phonological instruction during whole-class learning, which means they can't progress to the next learning phase. It's like being stuck on a learning treadmill: lots of effort but no forward movement.

So, what's the solution? How can we, as teachers, respond to Dr Bowers' call to action and show them another way?

Here's where it gets exciting. Did you know that when children with literacy learning difficulties receive morphological instruction, they improve in all areas of literacy (Goodwin & Ahn, 2010)? Even more intriguingly, children with dyslexia often make bigger gains than their non-dyslexic peers when given morphological training (Siegel, 2008).

This begs the question: are we limiting our students by sticking to one approach? What if we could offer them not just one but *four* different Linguistic Lenses through which to view and understand words?

As teachers, we have the power to transform our teaching approach. We can break the cycle of repetition and introduce fresh perspectives that truly resonate with the needs of our individual learners. Isn't it time we expanded our toolkit?

Remember, every challenge in our classroom is an opportunity for growth—not just for our students but for us as teachers too. Let's commit to being the teachers who say, "Let's try another way". After all, isn't that why we became teachers in the first place?

Embracing Flexibility in Literacy Instruction

As teachers, we find ourselves at the intersection of tradition and innovation, equipped with a plethora of literacy programs and instructional approaches—some mandated by school leaders and others mandated by the specific sector in which we work. While these resources can provide valuable structure and guidance, they often fall short of addressing the unique abilities of each student in our classrooms. Have you ever found yourself questioning how a one-size-fits-all program can truly meet the diverse needs of all your students? For instance, consider the range of abilities present in a typical classroom: some students may be advanced readers who entered school with strong literacy skills, having read every novel in the primary school library by Year 2, while others may require additional support and scaffolding to develop their skills. This diversity in our students' needs compels us to embrace flexibility in our teaching pedagogy, to tailor our instructional approaches to nurture each student's potential.

This realisation marked the beginning of my research journey. I recognised that the existing research on whole-class strategies for enhancing advanced literacy skills in older students is limited (Hutcheon et al., 2012) and that the quality of commercial programs varies significantly (Oakley, 2018). Consequently, I set out to advocate for a linguistically informed approach to instruction, emphasising the necessity for teachers to equip themselves with robust pedagogical and content knowledge. Recent studies have underscored the importance of this expertise, particularly highlighting the power of linguistic metalanguage in instruction (Daffern et al., 2024). As we stand on the cusp of educational transformation, it is our responsibility to weave flexibility into the very fabric of our literacy instruction, creating a rich tapestry of learning that honours the diverse needs of every student in our classrooms.

Psychologist Daniel Willingham offers an insightful perspective: "As one gets more distant from the desired level of analysis (the child in the classroom), the probability of learning anything useful diminishes." This principle emphasises the value of direct classroom experience in informing effective teaching practices. While educational theories provide a crucial foundation, their practical application in specific classroom contexts is where true learning occurs.

Just as sciences like chemistry and physics underpin cooking and driving respectively, study of them alone does not create master chefs or safe drivers. Similarly, effective teaching requires more than just theoretical knowledge—it demands practical application and adaptation. Evidence of best practice comes from the classrooms of grassroots educators (or the offices of school leaders). That is what you will find in this book. My real-world examples showcase students' capabilities and provide tangible models for effective teaching. By focusing on what works in actual classrooms, we can bridge the gap between theory and practice.

In classrooms often exceeding 26 students, differentiation is not merely beneficial—it's essential. Recognising and adapting to the varied needs, abilities and learning styles of our students while still maintaining a structured and effective literacy program ensures that every learner receives appropriate challenges and support.

This handbook will equip you, as a teacher or curriculum leader, with the knowledge and tools to implement a linguistic approach to word study. By integrating Linguistic Lenses into reading, writing and spelling instruction, we can embrace flexibility in our teaching and recognise the importance of implicit learning, creating an environment where students are empowered to make meaningful connections in their learning journey. This approach will enable you to provide a solid foundation in literacy skills while also adapting to the unique needs and abilities of each student in your diverse classroom.

What You'll Discover in This Book

This book is more than a guide—it's your passport to a new world of teaching and learning. Here, words come alive and every student becomes a linguistic explorer. Here, one-size-fits-all approaches are left behind, replaced by a rich, multifaceted understanding of the English language. I want you to witness what genuine literacy success can look like for all students. This book is designed to empower you to tailor your instruction to meet the unique needs of your learners and foster a deep, lasting understanding of language.

As you turn these pages, you're not just reading—you're gearing up for an expedition that will forever change how you and your students view words.

Vocabulary development isn't just *another* aspect of language learning— it's the cornerstone of academic success. A robust vocabulary will empower your students to:

- comprehend complex texts with ease
- express sophisticated ideas in writing
- spell effectively and confidently.

Research consistently demonstrates the profound impact of vocabulary knowledge on academic achievement. This book presents a new map for instruction, interweaving four essential linguistic elements that each act as a powerful Lens through which we can examine and understand language:

1. **Phonology** is the key to recognising and manipulating sounds in spoken words, enhancing pronunciation and listening comprehension.
2. **Orthography** is the bridge connecting sounds to written symbols, boosting spelling proficiency and reading fluency.
3. **Morphology** is the explorer of word building blocks, expanding vocabulary and illuminating word relationships.
4. **Etymology**, the time traveller, provides historical context and forges connections across languages and cultures.

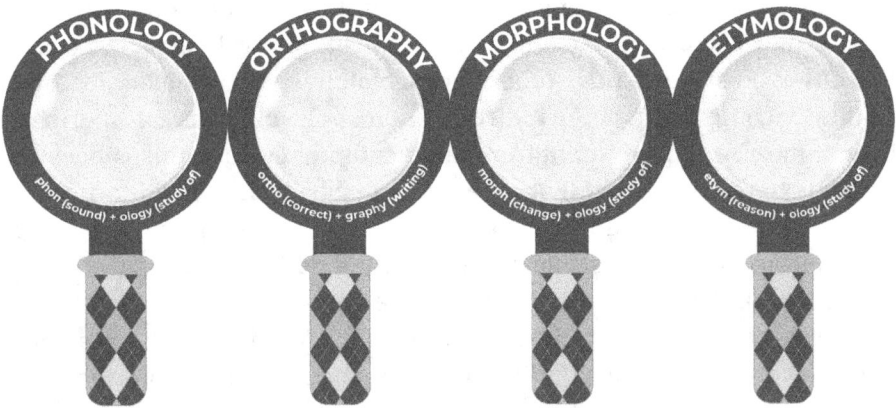

Picture yourself as an explorer, with this book as your map. Our expedition into the world of words will require preparation, direction and effort, but fear not—I've crafted the essential tools to ensure your success.

This book contains a chapter on each of the four Linguistic Lenses. Each of these how-to guides:

- sets learning intentions
- unpacks the Lens in detail
- identifies its Key Features
- includes comprehensive "Teachers' Toolkits" explaining all the components of each Key Feature
- follows the word "conscience" through each Linguistic Lens
- provides Guiding Questions to facilitate linguistic word study in your classroom
- illustrates application of the Guiding Questions through real-life Case Studies from my time in school leadership and as a classroom teacher
- demystifies metalinguistic terminology, explaining everything in detail

- concludes with "Contemplate and Consider!" reflection questions or activities to deepen your understanding and "Implement and Innovate!" suggestions to creatively apply your new knowledge, designed to build your confidence, spark collegial discussions and enact positive change within your school community.

Scattered throughout the book, you'll also find "Teaching Tip!" sections offering practical advice for immediate classroom implementation.

The Transformative Power of Linguistic Lenses

I've witnessed firsthand the incredible impact of incorporating Linguistic Lenses into classroom teaching. By embracing these Linguistic Lenses, I've observed skyrocketing student engagement with vocabulary learning as they become fascinated with words. Across all subject areas, there has been a marked improvement in reading comprehension. This is because students have an internal language and strategy in their head to unpack the meaning of words they might not recognise, meaning they are much less likely to just skip over them. Their writing skills have enhanced, with students confidently wielding more precise and varied vocabulary, taking creative risks and eagerly integrating newly acquired words into their written work. The understanding of which spelling choices are possible and plausible, as opposed to mere rote memorisation, has unveiled to them a logic to spelling, which has not only improved their accuracy but also encouraged them to experiment with new vocabulary.

Perhaps most significantly, there has been a surge in students' confidence when encountering unfamiliar words, both in academic settings and everyday contexts. The result? A rich, dynamic learning environment that illuminates the English spelling system.

Every Teacher's Role

In the Australian education setting, literacy isn't just the English department's domain—it's a team sport, and every teacher plays a fundamental role. The Australian Professional Standards for Teachers make this crystal clear: all educators, regardless of their subject specialty, are expected to be literacy champions (AITSL, 2014). But here's the thing: the foundational literacy skills our students build in primary school, coupled with what they learn in English classes as they progress through secondary school, often fall short of preparing them to tackle the specialised vocabulary and complex texts they encounter across different subjects (Moon et al., 2019). Think about it—the language of Shakespeare is a world apart from the jargon of cellular biology or economic theory.

This is where subject-specialist teachers become "literacy lighthouses". As your students progress through upper primary and secondary school, the academic language they encounter becomes increasingly complex. It's like climbing a linguistic Mount Everest, and every teacher needs to be a guide on this journey, ensuring all students have the tools to reach the summit regardless of their starting point. Yet, it is no secret that we're facing a bit of a challenge. Research suggests that about one-third of our teaching graduates are entering the classroom with only basic literacy teaching skills (Moon et al., 2019). It's like sending climbers up that mountain with incomplete maps and rusty equipment.

Teaching Tip!
- All teachers are literacy champions, not just the English department or primary school teachers!
- About one-third of teaching graduates have basic literacy teaching skills. Build collaborative teams with the English department and upper primary school teachers for cross-curricular strategies.
- Become a "literacy lighthouse" in your subject area by explicitly teaching subject-specific vocabulary and integrating Linguistic Lenses into your content instruction.

This book is your sherpa, guiding you through the challenges of integrating these key linguistic elements into your teaching. In it, I show you how to weave word study and vocabulary instruction seamlessly into your curriculum, no matter what subject you teach. Remember, every lesson is an opportunity to build literacy skills. Whether you're exploring ecosystems in science or analysing primary sources in history, you're not just teaching your subject—you're equipping your students with the tools they need to scale their own linguistic Everests.

So, are you ready to lead your students to new heights of literacy? Let's start this climb together. The view from the top is going to be spectacular!

CHAPTER 1

The Lay of the Land

"All words are spelled the way they are for a reason."
~ Lyn Stone

After engaging with this chapter, you will be equipped with these essential insights:

1. **Literacy Landscape:** Understand the current state of literacy development in Australian secondary and upper primary school education, including student achievement, the impact of this achievement data on public perception of teacher quality and how it shapes educational policies and programs.
2. **Linguistic Foundations:** Discover the critical roles of phonology, orthography, morphology and etymology in effective literacy instruction.
3. **Reading Framework Snapshot:** Learn how insights from the Simple View of Reading and Cognitive Foundations Frameworks can provide you with the knowledge to meet diverse student needs, especially struggling readers.
4. **Comprehensive Framework:** Gather the components of an integrated approach to vocabulary and word study instruction.

The Australian education system stands at a critical juncture, where student achievement, public perception of teacher quality and the development of education policies intersect in complex and often contentious ways. This chapter explores the intricate relationship between these elements, offering insights into the challenges and opportunities facing teachers in secondary and upper primary schools across the nation.

The average achievement of Australian students has become a focal point of public discourse and policy decisions in recent years. Contrary to some alarmist media reports, there is no strong evidence of a precipitous decline in student achievement over the past 25 years (Georgiou & Larsen, 2023). However, the persistent achievement gaps and mixed results in international assessments have fuelled ongoing debates about the effectiveness of the Australian education system. Recent data from various national and international assessments paints a concerning picture of our students' reading skills, particularly in secondary schools. International assessments such as PIRLS (Progress in International Reading Literacy Study), TIMSS (Trends in International Mathematics and Science Study) and PISA (Programme for International Student Assessment) consistently show a decline in reading skills in Australian students between Years 4 and 10. The PISA data is particularly alarming, indicating that nearly one in five adolescents are considered low achievers in reading. The NAPLAN (National Assessment Program – Literacy and Numeracy) testing trends reveal an even more troubling pattern: as students progress through school, the learning gap widens dramatically. By Year 9, there's a staggering eight-year difference in achievement levels among students. This growing disparity is evident in the following statistics:

- In Year 3, 11% of pupils have basic or below-basic reading skills.
- In Year 7, 15.4% fall into this category.
- In Year 9, the percentage increases to 24% (Stocker et al., 2023).

These figures highlight a critical issue: as our students advance through the education system, a large proportion are falling behind in their reading abilities. It is particularly concerning that despite numerous policy initiatives and increased government funding aimed at improving literacy achievements over the past two decades (Chamberlain & Medina, 2020), we're not seeing the desired results.

Public Perception of Teacher Quality

Information about students' average achievement significantly contributes to public perceptions of teacher quality (Mockler, 2022). This creates a complex dynamic where teachers' perceived effectiveness is often judged through the lens of student performance on standardised tests. The impact of these standardised assessments extends beyond mere statistics—they significantly influence the development of education policies, school improvement programs and teaching practices across Australia (McGaw et al., 2020).

This creates a challenging environment for educators. On one hand, teachers are expected to improve student outcomes as measured by standardised tests. On the other hand, they must navigate the complexities of individual student needs, diverse classroom environments and the broader goals of education that may not be captured by these assessments.

The Role of ACARA

The Australian Curriculum, Assessment and Reporting Authority (ACARA) plays a key role in this landscape. Their Measurement Framework for Schooling in Australia links national educational priorities to system accountability through standardised test results (2020). These assessments serve as Key Performance Measures, providing evidence of schooling outcomes and informing policy development. Australia's participation in international assessments such as PIRLS and TIMSS, alongside the national NAPLAN tests, provides valuable insights into student performance trends. Data from these assessments shows improvements in average basic skills scores over the last 25 years, particularly in primary school years. However, these gains must be viewed cautiously, as they might be partially attributed to increased familiarity with the tests rather than to substantive educational advancements (Thompson, 2013). While these standardised assessments provide important data, it's crucial to recognise their limitations—they offer a snapshot of student performance in specific areas but may not capture the full range of skills and knowledge that students acquire throughout their education. As educators, we must balance the insights gained from these assessments with a holistic view of student development and learning.

The Australian Education Research Organisation (AERO) 2022 report on writing development emphasises the importance of explicit instruction in writing skills. The report highlights that while there have been improvements in basic literacy skills, more complex writing tasks continue to challenge many students. This underscores the need for targeted interventions and professional development for teachers to enhance writing instruction across all subject areas. As students progress through secondary school, the demands of academic writing increase significantly. Teachers must be equipped with strategies to support students in developing these complex literacy skills, integrating writing instruction across the curriculum rather than treating it as a separate subject.

Challenges for High-Achieving Students

A persistent concern in the Australian education system is teachers' ability to challenge high-achieving students effectively. The 2022 AERO report highlights that while there have been improvements in supporting struggling students, high achievers often do not receive the level of challenge necessary for optimal growth. The phenomenon of "teaching to the test" can inadvertently lead to a narrowing of the curriculum, potentially disadvantaging high-achieving students who require more complex and challenging learning experiences (Larsen, 2024). This raises important questions about how to balance standardised assessment requirements with the need to provide rich, diverse learning opportunities for all students. As teachers, we must strive to create classroom environments that cater to the needs of all learners, including those who are performing above grade level. This must involve differentiated instruction and the integration of higher-order thinking skills across all subject areas.

Initial Teacher Education and Professional Development

The Australian Government has placed significant emphasis on improving initial teacher education (ITE) as a means to enhance student performance. Its Quality Initial Teacher Education Review (2021) identified several areas for improvement in ITE programs, particularly regarding evidence-based reading instruction, aligning with the broader push for evidence-based practices in Australian education. This involves a stronger focus on phonics in the early years of schooling and structured literacy approaches in teacher preparation programs. Yet, how to enact positive change in the secondary school classroom remains elusive.

The focus on improving teacher education should not end with ITE programs. Ongoing professional development is key for teachers to stay abreast of current research, refine their instructional strategies and adapt to the changing needs of their students. Despite the recognised importance of ongoing professional development for teachers, many schools face significant challenges in providing effective training for new and experienced educators alike, creating a gap between policy aspirations and classroom realities (Stocker et al., 2023). Schools often struggle to implement new initiatives or provide the level of support necessary for teachers to continually enhance their skills and knowledge. Addressing these resource limitations is crucial for the ongoing improvement of the Australian education system. Schools and education departments must prioritise professional development opportunities that are evidence-based, relevant to teachers' needs and directly applicable to classroom practice.

Literacy Instruction: Knowledge and skills

To address the literacy challenges faced by Australian students, a comprehensive approach to word study and vocabulary instruction is essential. This must include the linguistic foundations that are the critical components of word knowledge, underpinning effective literacy instruction: phonology, orthography, morphology and etymology. By implementing a multifaceted approach to vocabulary and word study, we can equip students with the tools they need to become proficient readers and writers.

Here's the knowledge the research says is important:

- **Phonology**, the study of sound systems in language, forms the foundation of literacy skills. Strong phonological skills are essential for decoding words when reading (translating the written symbols into sounds) and encoding them when spelling (converting the sounds into written symbols), even in secondary school (Kilpatrick, 2016), and it plays a role in reading proficiency at upper primary and secondary levels (Wolter & Pike, 2015).
- **Morphology** instruction has been shown to significantly boost vocabulary growth and reading comprehension, especially for academic language (Carlisle, 2010). Understanding morphology—the structure of words—enables students to break down words into their component parts (prefixes, suffixes and bases), facilitating decoding unfamiliar words, understanding their meanings and making connections between related terms (Bowers et al., 2010). Explicit instruction in morphology can significantly improve reading comprehension and vocabulary acquisition (Bowers & Kirby, 2010). This is particularly valuable as students encounter increasingly complex texts in their secondary school years.
- **Orthography** involves understanding spelling patterns and conventions. By helping students recognise and internalise these patterns, we can improve their spelling accuracy and boost their confidence in written expression. Research has highlighted the importance of integrating orthographic knowledge with phonological and morphological awareness for improved spelling outcomes (Daffern, 2017). Mastering English orthography is also crucial for reading fluency and comprehension (Treiman & Kessler, 2004);

students who understand spelling conventions read more quickly and accurately, leading to improved comprehension (Ehri, 2014).
- **Etymology**, the study of word origins and historical development, can deepen understanding of new vocabulary and aid its retention (Nagy & Townsend, 2012), and also fosters a deeper appreciation for language among students (Rasinski et al., 2011).

Recent research has found that "multi-component approaches make good sense, because successful reading, spelling and reading comprehension require more than just morphology instruction", but here's the catch: we still need to understand "the mechanisms or 'key ingredients' of morphology instruction itself, and why they are important" (Colenbrander et al., 2024).

So, what if we had a comprehensive framework that not only emphasised morphology but also illuminated the essential "key ingredients" of all four knowledge areas in linguistics? We do! Linguistic Lenses is a framework I've developed to enhance literacy instruction by providing a comprehensive approach to the four core components. This framework does something remarkable: it identifies the four core Knowledge Components of linguistics, breaks each one down into its Key Features and provides Guiding Questions for each Lens. These Guiding Questions are the 'key ingredients' we've been looking for—essential tools for studying words effectively.

But what skills and strategies does the research highlight as important for language learning, and how can you implement them in your classroom?

- Building semantic networks is a powerful strategy for deepening students' understanding of vocabulary. This emphasises the importance of rich and varied contexts for vocabulary learning (Nagy & Scott, 2000). By encouraging students to make connections between words and concepts, we help them build a more robust and flexible understanding of language. This enhances not only their comprehension but also their ability to use words effectively in their own writing and speaking.
- Teaching students how to use context clues, word parts and reference materials effectively empowers students to become independent learners, capable of expanding their vocabulary beyond the confines of the classroom (Graves, 2006). Implementation includes teaching specific strategies for using context clues to determine word meanings and guiding students in using dictionaries and other reference materials effectively.

- Providing opportunities for students to encounter and use new vocabulary in meaningful contexts across various subject areas is essential for reinforcing learning. This cross-curricular approach to vocabulary instruction helps students see the relevance of new words in different contexts and increases the likelihood of retention and active use. Implementation strategies include collaborating with colleagues to identify and teach key vocabulary across subject areas, creating authentic writing and speaking tasks that require the use of target vocabulary and incorporating vocabulary-rich texts across all areas of the curriculum.

Teaching Tip!

Focus on linguistic foundations:

- **Phonology:** Teach sound manipulation skills.
- **Orthography:** Teach spelling patterns and conventions.
- **Morphology:** Introduce word parts and formation.
- **Etymology:** Use word origins to enhance understanding.

Develop teaching strategies:

- Build semantic networks using word webs and concept maps.
- Teach context-clue strategies for inferring word meanings.
- Implement cross-curricular vocabulary instruction.
- Use multisensory approaches in word study.
- Provide explicit instruction and modelling of word analysis.
- Differentiate instruction based on students' literacy levels.
- Conduct regular assessments and provide feedback.
- Encourage collaborative learning for vocabulary development.

The case studies in this book are full of examples of what this actually looks like in practice!

From a Simple View to Cognitive Foundations

Do you remember a time when a struggling student finally had that lightbulb moment? That's the magic that we teachers are always after, and so understanding the science behind reading can help us create more of those memories. There are two powerful frameworks that can help transform your understanding of effective literacy instruction: the Simple View of Reading and the Cognitive Foundations Framework. Let's dive into them.

The Simple View of Reading, first proposed by psychologists Philip Gough and William Tunmer in 1986, has been a cornerstone of literacy instruction in primary education for decades. This model posits that reading comprehension is the product of two essential components: decoding and language comprehension. While initially developed with primary education in mind, its principles remain relevant and valuable for secondary school students. In the Simple View of Reading, decoding refers to the ability to recognise and read words accurately and fluently. Language comprehension, on the other hand, encompasses the broader skills of understanding spoken language, including vocabulary knowledge and grammatical structures. The model suggests that both components are necessary for successful reading comprehension—a deficit in either area will result in poor overall reading ability. For upper primary and secondary school teachers, understanding the Simple View of Reading provides a foundation for addressing literacy challenges. As we have already established, many students enter secondary school with unresolved issues in either decoding or language comprehension that can significantly impact their ability to engage with increasingly complex texts across various subjects. By recognising these core components, you can more effectively identify and address the root causes of reading difficulties.

However, as students progress through secondary school, the demands on their reading skills become more sophisticated. This is where the Cognitive Foundations Framework, developed by Tunmer and Wesley Hoover (2019), comes into play. This framework expands upon the Simple View of Reading, offering a more in-depth understanding of the cognitive processes involved in skilled reading. Think of it as the Simple View's more sophisticated cousin, breaking down the reading process into six key elements that contribute to reading comprehension:

1. **Phonological awareness**, while often associated with early reading instruction, remains relevant in secondary education. Students who struggle with this skill may have difficulty with complex multisyllabic words common in academic texts. The Phonology Lens will show you how you can support these students by focusing on syllable patterns and stress in more advanced vocabulary.
2. **Alphabetic coding skill**, closely related to the decoding component of the Simple View, involves the ability to map sounds to letters and blend them into words. In secondary contexts, this skill becomes particularly important when encountering specialised vocabulary in subjects like science or mathematics. You can support your students

by explicitly using the Orthography Lens as a strategy for decoding unfamiliar words within your subject areas.

3. **Orthographic knowledge** refers to the understanding of conventional spelling patterns. This extends to recognising and using Greek and Latin roots, prefixes and suffixes common in academic language. For example, your colleague, the biology teacher, might focus on the orthographic patterns in terms like "photosynthesis" or "mitochondria", helping students to recognise these patterns across related words. This is where the key terminology in the Etymology Lens comes in handy.

4. **Vocabulary knowledge**, a critical component of both frameworks, takes on increased importance in upper primary and secondary schooling. The academic vocabulary demands across subject areas increase significantly, and your students will need strategies for independently expanding their word knowledge. We know that effective secondary teachers (should) integrate vocabulary instruction into their content areas, using techniques such as semantic mapping and word analysis to deepen students' understanding of key terms. The Morphology Lens supports you to make this possible.

5. **Morphological awareness** becomes relevant as texts become more complex and your students encounter a greater number of multimorphemic words. A history teacher, for instance, might break down terms like "industrialisation" or "deforestation" to help their students understand how the base words, prefixes and suffixes contribute to meaning. Knowing how to do this can be difficult without the Morphology Lens there as an instructional guide.

6. **Sentence processing skill**, the ability to understand increasingly complex syntactic structures, is vital for comprehending academic texts. Older students often struggle with the dense, information-packed sentences common in textbooks and scholarly articles. You and your colleagues across subject areas can support this skill by guiding your students through the unpacking of complex sentences, identifying main clauses, subordinate clauses and embedded phrases.

By understanding and applying the Cognitive Foundations Framework, you will be able to move beyond the basic decoding and comprehension dichotomy of the Simple View of Reading.

Consider, for example, one of your Year 9 students struggling with the vocabulary in a science textbook. The Simple View might suggest that the student has either decoding or comprehension issues. However, the

Cognitive Foundations Framework will enable you to pinpoint more specific areas of difficulty. Perhaps the student has strong phonological awareness and basic decoding skills but lacks the orthographic and morphological knowledge to efficiently process scientific terminology. With this understanding, you, or their science teacher, can use the Morphology Lens to build the student's knowledge of common bases and affixes in scientific language. Similarly, an English teacher working with a Year 11 class on a complex literary text might use this knowledge to support students' comprehension. While many students at this level have mastered basic decoding, they may struggle with the sophisticated sentence structures and figurative language common in advanced literature. By focusing on sentence processing skills and deep vocabulary knowledge, the teacher can help students navigate these challenging texts more effectively. So many teachers always ask me, "But how do I actually do this in my own classroom?" Well, the Linguistic Lenses Framework structures this approach for you.

It's important to note that while the Cognitive Foundations Framework provides a more detailed model of reading processes, it doesn't negate the value of the Simple View of Reading. Rather, it builds upon and refines our understanding of how to support skilled reading. What if we used both models in conjunction: the Simple View as a quick diagnostic tool to identify broad areas of difficulty and the Cognitive Foundations Framework to drill down into specific cognitive processes that may need support?

Teaching Tip!

The Simple View of Reading is a quick diagnostic tool: reading equals decoding plus language comprehension. It allows us to identify broad areas of difficulty. The Cognitive Foundations Framework provides more in-depth analysis.

Combine knowledge of both frameworks for comprehensive support. Apply strategies across all subject areas, using Linguistic Lenses as your instructional tool (and this book as your guide), and tailor interventions to individual student needs.

But *how* can we translate the theory of these frameworks into practical and tangible tools to support our learners in the classroom? That is exactly what this book is about.

CHAPTER 2

The New Map—the Power of Four Lenses

"Students should be given opportunities to learn about not just the phonological aspects of spelling, but also the morphological aspects of spelling. And even what I described as the orthographic aspect of spelling. That should start early as well."
~ Dr Tessa Daffern

After diving into this chapter, you'll emerge with these big-picture understandings:

1. **Master the Linguistic Lens Framework:** Learn how Linguistic Lenses can enhance literacy instruction and student learning.
2. **Navigate the Four Lenses:** Distinguish between the Phonology, Orthography, Morphology and Etymology Lenses.
3. **Grasp Lens Essentials:** Outline the knowledge and Key Components unique to each Linguistic Lens.
4. **Understand Guided Inquiry Techniques:** Be ready to apply Guiding Questions associated with each Linguistic Lens to facilitate and deepen word study.
5. **Embrace Equity Through Linguistics:** Recognise how Linguistic Lenses can create equitable learning environments by empowering diverse learners to overcome socioeconomic, cultural and geographical barriers through explicit language instruction.

To effectively implement a comprehensive approach to literacy instruction, we as teachers must be well prepared and well versed in phonological awareness, alphabetic coding skill, orthographic knowledge, vocabulary knowledge, morphological awareness and sentence processing skill (Stocker et al., 2023). This book provides a professional development opportunity for you—whether you are a teacher or pre-service university student—and your colleagues to deepen your understanding of the cognitive processes involved in reading comprehension, providing practical strategies for integrating word study and vocabulary instruction across the curriculum. It also aims to offer guidance on assessing and addressing individual student needs in each component of literacy.

The research is clear that explicit teaching of phonology, orthography, morphology and etymology bolsters not only reading comprehension but spelling accuracy and writing proficiency, improving our students' literacy. So, these Lenses serve as essential instructional instruments, explaining complex linguistic elements through tangible strategies that explicitly unpack the English spelling system at a metalinguistic level.

Equity Through Linguistic Lenses: Addressing our greatest challenge

I believe that one of our greatest challenges lies in creating a truly equitable learning environment for all students, regardless of their socioeconomic status, cultural background or geographical location. Linguistic Lenses can address these disparities and level the playing field in our classrooms. By explicitly teaching the fundamental components of the English spelling system—phonology, orthography, morphology and etymology—we can empower students from all walks of life with the tools they need to succeed. Through these Lenses, I aim to reshape our educational landscape, ensuring that every student has the opportunity to thrive, regardless of their starting point. Here are three points to consider:

- **Socioeconomic disparities:** Consider Sarah, from a family of university graduates, and Tom, whose parents didn't complete high school. Statistically, Tom may lag two years behind Sarah academically. However, this gap can be narrowed through a comprehensive approach to language instruction. A deep understanding of phonology, orthography, morphology and etymology has been shown to significantly enhance vocabulary development, reading comprehension and written composition skills (Adoniou, 2022). Aligning with repertoire theories of spelling, which advocate for integrated instruction, Linguistic Lenses help to create a level playing field that transcends socioeconomic backgrounds.

- **Supporting First Nations learners:** One-third of First Nations students require additional literacy and numeracy support. Utilise Linguistic Lenses to integrate culturally responsive teaching methods that honour First Nations knowledge and history. Use the Etymological Lens to explore language origins, fostering a deeper connection between First Nations languages and English, thereby enhancing comprehension and engagement.
- **Overcoming geographic barriers:** Half of students in very remote areas need extra assistance. For these students, implement Linguistic Lenses through innovative digital platforms. Focus on phonological and orthographic patterns that may be challenging for remote learners, creating targeted online resources that address these specific needs. You can find these at www.linguisticlenses.com.

By adopting a repertoire approach, whereby skilled literacy learners draw upon multiple sources of knowledge rather than relying solely on memorisation or simple sound-to-letter correspondences, students can recognise that the English spelling system involves a complex interplay of phonology, orthography, morphology and etymology. The Linguistic Lenses framework applies this by offering structured ways to explore and understand each of these linguistic components:

1. **Phonological awareness:** Explicitly teaching sound structures helps level the playing field for students from diverse linguistic backgrounds, particularly benefiting those from non-English-speaking homes or areas with limited exposure to standard English.
2. **Orthographic knowledge:** Focusing on spelling patterns and conventions provides a systematic approach to literacy, supporting students who may not have access to rich print environments at home.
3. **Morphological understanding:** Teaching word formation and structure increases vocabulary and comprehension, which is imperative for students with limited exposure to academic language.
4. **Etymological exploration:** Investigating word origins not only enriches language learning but also validates diverse cultural and linguistic heritages, fostering inclusivity.

This pedagogy serves as a powerful equaliser, providing all students, regardless of their background, with the tools to decode, comprehend and engage with complex texts. By implementing these Linguistic Lenses across our educational system, we can create a more equitable learning environment that addresses the diverse needs of our student population, and work towards closing the achievement gap and fostering a more equitable educational landscape.

Your 'Big-Picture' Guide to each Linguistic Lens

The Four Linguistic Lenses are as follows:

1. **The Phonology Lens** focuses on the auditory aspects of language, encompassing phoneme awareness, phonological sensitivity and phonetics. It's an oral language tool that sharpens our perception of the sounds present in spoken and heard words.
2. **The Orthography Lens** delves into the visual representation of language. This Lens examines graphemes and their positions, combinations and sequences within written words. It encompasses the alphabetic principle, orthographic knowledge and the conventions that govern our writing system.
3. **The Morphology Lens** unveils the architecture of words, studying morphemes—the smallest units of meaning. It explores word structure, semantic relationships and grammatical forms, serving as a crucial link between orthographic patterns, pronunciations and word meaning.
4. **The Etymology Lens** traces the historical journey of words, illuminating their origins and relationships to other words sharing the same roots. Etymology has the remarkable power to elucidate numerous aspects of spelling in a memorable and engaging manner.

Each Lens offers a unique perspective on word analysis, collectively enhancing students' ability to form strong, lasting memories of words and their associated meanings.

A breakdown of each Linguistic Lens

Each Linguistic Lens has unique properties.

The front of each Lens highlights:

- the name of the Knowledge Component
- an Explanation of Terminology—what those words mean.

The back of each Lens signposts:

- the significant Key Features needed for word study, which have been translated into a comprehensive process of...
- Guiding Questions, which form the foundation of word study.

Linguistic Lenses offer a comprehensive framework for literacy instruction, integrating four essential Knowledge Components that collectively foster word consciousness in students. These Knowledge Components work synergistically, and when faced with time constraints and a crowded curriculum, words can be analysed through a focal Lens to allow for more efficient instruction.

Each Knowledge Component is broken down into Key Features, which are then elaborated through specific Guiding Questions. These questions are designed to facilitate deeper understanding and engagement with the Linguistic Lenses framework through classroom discussion and word structure analysis. They incorporate essential linguistic terminology to support instruction and guide word study. By promoting critical thinking and encouraging language concept exploration, these questions will help you and your students develop a deeper understanding of language complexities. Adaptable to various age and proficiency levels, they serve as springboards for discussions, activities and further inquiry into each aspect of the Linguistic Lenses framework.

Navigating Linguistic Lenses: A flexible approach to word analysis

Just as every student in your classroom is unique, so too is every word in our language. This diversity is what makes vocabulary and word study so exciting, but it can also present challenges when we're trying to teach with scripted rules. Linguistic Lenses are powerful instructional tools to support you in unpacking the intricacies of words alongside your students, no matter the context or content area you find yourselves in. However, it's important to understand that not every word will tick all the boxes or fit neatly into every category—and that's perfectly okay! In fact, it's part of what makes this process so engaging.

So, here's how you can approach this flexibly:

1. Start with the Guiding Questions of each Lens.
2. As you read each question, ask your students: "Is this relevant to the word I'm analysing?"

3. If yes, dive in and explore. If no, simply acknowledge that and move on. Remember, a "no" is just as informative as a "yes" in linguistic analysis!

Teaching Tip!

Think of the Guiding Questions as tools in a toolbox: you don't need to use every tool for every job, but it's valuable to know how each one works when you do need it. By the end of this journey, you'll have a well-rounded understanding of how to apply these Lenses flexibly and effectively in your teaching.

The next four chapters unlock the power of each Linguistic Lens one by one.

Setting up for Your Word Study Using the Linguistic Lens Graphic Organiser

To help you start your word study journey, I'd like to introduce you to a valuable tool: the Linguistic Lenses Graphic Organiser (LLGO). While you can conduct word studies using your preferred method (such as freehand, posters, drawings, diagrams or anchor charts), I highly recommend starting with the LLGO, especially if you're new to linguistic analysis.

The LLGO serves as an excellent support for learning and using specialised linguistic terminology, or "metalanguage". Importantly, it also helps to structure your thinking, making it easier to navigate complex linguistic concepts and ensuring you cover all essential aspects of word analysis. It provides a clear visual map of word relationships and concepts, helping students make cognitive connections between new vocabulary and existing knowledge. Graphic organisers in general are powerful visual tools that can significantly enhance instruction and study, improving retention and promoting deeper understanding.

And great news! All the images in this book are readily available as both printable blackline masters and digital templates for free at www.linguisticlenses.com. Feel free to download and use them to enhance your teaching experience.

When used in conjunction with the Guiding Questions, the LLGO promotes deeper linguistic analysis. It encourages students to think critically about words and their structures, fostering analytical skills that extend beyond vocabulary acquisition. Moreover, together these tools are highly adaptable to various learning styles and abilities, making them ideal for diverse classrooms. This flexibility allows you to differentiate instruction effectively, ensuring that all students can engage with and benefit from the word study process.

Implementing the LLGO in your classroom can be a smooth process if approached thoughtfully. I recommend starting gradually, introducing the organiser step-by-step to avoid overwhelming students; that's exactly what we will do here, chapter by chapter, Lens by Lens. Encourage active participation by allowing students to fill out the organiser themselves. This hands-on approach can increase engagement and deepen understanding. Feel free to customise the LLGO as needed to suit your specific lesson objectives or student needs.

Remember, the ultimate goal is to make word study both rigorous and engaging. The LLGO serves as a scaffold, supporting both you and your students as you delve into the intricacies of language analysis. As you become more comfortable with linguistic analysis, you may find yourself relying less on the LLGO, but it will have provided a solid foundation for more advanced freeform word study techniques.

Now, let's get practical. Want to set up your classroom for some awesome word study using Linguistic Lenses and the LLGO? Here's how:

1. Fire up your interactive whiteboard and display the LLGO digital template. (Remember, it can be found at www.linguisticlenses.com.)
2. Grab each Lens magnet and stick it right next to the relevant section on the board.
3. Write the vocabulary word in the centre of the LLGO.

And just like that, you're all set for some engaging word study action. Here we go!

CHAPTER 3

Your Guide to the Phonology Lens

"From the time a Latin alphabet was imported to record our spoken English, the quest for phonological consistency was doomed."
~ *Dr Misty Adoniou*

By the end of this chapter, you will have gained the following key understandings:

1. **The enigma of English orthography:** Uncover the discrepancies between English spelling and pronunciation challenging the notion of English as a purely phonetic language.
2. **The 44 phonemes:** Explore the core set of 44 distinct sounds that comprise spoken English and examine how these phonemes navigate the constraints of a 26-letter alphabet.
3. **Consonant phonemes:** Analyse the 24 consonant phonemes that provide the skeletal structure of English pronunciation, understanding their articulation and role in word formation.
4. **Vowel complexity beyond the basic five:** Investigate the intriguing disparity between the five traditional vowel letters and the 20 vowel phonemes in English, appreciating the nuances of vowel sounds in our language.
5. **A new pedagogical perspective:** Develop a refined approach to teaching Phonological Sensitivity, Phoneme Awareness and Phonetics, enhancing your ability to guide students through the subtleties of English sounds.

6. **Phonology in context:** Gain insight into how phonology interacts with other linguistic components, understanding its key role within the broader tapestry of language study.

Introducing the Phonology Lens

So, here's the scoop: current literacy programs often overemphasise a simplified version of phonological knowledge, teaching it in isolation from the broader linguistic context. This approach proves effective for younger children grappling with simpler words, but it begins to falter as students encounter more complex language, primarily because English spelling isn't as predictable as these programs might suggest.

A massive study with over 2000 teachers in England found that phonics teaching is most effective for five- and six-year-olds (Wyse & Bradbury, 2022). This means we just might need to adapt our approach from Year 1 onwards. Phonological knowledge only really helps with spelling in the first two years of school (Adoniou, 2019). And here's the kicker—teaching the alphabetic code (that letters and sounds have a one-to-one match) in isolation from reading context could be risky business because it can disconnect spelling from meaning, which is integral for reading comprehension (Wyse & Bradbury, 2022). It's like trying to solve a puzzle with only half of the pieces. It oversimplifies the complex nature of English orthography and can lead to misconceptions, such as the idea of "silent letters", which fails to recognise the important functions these letters serve in words.

So, while phonics certainly has its place, especially in those early years, it's time we expanded our toolkit. By providing students with a richer, more accurate understanding of English spelling, we're not just teaching them to read and write—we're setting them up for a lifelong journey of language exploration and appreciation. Now that's a plot twist worth tuning in for!

Let's think of phonology as *one* piece of a big, colourful mosaic. Each piece represents a different aspect of our language. When you're exploring vocabulary with your students, imagine this mosaic coming to life—each word a unique blend of colours and patterns. That's where Linguistic Lenses come in handy. They help us see how each piece fits into the bigger picture of English spelling.

It is now time to unveil the Phonology Lens, the compass guiding our voyage through the intricate seas of language sounds. This Lens is replete with

Key Features designed to expertly navigate you and your students through phonological study. Additionally, my curated set of Guiding Questions promises to make your journey through phonology as engaging and enjoyable as a catamaran journey through Australia's Great Barrier Reef.

The front of the Lens is where the party starts. It's got the big-picture stuff—what phonology is all about. Fun fact: <phon-> means "sound" and <-ology> means "the study of". You can drop that at your next staff meeting!

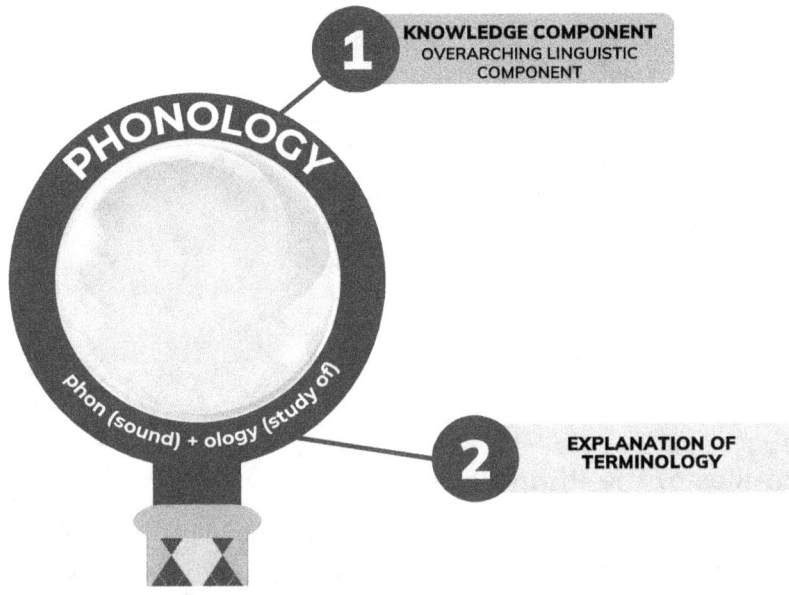

So, phonology is the branch of linguistics that deals with sound patterns in language. Think of it as the soundtrack to our words—how they sound, how we pronounce them and how that relates to spelling.

Why should we care about phonology beyond the early years? Well, it's not just for the little ones:

- It helps crack the code of those jaw-breaking, complex, multisyllable words.
- It turbocharges reading fluency—your students will be zipping through complex texts in no time.
- It's great for clear communication—no more mumbling through big words!
- It's a lifesaver when learning new languages or tackling scientific vocabulary.

The back of the Lens is where we get into the nitty-gritty. It's got all the **Key Features** you need for phonological study, broken down into easy-to-follow **Guiding Questions**.

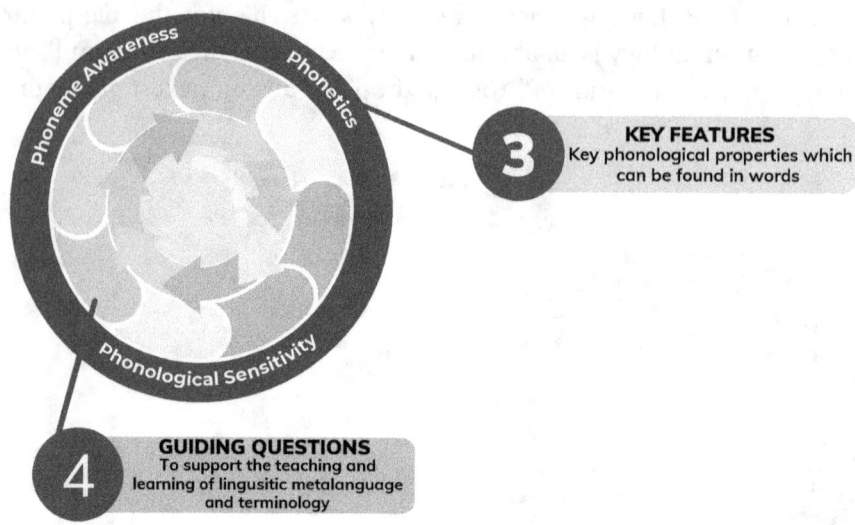

Key Features of the Phonology Lens

Imagine phonology as a grand orchestra, with each sound playing a crucial role in the melody of communication. The Phonology Lens is our backstage pass to this linguistic concert, allowing us to explore the intricate world of speech sounds, from the sweeping crescendos down to the tiniest notes.

Let's tune into the three Key Features that make up this auditory adventure:

1. **Phonological Sensitivity:** This is our innate ability to groove with the music of language. Like an Ibiza DJ manipulates tracks, phonological sensitivity allows us to manipulate phonemes, transforming "cat" into "bat" with a sonic sleight of hand. We recognise onset and rime, feeling the beat in words like "c-at", "b-at" and "r-at". Our inner rhythm helps us clap out syllables, from the solo beat of "dog" to the verbal percussion of "hip-po-pot-a-mus". We tune into rhymes, linking "moon" with "June" in a poetic dance. It's about developing a sixth sense for the sound patterns that give language its irresistible rhythm and flow.

2. **Phoneme Awareness:** Here, we zoom in with our audio microscope to the individual instruments—the distinct speech sounds that form the building blocks of words. This virtuoso skill allows us to segment and blend phonemes, breaking "stop" into /s/, /t/, /o/ and /p/, and fusing them back together. We distinguish between consonants and vowels, the backbone and melody of our word symphony. Our refined ear feels the difference between voiced and unvoiced phonemes, the vibrato in "zoo" versus the whisper in "sue". We unravel non-phonetic spelling mysteries to explore diphones and understand why "knight" doesn't sound as it looks. It's the ability to manipulate these sonic elements with the precision of a linguistic conductor.

3. **Phonetics:** This is where we don our lab coats and study the physical choreography of speech. We master pronunciation and articulation, executing the dance of lips, tongue and vocal cords. Our scientific curiosity helps us decode the International Phonetic Alphabet (IPA), a universal notation system for speech sounds. We learn to recognise the elusive schwa, that chameleon vowel lurking in unstressed syllables. It's about understanding the mechanics of each instrument in our language orchestra, revealing how we physically create the rich tapestry of human speech.

Together, these Key Features of the Phonology Lens offer us a comprehensive view of the sound system of language. They transform our perception of spoken words from a simple stream of sound into a rich, multilayered experience. It's like upgrading from a basic radio to a state-of-the-art sound system.

Are you ready to unpack each of these Key Features? Tune in, turn up the volume and prepare to be amazed by the symphony of sounds that create the music of language. Let the linguistic concert begin!

Components of Phonological Sensitivity: The Teachers' Toolkit

Think of phonological sensitivity as students recognising and manipulating sound units in spoken language. For older students, it's about developing a nuanced understanding of words that can enhance reading, writing and linguistic analysis skills.

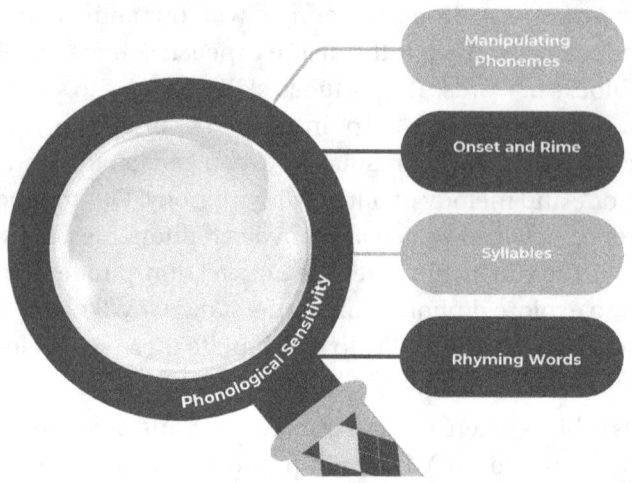

1. **Manipulating Phonemes** means identifying, isolating and altering individual sounds (phonemes) in words. It is comprised of several skills:
    a. Sound identification—recognising all the phonemes in a word
    b. Sound changing—altering specific phonemes to create new words
    c. Sound deletion—removing specific phonemes from words
    d. Sound addition—inserting new phonemes into words.

> **Teaching Tip!**
>
> Think of phonemes as linguistic Jenga blocks—they can be identified, removed, added or swapped to build different words. For example, challenge students to change "catastrophe" to "apostrophe", or "photosynthesis" to "psychosis".

2. **Onset and Rime** are the two parts of a syllable—the onset is the initial consonant (or consonants) and the rime is the rest of the syllable, comprising the vowel and any following consonants. For example, in "street", <str-> is the onset and <-eet> is the rime. Note that the onset can be absent in some syllables, such as in the first syllable of "absent".

Teaching Tip!

Think of onset and rime as the "handshake and hug" of a syllable—the onset introduces, the rime embraces the rest.

Analyse how onset and rime patterns change in morphological word families. Compare "sign" with the first syllables of "signature" and "signify".

3. **Syllables** are units of pronunciation that typically consist of a vowel sound with or without surrounding consonants. Complex words often have multiple syllables. Syllables can be stressed (emphasised) or unstressed, and unstressed syllables often contain a schwa.

Teaching Tip!

Imagine syllables as the "heartbeats" of words—some strong, some weak—creating the rhythm of language.

4. **Rhyming Words** have the same or similar ending sounds. They can have a single syllable or multiple.

Teaching Tip!

Think of rhymes as "sound echoes" at the end of words. Focus on sound, not spelling—for example, "through" and "blue" rhyme.

Remember, for older students, understanding these components isn't just about basic word skills—it's about developing a deeper appreciation for the structure and musicality of language. By mastering these components, students gain a toolkit for dissecting, analysing and manipulating language at a sophisticated level, applicable across various subjects and real-world communication scenarios.

Components of Phoneme Awareness: The Teachers' Toolkit

Teaching Tip!

I will use the IPA when discussing phonemes. A reference chart can be found on page 43.

A phoneme is the smallest unit of sound in a language—for example, "cat" has three phonemes: /k/, /æ/ and /t/. Phoneme awareness is the sophisticated ability to recognise, isolate and manipulate the individual sound units (phonemes) in spoken language. For older students, this skill is key to decoding unfamiliar words and enhancing their writing style.

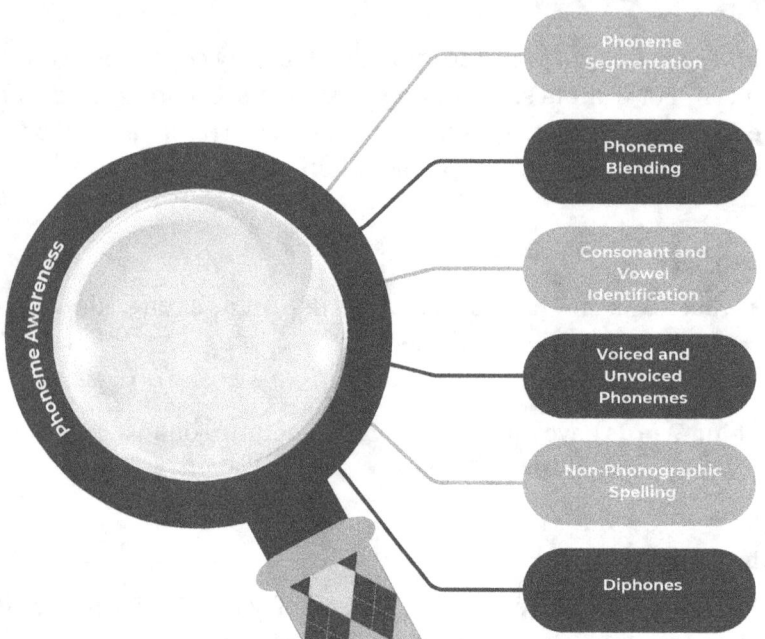

1. **Phoneme Segmentation** is the ability to break words into individual phonemes. This skill is important for spelling and decoding unfamiliar words.

Teaching Tip!

Think of this as "sound dissection". It's about hearing and isolating each distinct sound in a word, not just the letters.

Move beyond simple words to multisyllabic, academic vocabulary—for example, challenge your students to segment "photosynthesis" into its component phonemes.

2. **Phoneme Blending** is the reverse of segmentation—it's the process of combining individual phonemes to form a complete word. For

example, blending the phonemes /s/, /k/, /uː/ and /l/ creates the word "school". This skill is essential for reading fluency and word recognition.

Teaching Tip!
Imagine this as "sound fusion". It's like mixing ingredients to create a word "smoothie".

3. **Consonant and Vowel Identification** involves recognising and distinguishing between consonant and vowel phonemes in words. Consonant phonemes involve some obstruction of airflow; vowel phonemes don't. English has 24 consonant phonemes and 20 vowel phonemes with 44 phonemes altogether. Therefore, not all letters can correspond to just one sound.

Teaching Tip!
Think of consonants as "sound shapers" and vowels as "sound carriers".

Move beyond basic identification to understanding how consonant and vowel phonemes interact in complex words—for example, analysing how the vowel sounds differ in the words "photograph" and "photographer".

4. **Voiced and Unvoiced Phonemes** are those sounds produced with vocal cord vibration (voiced) and those without (unvoiced). Voiced phonemes include /b/, /d/, /g/, /v/, /z/ and /dʒ/; feel the vibration in your throat when you articulate these phonemes. Unvoiced phonemes include /p/, /t/, /k/, /f/, /s/ and /tʃ/.

Differentiating between these sounds is crucial for correct pronunciation.

Teaching Tip!
It's all about the "buzz". Voiced phonemes make your vocal cords vibrate; unvoiced don't.

Focus on how this distinction affects meaning and pronunciation in advanced vocabulary.

5. **Non-Phonographic Spelling** is when a phoneme exists in pronunciation but isn't represented by a letter (grapheme) in spelling.

A common example is the schwa sound /ə/ in unstressed syllables—for example, the second syllable in "rhythm" contains a schwa sound not represented in spelling. The IPA helps identify these "hidden" sounds.

Teaching Tip!
Think of these as "invisible" sounds. They're heard but not seen in spelling.

6. **Diphones** are single letters or "graphemes" that represent two distinct phonemes, challenging the idea of one-to-one phoneme–grapheme correspondence. They are common in English orthography. Examples include the <x> in "box" (/k/ + /s/) and the <u> in "cute" (/j/ + /u:/)

Teaching Tip!
Consider these "two-for-one" sound deals in spelling.

Remember, understanding these concepts deeply yourself is key to helping your students grasp them. As students get older, phoneme awareness isn't just about basic sound recognition—it's about developing a sophisticated understanding of language structure that can enhance reading, writing and linguistic analysis skills across all subjects.

Components of Phonetics: The Teachers' Toolkit

Phonetics is all about how we produce those 44 English speech sounds. Phonics is how they relate to the letters we see on the page. And trust me, it's way more complex (and cool) than it sounds.

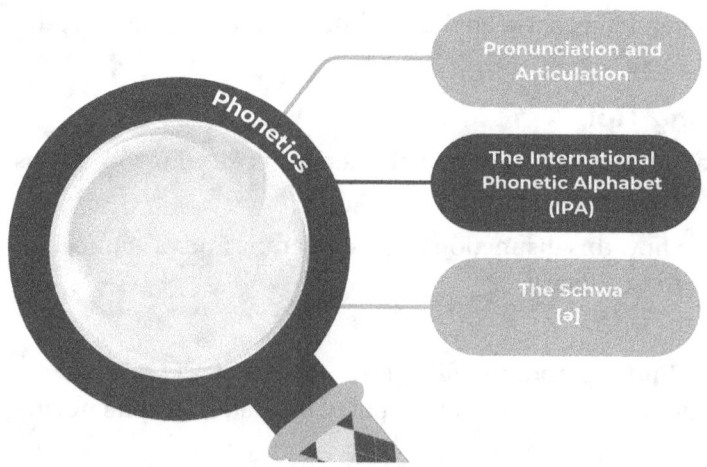

1. **Pronunciation and Articulation** are different but closely related concepts in speech production. Articulation refers to producing individual speech sounds by moving your lips, tongue and teeth, like playing single notes on an instrument. Pronunciation, however, is more comprehensive: it includes articulation but also encompasses how you combine sounds into words, where you place stress (emphasis) in words and sentences, and the intonation (pitch patterns) of your speech. While articulation focuses on clear, correct sounds, pronunciation is about using those sounds to speak naturally and understandably in a particular language.

Teaching Tip!
Think of the vocal tract as a musical instrument, with different parts creating different sounds.

2. **The International Phonetic Alphabet (IPA)** is a standardised set of symbols representing speech sounds across languages. It is an essential tool for understanding non-phonographic spelling, bridging the gap between spelling and pronunciation. Throughout this book, I will utilise IPA notation when discussing sounds in words rather than the written letters.

Teaching Tip!
The IPA is like a "sound map" for languages, showing the terrain of pronunciation.

3. **The Schwa** is a neutral vowel phoneme common in English. It is represented by the symbol [ə] in IPA. It often occurs in unstressed syllables, such as the <a> in "about", and is often a "hidden" sound not represented in spelling. It is key to natural rhythm and flow in English speech.

Teaching Tip!
The schwa is a linguistic chameleon—it blends into words, often unnoticed but paramount for natural speech.

Remember, understanding phonetics deeply can transform how you approach teaching pronunciation, spelling and even literature analysis. It's not just about correct pronunciation—it's about understanding the very fabric of spoken language. This knowledge can enhance students' language skills across all subjects, from sciences (pronouncing technical terms) to literature (analysing poetic sounds) and beyond.

Exploring "Conscience" Through the Phonology Lens

Picture this: You're in the middle of a gripping novel, or perhaps you've stumbled upon a spelling mishap in your students' writing. Maybe you're exploring subject-specific vocabulary. Suddenly, the word "conscience" appears, begging to be decoded. What do you do?

Begin by writing "conscience" at the centre of your LLGO. This serves as the focal point for our analysis.

Navigate the Lens clockwise, verbalising the Guided Questions to demonstrate the process for your students.

Navigating the Phonology Lens: A clockwise journey through 15 Guiding Questions

Structured as a clockwise journey through 15 Guiding Questions, this approach transforms complex linguistic concepts into an accessible, conversation-style exploration of the phonology of words, setting you up for success in your classroom. The Phonology Lens' user-friendly design, featuring a circular layout with a clear starting point and progression, makes it easy for both you and your students to adopt. By consistently applying this approach, you will help your students internalise a systematic approach to phonological word analysis, developing their ability to independently explore and understand unfamiliar vocabulary.

Here's how to use this tool:

1. Start at the top. See the box "What phonemes can you hear?" That's your launchpad.
2. Work your way around clockwise. It's like a word treasure hunt!
3. Once you've circled the outer rim, follow the arrow inward to "How many syllables?" and work through the inner rim.

Here's how to make it work in your classroom:

- **Consistency is key.** Use these questions regularly. It might feel a bit weird at first, but soon it'll be second nature.
- **Some words are party animals**—they'll spark great discussions. Go with it! That's where the real learning happens.
- **Other words are wallflowers**—they might not need as much attention. That's okay too.

The grand goal is for your students to internalise these questions. Imagine them having a little word detective in their heads, asking these questions whenever they stumble upon a tricky word. How great would that be?

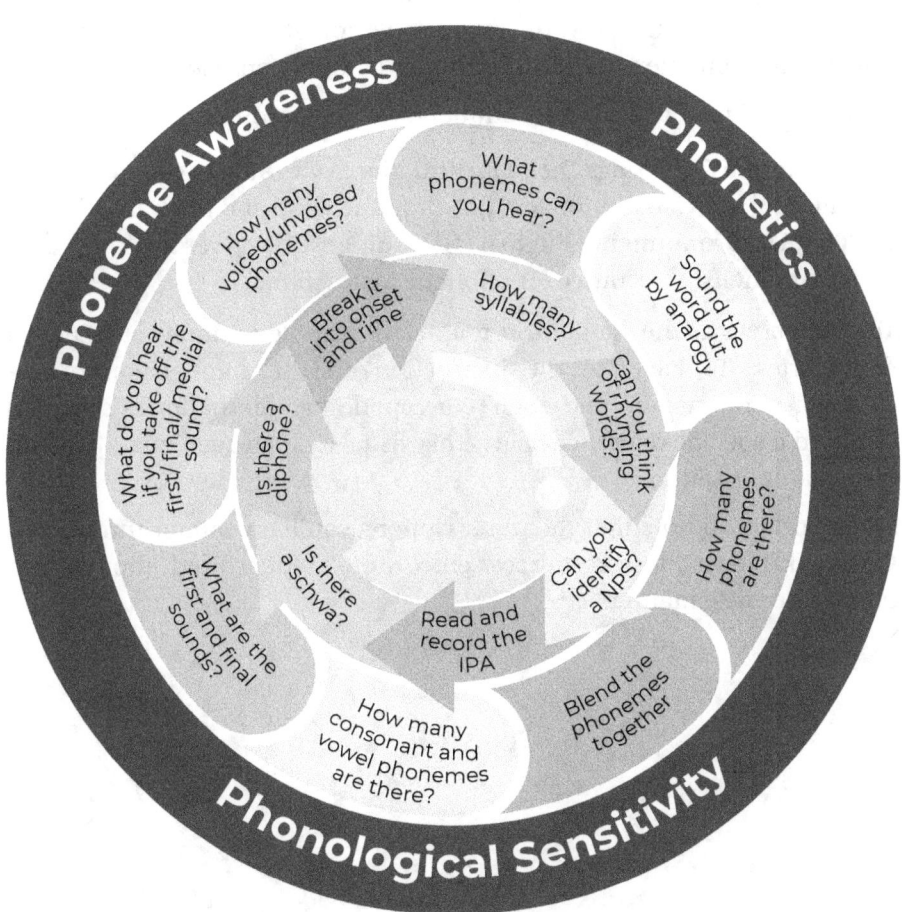

In my experience leading literacy and curriculum initiatives in schools, I've always placed a strong emphasis on fostering a word-conscious culture (Cullen & Townsin, 2024). This approach has been a cornerstone of my whole-school structured literacy strategy, with leadership providing ongoing support and guidance to ensure consistency in instruction.

My own research has shown a strong link between teacher professional development and the instructional tools used in classrooms (Cullen & Townsin, 2024). Recognising this connection, I have implemented consistent professional learning and mentoring programs to ensure all teachers utilised the same reference tools for literacy instruction. This school-wide consistency reinforced our structured approach effectively.

Specifically, I have used and recommend two key resources:

1. **The online** *Cambridge Dictionary* **(dictionary.cambridge.org):** This tool is invaluable for accurate pronunciation and IPA transcription.
2. **THRASS Pronouncing English (IPA Guide):** This serves as a comprehensive resource for phonetic instruction.

The IPA serves as the standard pronunciation guide in numerous English dictionaries. To facilitate the instruction and comprehension of the 44 English phonemes and their corresponding international symbols, I utilised a specific reference chart. This visual aid has been included with proper authorisation.

It's important to note that the transcriptions you'll encounter throughout this book reflect these resources, ensuring a standardised approach to phonetic representation.

IPA SOUNDS AND SYMBOLS

CONSONANTS

Plosives
b	as in bird	(bɜːd)
k	as in cat	(kæt)
d	as in dog	(dɒg)
g	as in gate	(geɪt)
p	as in panda	('pæn.də)
t	as in tap	(tæp)

Fricatives
f	as in fish	(fɪʃ)
h	as in hand	(hænd)
s	as in sun	(sʌn)
ʒ	as in treasure	('treʒ.ə)
ʃ	as in shark	(ʃɑːk)
θ	as in thumb	(θʌm)
ð	as in feather	('feð.ə)
v	as in voice	(vɔɪs)
z	as in zip	(zɪp)

Affricates
tʃ	as in chair	(tʃeə)
dʒ	as in jam	(dʒæm)

Nasals
m	as in mouse	(maʊs)
n	as in net	(net)
ŋ	as in king	(kɪŋ)

Liquids
l	as in leg	(leg)
r	as in rain	(reɪn)

Semi-vowels
w	as in water	('wɔː.tə)
j	as in yawn	(jɔːn)

VOWELS

Short monophthongs
æ	as in ant	(ænt)
e	as in bed	(bed)
ə	as in teacher	('tiː.tʃə)
ɪ	as in tin	(tɪn)
ɒ	as in frog	(frɒg)
ʊ	as in book	(bʊk)
ʌ	as in bus	(bʌs)

Long monophthongs
ɑː	as in car	(kɑː)
iː	as in me	(miː)
ɜː	as in fern	(fɜːn)
uː	as in moon	(muːn)
ɔː	as in fork	(fɔːk)

> ː is used to indicate a long vowel (long monophthong)

Diphthongs
eɪ	as in baby	('beɪ.biː)
eə	as in hair	(heə)
ɪə	as in ear	(ɪə)
aɪ	as in tiger	('taɪ.gə)
əʊ	as in nose	(nəʊz)
ɔɪ	as in coin	(kɔɪn)
ʊə	as in lure	(lʊə)
aʊ	as in cow	(kaʊ)

> ' is used to indicate the stressed syllable e.g. (pæn.) in ('pæn.də)

> . is used to indicate the the break between syllables.

The THRASS Phonics Word Bank © THE THRASS INSTITUTE Australasia & Canada

1. What phonemes can you hear?

We're going to break down our word "conscience" into all its individual sounds. Remember, we're listening for sounds, not looking at letters!

Let's start with our thumb and work our way through. I'll say the sounds and you raise a finger for each one you hear. Ready?

> **Teaching Tip!**
> - **Colour coding:** Use blue for consonants and red for vowels. This visual distinction helps in recognising the structural components of the word.
> - **Sequential analysis:** Always initiate your phoneme count with your thumb. This ensures a consistent and organised approach.
> - **Phoneme–Grapheme Correspondence:** Match each identified sound with its corresponding grapheme (letter, or combination of letters). This bridges the gap between auditory perception and written representation.

I'm going to use IPA symbols here to reference that we are talking about the sounds in the word, not the letters! Here we go: /k/, /ɒ/, /n/, /ʃ/, /ə/, /n/, /s/.

How many fingers do you have up? That's right, seven! "Conscience" has seven phonemes.

Case study: Hanna's journey

Meet Hanna, a bright-eyed student in the first year of formal schooling with an insatiable appetite for reading. At just five years old, Hanna was already devouring books at a Year 2 level, leaving her teachers puzzled about how to support her advanced literacy skills.

Hanna's parents, recognising their daughter's unique learning profile, sought guidance from me during their school tour. (No, Hanna was not yet attending my school!) They shared their concerns: despite Hanna's readiness for novels, she was being held back by what they believed was a linear approach to learning, where her teachers were focusing on her age rather than her stage of learning. This scenario can be all too common in our education system, where gifted learners often find themselves restricted by age-based expectations.

In response to Hanna's situation, I provided her parents with a novel challenge to nurture her love for reading. More importantly, I shared key research-based insights to empower them in advocating for their daughter's learning. These included the importance of understanding English orthography as a morphophonemic system, teaching how spellings represent sounds, meaning and history. I also emphasised the need for instruction without age restrictions or a one-size-fits-all approach and highlighted the risks of limiting young, advanced readers, potentially stunting their writing development and overall literacy growth.

Fast-forward one year and Hanna's educational assessment revealed what we had suspected: she was intellectually gifted. At six years old, Hanna's IQ scored in the superior range (97th percentile), with her literacy skills two to three years above her chronological age.

However, the assessment also highlighted a critical issue in our current approach to literacy evaluation. During the "pseudoword decoding" subtest, Hanna, an advanced reader, was penalised for attempting to make sense of nonsense words. For instance, she read "stight" as "straight"—a logical interpretation for a child accustomed to meaningful reading.

The assessment noted that Hanna struggled with "long and complex" words, often giving up or doubting her abilities. But what if Hanna had been equipped with morphological and etymological strategies? Would these words still seem as daunting?

Despite her "excellent phonic knowledge" and "advanced decoder" status, Hanna consistently had to override her instinct to make meaning—the very essence of reading—to conform to the test's expectations.

This raises the question: why are we testing capable readers on their ability to decode nonsense words when the ultimate goal of reading is comprehension?

I believe we need to recognise that phonics, while important, is just one piece of the literacy puzzle. Extensive research has found that introducing morphological and etymological skills earlier, rather than reserving them for upper primary and secondary school, would be beneficial (Bowers, 2018; Daffern, 2024; Adoniou, 2019). We should also develop assessment methods that value meaning making and comprehension, not just decoding skills, and provide differentiated instruction that allows gifted learners like Hanna to thrive without artificial constraints.

As teachers, shouldn't we question practices that prioritise nonsense over meaning? Our goal isn't to create students who can read nonsense words; it's to develop learners who can navigate the complexities of language with confidence and understanding. Hanna's story reminds us that sometimes the most counterproductive thing we can do is to insist on teaching nonsensical elements like pseudowords, especially to advanced readers who are already seeking meaning in text.

2. Sound the word out by analogy

You're not just teaching words; you're building bridges between what your students already know and the new linguistic territories they're about to explore. That's analogous learning in a nutshell. It's like giving your students a pair of X-ray goggles for words. Suddenly, they're seeing connections everywhere. And those tricky new terms? They're not so scary anymore.

> **Teaching Tip!**
>
> Analogous learning is your classroom game-changer. Imagine teaching "photosynthesis" by turning leaves into tiny factories: sunlight, water and CO^2 go in; glucose and oxygen come out. Boom! A complex process just became relatable. Want to make "tenacious" stick? Bring in the image of a determined little dog refusing to let go of its favourite chew toy. Your students will never forget it (and might even chuckle in the process)! Turn your class into word detectives by exploring the <bio–> family: biology, biography, biodegradable... suddenly, students are seeing patterns across subjects like never before. Ready for some phonetic fun? Introduce the <–ight> gang: light, fight, sight and night. Watch as your students crack the code of English spelling.

This approach is helpful for several reasons. It's like creating a mental spider web of connections, making new words stick because they're linked to familiar concepts. Say goodbye to glazed-over eyes—analogous learning turns vocabulary lessons into exciting explorations. Students aren't just memorising; they're analysing, comparing and making connections using higher-order thinking skills. Plus, this approach works across the board, from science terms to literary devices. But don't just take my word for it. The big guns in educational research are backing this up, showing it activates prior knowledge like a charm (Graves & Prenn, 1986). Analogous learning is a superstar for tackling complex and abstract terms (McKeown et al., 1985) and outperforms traditional methods in vocabulary development (Graves, 1986). Applying this to the Phonology Lens is like giving your students a secret decoder ring for the English language—they'll start seeing patterns in sounds and spellings that they never noticed before.

Teaching Tip!

Drawing an analogy to a phonics chart in your classroom will be helpful, but ensure that it accurately represents the complexity of English phonology. Your chart should include all 44 phonemes (sounds), not just the 26 letters of the alphabet and a single letter–sound correspondence. This way, you will provide your students with a more accurate representation of phonology, creating sustainable links between letters and sounds.

Now, let's map these phonemes (sounds) to their graphemes (letters). Remember to use blue for consonants and red for vowels.

Say to your students, "Time to sound out this word by analogy!" Remind them that we're focusing on phonemes (sounds), not letter names. We're acoustic analysts today!

Using the "conscience" example, you would hear and say aloud the first sound: /k/ as in "cat". Then, write down the grapheme, our visual representation of that /k/ sound: <c>. Colour coding time: use blue for this letter because it's representing a consonant phoneme. Blue for consonants, always.

Next, write the analogous word connection "cat" under the grapheme "c", bridging new information with existing information for students. The letter <c> in "conscience" is the same as the <c> in "cat".

Continue sounding out the phonemes in the word "conscience" using your "phoneme fist". Second finger, take the stage! You're representing our next phoneme.

Say /o/ as in "octagon". Write down the grapheme which represents this phoneme: <o>. Record it in red, because it is a vowel phoneme.

Let's keep our "phoneme fist" going. Now, raise your third finger. This represents our third phoneme: /n/ as in "night". Let's write down the grapheme for this phoneme: it's the letter <n>. Remember to use blue for consonant phonemes.

Okay, fourth finger up! We're onto our fourth phoneme: /ʃ/ as in "conscious".

In "conscience" the letters <s>, <c> and <i> (say the letter names) team up to make the sound /ʃ/, like in the word "conscious". Here, three letters are working together to make that one sound. Three letters making one sound is what we call a "trigraph".

Even though it's three letters, we would still use blue to write it down, because this /ʃ/ sound is a consonant, but let's also underline it.

Now, let's get that fifth finger up! We're tackling the fifth phoneme: /ə/ as in the final syllable of "teacher". Did you catch that subtle sound? We've got something special here: the schwa. It's that neutral unstressed vowel sound. I'm going to pop the IPA symbol above it as a little reminder for us.

Do you notice where this schwa is placed in the word? It's neutral in the final unstressed syllable. Even though it's neutral, our schwa is still the vowel, so I break out the red pen for this one. Red for vowels!

We've run out of fingers on one hand! Let's bring in the other hand and use that thumb for our sixth phoneme: say /n/ as in "night". Sound familiar? We've met this sound before. Let's record this; the grapheme for this phoneme is the letter <n>.

Now, what colour do you think you should use? That's right, blue! Remember our colour code: blue is for consonants.

We're not done yet! Keep that other hand up, and let's add another finger. We're on to our seventh phoneme: /s/ as in "ace".

Now, here's where it gets interesting. In "conscience" the letters <c> and <e> are teaming up. Together, they're making the /s/ sound, just like in the word "ace". Clever, right? When two letters work together to make one sound, we call it a "digraph". Underline it on the graphic organiser.

Even though it's two letters, use your blue pen. Why? Because this /s/ sound is still a consonant phoneme.

48 Using Linguistic Lenses to Journey into Words

3. How many phonemes are there?

As teachers, we're constantly seeking effective strategies to enhance our students' linguistic capabilities. One such powerful tool in our repertoire is the repeated "sounding out" of phonemes. This technique isn't just about pronunciation; it's about equipping our students with a vital skill set for independent learning. By guiding students to break words into individual sounds repeatedly, we're providing them with a robust strategy for both spelling during independent writing and decoding during silent reading. This practice aligns perfectly with the core philosophy of Linguistic Lenses: to provide students with tools they can wield autonomously.

When teaching phoneme segmentation, repeating the process three times is crucial for effective explicit instruction. The first demonstration allows the teacher to clearly segment the phonemes for the entire class, providing a model for all students. The second demonstration benefits students who may have missed or not fully grasped the initial instruction. The final repetition ensures that every student has had ample opportunity to observe and understand the teacher's explicit demonstration. This three-step approach to repetition is essential because it reinforces the concept for quick learners, provides additional chances for students who need more time to process, and ensures comprehensive coverage of the skill for the entire class.

Teaching Tip!
Contextual repetition consistently supports word learning and reading fluency development across various instructional approaches.

Let's delve into the research-backed benefits of repetition:

- **Contextual reinforcement:** Repeated exposure to words within the same context helps students focus on target vocabulary, reducing the cognitive load associated with word learning (Horst, 2013). It's like giving them a familiar map to navigate new linguistic territory.
- **Enhanced retention:** Studies indicate that children exposed to repeated stories retain word-object associations more effectively than those hearing diverse stories, even with equal word exposure (Horst, 2013). Repetition, it seems, is the key to locking words into long-term memory.

- **Automaticity development:** Repeated reading builds both accuracy and speed in word recognition, freeing up cognitive resources for comprehension (Shanahan, 2017). It's about making decoding second nature, allowing students to focus on meaning.
- **Skill application practice:** For students who understand phonics patterns but struggle with fluent application, repeated reading offers crucial practice (Shanahan, 2017). It bridges the gap between knowledge and practical application.
- **Boosted comprehension:** While the primary focus might be on reading words, repeated reading has shown to enhance both oral reading fluency and comprehension (Shanahan, 2017). It's a two-for-one deal in reading proficiency.
- **Universal efficacy:** Research suggests that repeated reading benefits both struggling readers and those in mainstream classrooms (Shanahan, 2017). It's a versatile tool that can be tailored to diverse learning needs.

Now, here's the big question: how many phonemes are there in the word "conscience"?

Let's double-check our work. We're going to use our "phoneme fist" three more times. Ready? Let's sound it out together: /k/, /ɒ/, /n/, /ʃ/, /ə/, /n/, /s/.

One more time: /k/, /ɒ/, /n/, /ʃ/, /ə/, /n/, /s/.

And once more for good measure! /k/, /ɒ/, /n/, /ʃ/, /ə/, /n/, /s/.

Now, the moment of truth: let's count those fingers: One, two, three, four, five, six, seven. Fantastic! We've discovered that there are seven phonemes in the word "conscience"—seven sounds working together to create one powerful word. Let's write that down.

You know, I want to share something interesting with you. As we grow older, sounding out words can sometimes become trickier. It's like a muscle—if we don't exercise our language skills and phoneme awareness regularly, they might get a bit rusty. That's why what we're doing right now is so important.

Contemplate and Consider!

Before you guide your students through this, it's important to sharpen your own skills. So, teachers, are you ready for a phoneme-counting challenge?

1. Read each word in the list below silently.
2. Close your eyes. (It helps you focus on sounds.)
3. Say the word aloud s-l-ow-l-y, focusing on each individual sound.
4. Count the phonemes. (Remember, we're counting sounds, not letters!)
5. Write down your answer.
6. Compare with a colleague—did you get the same count?

Let the phoneme hunt begin!

1. <necessary>
2. <accommodation>
3. <nutritious>

Bonus challenges:

- Identify the sneaky schwa sounds in these words.
- Find any phonemes represented by multiple letters (digraphs or trigraphs).

Remember:

- Phonemes are the smallest units of sound in spoken language.
- The number of phonemes often differs from the number of letters.
- Some sounds (like the schwa) can be tricky to spot!

After completing the activity, discuss with your colleagues:

- Which word was the hardest to sound out?
- Did you notice any patterns or interesting features in these words?
- How might this exercise help you empathise with your students' experiences?

By honing our own phoneme awareness, we're better equipped to guide our students through this skill!

Answer Key

1. <necessary>: 8 phonemes
   /n/ /e/ /s/ /ə/ /s/ /e/ /r/ /iː/
2. <accommodation>: 10 phonemes
   /ə/ /k/ /ɒ/ /m/ /ə/ /d/ /eɪ/ /ʃ/ /ə/ /n/

3. <nutritious>: 9 phonemes
    /n/ /j/ /u:/ /t/ /r/ /ɪ/ /ʃ/ /ə/ /s/

Note: the exact number of phonemes may vary slightly depending on the specific accent or pronunciation guide used. This answer key is based on standard Australian English pronunciation.

Bonus challenges:

- In <necessary>, the second <e> is pronounced as a schwa /ə/. In <accommodation>, the first letter <a>, seventh letter <o> and the final <o> are pronounced as schwas /ə/. In <nutritious>, the <ou> is pronounced as a schwa /ə/.
- In <necessary>, the <ss> digraph represents the /s/ sound. In <accommodation>, the <cc> digraph represents the /k/ sound and the <mm> digraph represents the /m/ sound. In <nutritious>, the <ti> digraph represents the /ʃ/ sound.

4. Blend the phonemes together

As students progress through their academic journey, the ability to blend phonemes becomes an increasingly powerful tool in their linguistic toolbox. Far from being a basic skill reserved for early readers, phoneme blending is a sophisticated technique that can significantly enhance reading fluency, vocabulary acquisition and spelling accuracy for upper primary and secondary students:

- **Reading fluency:** Imagine your students effortlessly gliding through complex texts, their reading as smooth as silk. This is the power of phoneme blending in action. By practicing the skill of combining individual sounds swiftly and accurately, students develop a reading fluency that allows them to focus more on comprehension and less on decoding.
- **Vocabulary expansion:** In the face of unfamiliar vocabulary—a common challenge in advanced novels and secondary-school texts—phoneme blending becomes a secret weapon. When students encounter a new word, instead of reaching for a dictionary or skipping over it entirely, they can break the word down into individual phonemes, segmenting each phoneme and blending the phonemes back together. This process not only helps them pronounce the word correctly but also provides a foundation for understanding its meaning through context or word parts.

- **Spelling accuracy:** Segmenting and blending isn't just for reading—it's a two-way street that leads to improved spelling as well. When writing, students can segment the word they want to spell into individual phonemes, identify the graphemes that represent each sound and record them to form the correct spelling. This approach transforms spelling from a memorisation challenge into a logical process, boosting both accuracy and confidence.

We're going to blend the phonemes of "conscience" together. Are you ready?

Now, when I say "blend", we're going to merge or push these sounds together, like we're zipping up a jacket. We're creating one smooth word from all these individual sounds.

Start with the first phoneme, /k/, and then slide your finger across the phoneme boxes. It's like creating a sound train, with each phoneme as a new cart.

Here we go! /k/, /ɒ/, /n/, /ʃ/, /ə/, /n/, /s/. Did you hear how those individual sounds came together to form our word "conscience"?

That's the power of phoneme blending. This is how we build words from their smallest sound parts.

5. How many consonant and vowel phonemes are there?

First, let's talk about consonants. These are the sounds we make when we partially close our mouths or obstruct airflow with our lips, teeth, or tongue. It's like creating little sound barriers! Some consonants are voiced—that means our vocal cords vibrate when we make them. Others are unvoiced—just a push of air, no vibration.

Now, here's a question for you: how many consonant phonemes are there in our word "conscience"?

Let's go back to page 48 and count them together. We'll mark each consonant phoneme with the letter <c> underneath. Ready?

We've found five consonant phonemes. Can you believe it? Five out of seven!

Here's a fun fact to remember: there are 24 consonant phonemes in English. That's a lot of sounds to play with!

Now, let's switch to vowels. Vowel phonemes are like the free spirits of sounds: they flow freely without any significant obstruction. When we make vowel sounds, it's almost like we're singing.

So, here's our next challenge: how many vowel phonemes are there in "conscience"?

Let's mark each vowel phoneme with a <v>. Count with me...

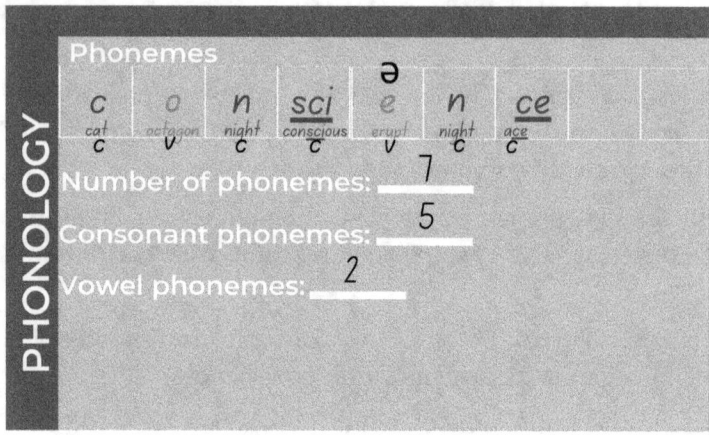

Excellent! We've found two vowel phonemes.

Remember this: there are 20 vowel phonemes in English. And those letters <a>, <e>, <i>, <o> and <u>? They're only vowel indicators.

Now, here's something to notice. How many vowels did we find? Two. And how many syllables are in "conscience"? Also two! That's not a coincidence. Every syllable needs to have a vowel. It's like each syllable has a vowel heart.

As children progress in their literacy journey, they may find it increasingly difficult to process and manipulate the sounds of language. This challenge arises from several factors: the growing complexity of vocabulary, a shift towards whole-word recognition, higher expectations for reading fluency and, sometimes, a reduced emphasis on explicit phonological instruction in later years. However, this is precisely why continuing to exercise our language muscles is beneficial, with a particular focus on phonological awareness and phoneme sensitivity.

Teaching Tip!

To reinforce the key concepts of English phonology and help both you and your students remember the distinctions between graphemes and phonemes, consider using this concise breakdown:

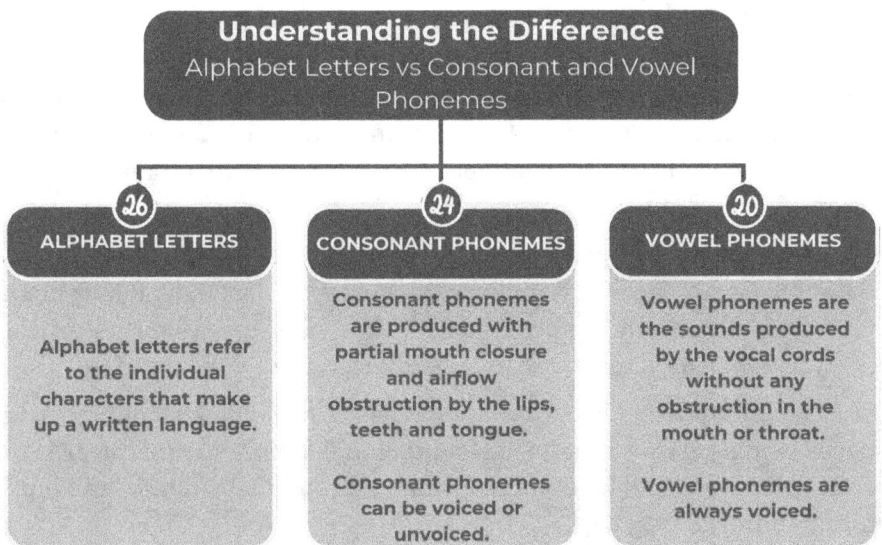

Letters of the alphabet represent written characters, while phonemes represent sounds.

Case study: challenging phonetic conventions—the Eugenie effect

As teachers, we often encounter moments that challenge our established teaching practices and push us to reconsider our approach. This case study explores one such pivotal moment that occurred during my first week as a curriculum leader at a new school and demonstrates how a simple classroom activity can spark a re-evaluation of our consideration of consonants and vowels.

Picture a vibrant Year 1 classroom buzzing with energy as I prepared to deliver a demonstration literacy lesson. The room was filled with eager students and observant teachers, all ready to engage in what seemed like a routine phonics exercise. Little did we know that a simple ice-breaker activity would lead to a profound learning opportunity for everyone present.

The activity involved students volunteering to "jump" around a phonics chart—displaying the 44 phonemes, divided into 24 consonants and 20 vowels—to sound out the phonemes in their name.

The rules were simple: crossing the middle line meant moving from consonants to vowels, and each jump across the middle line signified a syllable in a word. It was a creative way to visualise the structure of words and engage kinaesthetic learners.

The first student to volunteer was a Year 1 student named Eugenie. Her enthusiasm was palpable, but her name immediately sparked murmurs among the observing teachers. Why? Because Eugenie's name presented a unique challenge to the conventional rules of phonics that many teachers rely on.

If we adhered to the common teaching that <a>, <e>, <i>, <o>, <u> and sometimes <y> represent vowels, Eugenie's name would contain five vowels. This would imply that her name had five syllables—a clear contradiction of its actual three syllables: Eu/ge/nie.

This scenario perfectly illustrates the pitfalls of teaching absolute rules in English without a strong linguistic foundation. It's a prime example of how oversimplification can lead to confusion and potentially hinder students' understanding of language.

Embracing linguistic complexity instead of relying on rigid rules, I guided Eugenie through a more sustainable approach to learning:

1. **Sound identification:** We focused on identifying the actual sounds (phonemes) in her name, rather than just the letters.
2. **IPA:** I introduced the use of IPA symbols to accurately represent the sounds, demonstrating how this method can bridge the gap between spelling and pronunciation.
3. **Analogy and context:** We explored how the same letters can produce different sounds in various words, using Eugenie's name as a starting point:
    - <e> = consonant sound /j/ (as in "neutral")
    - <u> = vowel sound /uː/ (as in "flu")
    - <g> = consonant sound /ʒ/ (as in "genre")
    - <e> = vowel sound /eɪ/ (as in "café")
    - <n> = consonant sound /n/ (as in "net")
    - <ie> = digraph making the vowel sound /iː/ (as in "movie").

Here are the key takeaways for teachers:

1. **Avoid oversimplification:** Teaching absolute rules in English can set students up for confusion and failure.
2. **Embrace linguistic complexity:** Equip students with the understanding that letters are just letters until they are in a word.
3. **Utilise tools like IPA:** Introduce more advanced linguistic concepts to provide students with a deeper understanding of language structure.
4. **Personalise learning:** Use students' names and familiar words to make phonic concepts more relatable and memorable.
5. **Engage in continuous learning:** As teachers, we must constantly update our own understanding of language to provide accurate and comprehensive instruction.

The case study of "Eugenie" brilliantly illustrates the complexity of English vowels and the potential pitfalls of oversimplified teaching. While it's commonly taught that <a>, <e>, <i>, <o>, <u> and sometimes <y> represent vowels in English, Eugenie's name demonstrates why this approach can be misleading. In reality, these letters are vowel indicators in writing, but they don't accurately represent the full range of approximately 20 distinct vowel phonemes in spoken English. Eugenie's name, despite containing several of these vowel indicators, is pronounced with only three syllables, not the five that a simplistic application of vowel rules might suggest. This discrepancy highlights the crucial difference between written vowel indicators and actual vowel sounds. The case study also shows how the letter <e> in "Eugenie" can represent both a consonant sound (/j/ like in "yellow") and different vowel sounds (/eɪ/ as in "café" and /iː/ as in "movie").

By using the IPA, Linguistic Lenses advocates for a more sustainable strategy to teach consonants and vowels. The Phonology Lens not only clarifies the true nature of vowels in English but also equips students with a more accurate and flexible understanding of language structure, better preparing them to navigate the perceived complexities of English pronunciation and spelling.

Contemplate and Consider!

What is the difference between alphabet letters, consonant phonemes and vowel phonemes?

Take a few minutes to contemplate the following points. Jot down your thoughts and then discuss with a colleague or in a small group.

Contemplate:

- how letters are visual representations, while phonemes are sounds
- the number of each (26 letters versus 44 phonemes in English)
- how one letter can represent multiple phonemes and vice versa.

Consider:

- how this section has challenged your thinking of consonant and vowel phonemes
- any misconceptions you might have had
- new insights you might have gained about the complexity of English phonology
- how this knowledge might impact your teaching approach.

Share your reflections with colleagues. What new perspectives did you gain from others' insights?

Implement and Innovate!

This activity prepares you to effectively communicate complex phonological concepts to a non-specialist audience.

Imagine you're tasked with explaining to parents or colleagues why the traditional explanation that <a>, <e>, <i>, <o>, <u> and sometimes <y> represent vowels is inadequate for understanding English phonology:

1. Brainstorm your explanation strategy. Consider using analogies, visual aids or interactive demonstrations, such as a sound-symbol chart to show multiple sounds for each vowel letter.
2. Develop a list of examples that highlight the complexity of English vowel sounds, such as of how context changes vowel sounds in words.
3. Practice your explanation with a colleague, getting feedback on clarity and engagement.

Here are some example points you could raise:

- Graphemes can be used to represent a number of phonemes. Consider the graph <a>, which can represent multiple sounds: /æ/ as in "cat"; /eɪ/ as in "cake"; /ɑː/ as in "father"; /ə/ as in "about". Also, compare the digraph <ea> in "head" versus in "bead" and the quadgraph <ough> in "through" versus in "thought".

- The letter <y> can represent both consonants and vowels: /j/ as in "yellow" (consonant); /i:/ as in "happy" (vowel); /aɪ/ as in "fly" (vowel).
- The schwa /ə/ can be represented by many graphemes: <a> in "about"; <e> in "taken"; <i> in "pencil"; <o> in "lemon"; <u> in "supply"; <y> in "vinyl".

6. What are the first and final sounds?

Have you read any Roald Dahl? He's the genius behind *Charlie and the Chocolate Factory* and *Matilda*. Well, Dahl was a master of playing with sounds to create hilarious and unforgettable words. Imagine if we could twist and turn sounds like Dahl did. We could turn "human being" into "human bean" or invent delicious-sounding treats like "snozzberries"!

This technique is called "phoneme manipulation". It's when we change the order of sounds, swap one sound for another, or even add or remove sounds. When we read Dahl's books, we're not just enjoying a story—we're exploring how flexible and fun our language can be.

Now, let's play with some sounds ourselves. We're going to focus on our word "conscience". Are you ready?

Here's our first challenge: What's the first sound in the word "conscience"? It's /k/ as in "cat".

Now for our second challenge: What's the final sound in the word "conscience"? It's /s/ as in "ace". Notice how it's like a little hiss at the end of the word?

Isn't it amazing how we can break words down into these tiny sounds and then build them back up again?

7. What do you hear if you take off the first, final or medial sound?

We're going to play a game with our word "conscience".

Here's the first challenge: what do you hear if we take off the first sound? Let's try it together. Cover up the /k/ sound at the beginning. Now, let's sound out what's left... Did you hear that? Without the /k/, we get something like "onscience". It's not a real word, but it sure sounds funny!

Here's the next challenge: what do you hear if we take off the final sound? Cover the /s/ at the end. Let's sound it out... Wow! Without the /s/, we get something like "conscien". Again, not a real word, but isn't it interesting how different it sounds?

Now for our trickiest challenge: what do you hear if we take out the middle sound? Cover the /ʃ/ sound in the middle of the word. Let's try sounding it out without it... That's a tough one, isn't it? We get something like "conence".

Isn't it amazing how changing just one sound can make such a big difference? By noticing how each sound contributes to the word, we're training our brains to pay attention to all the little details in words.

This is exactly the kind of thing that authors like Roald Dahl do when they're inventing funny new words. They play around with sounds, just like we're doing!

8. How many voiced and unvoiced phonemes are there?

Place your fingers gently on your voice box. Can you feel it? That's where the magic happens!

We're going to play a game called "Voiced or Unvoiced?". It's like being a sound detective and a human buzzer all at once!

Here's how it works: sound out the word "conscience" again, but this time, pay attention to what's happening in your voice box. If you feel a buzz or vibration under your fingers when you make a sound, that's a voiced phoneme. It's like your voice box is giving you a tiny massage. If you don't feel any vibration and just feel a push of air, that's an unvoiced phoneme. It's like your voice box is taking a little nap.

Are you ready?

- /k/: Did you feel anything? No vibration, just air, right? That's unvoiced!
- /ɒ/: Oh, a big vibration there! That's voiced.
- /n/: Another vibration! Voiced again.
- /ʃ/: Just air this time. Unvoiced.
- /ə/: A little vibration. Voiced!
- /n/: Vibration again. Voiced.
- /s/: Just air. Unvoiced.

Record the number of voiced and unvoiced phonemes on the LLGO.

Isn't it amazing how some sounds make our voice box buzz while others don't? It's like each sound has its own personality! This is actually how we make different sounds in our language. Some sounds need our vocal cords to vibrate, while others just need air.

Next time you're saying a word, try feeling your voice box. You'll be amazed by how much is going on in there!

Case study: Edie's prose

The case of Edie, a six-year-old student in her first year of primary school, serves as a compelling example of how a truthful approach to language instruction can yield remarkable results.

Picture a bustling classroom in early October, the air thick with the excitement of new learning. Amid the chatter and rustling of papers, we focus on Edie, an "average" student with an extraordinary gift for language. What sets her apart isn't innate talent but, rather, having been taught a logical approach to the truth of English orthography from the beginning of her schooling.

The following piece of writing, independently produced by Edie at the start of Term 4, defies the expectations typically held for a student her age. The sophistication of her vocabulary and sentence structure prompted many teachers to want to understand the pedagogical approach that fostered such impressive results.

> I see a ruby crevice, it looks moist. I see rosey/red lumpy crevices things there bunched up like a peloton of bibe riders riding in a race I see horifiing things that make me want to throwup with sickness I see desckusting bumpy maroon things that I think they are squishy I think they are inside our mouth as tonsills. I wonder if its our bumpy lips I wonder if its inside our legs that put presher on them to help us walk. I wonder if it is our cryativ brain. I think it is strange that is a rose petile. It is strange that it dosen't look bumpy but it is. I wonder why it is lumpy.

Challenging the notion that spelling follows a rigid developmental trajectory, Edie's instruction exposed her to all 44 phonemes of the English language simultaneously. This approach aligns with recent research in cognitive science, particularly the work of Mark Seidenberg, whose "triangle" model of reading highlights the interconnected nature of orthography, phonology and semantics in skilled reading (Seidenberg & McClelland, 1989). Introducing all phonemes concurrently taps into the brain's capacity for statistical learning, allowing students to implicitly learn patterns in the relationships between spellings, sounds and meanings of words (Seidenberg, 2017). As teachers, we know that flexibility in our instruction is key, so this approach allows us to balance explicit instruction (teaching the phonemes and spelling patterns directly) with implicit learning (allowing students to discover and internalise patterns through their creative process). This balance is important, as while most learners need some explicit instruction, it must be thoughtfully balanced with implicit learning opportunities (Seidenberg, 2023). Explicit instruction serves to scaffold statistical or implicit learning.

It's important to note here that this approach doesn't disregard the value of systematic phonics instruction, which has been shown to be effective (National Reading Panel, 2000). Instead, it enhances it by embedding phonics within a richer context of language exploration, aligning with Seidenberg's critique of "whole language" approaches and his advocacy for evidence-based reading instruction that incorporates insights from cognitive science (Seidenberg, 2017).

Returning to Edie's work, one particular spelling error provides a fascinating insight into her linguistic development: the word "disgusting" appears as "desckusting", revealing a subtle but significant phoneme confusion.

We can analyse this through multiple lenses:

1. **Phoneme awareness:** Edie demonstrates a sophisticated grasp of phonemes, making plausible grapheme choices for most sounds she hears. However, her error highlights a specific challenge in distinguishing between voiced and unvoiced consonant pairs.
2. **Voiced versus unvoiced phonemes:** The crux of Edie's misspelling lies in the substitution of the unvoiced /k/ (represented by <ck>) for the voiced /g/. This substitution is particularly interesting because /k/ and /g/ are phonemic pairs, identical in all aspects except for voicing.
3. **Phonological analysis:** Edie's spelling suggests she's pronouncing the word as /dɪskʌstɪŋ/ instead of the correct /dɪsgʌstɪŋ/. This

indicates she's not yet fully differentiating between the voiced /g/ and its unvoiced counterpart /k/ in this word context. It's a common developmental stage where children may struggle to perceive or produce the subtle difference in voicing. However, it's important for me to note that this particular word presents a unique challenge: the /g/ in "disgusting" immediately follows /s/, an unvoiced sound, which can naturally lead to assimilation—a process where the voicing of one sound influences adjacent sounds. This means Edie's pronunciation could be seen as a result of a natural phonological process rather than solely a developmental error. As teachers, we can use this insight to inform our instruction. Here, my focus was on helping Edie distinguish between voiced and unvoiced consonants, especially in challenging contexts like this.

4. **Morphological awareness:** Despite the phoneme confusion, Edie correctly applies the <-ing> suffix, demonstrating a solid understanding of basic morphological principles. This shows her ability to recognise and manipulate word structures even when grappling with phoneme challenges.
5. **Etymology:** This error presents an excellent opportunity to explore the word's French origins, linking *des-* (opposite of) with *gouster* (taste). Discussing etymology can reinforce the correct pronunciation and spelling, emphasising the voiced /g/ sound in its historical context.

Here are some practical takeaways from this case study:

- Utilise writing samples as diagnostic tools to understand students' instructional needs.
- Introduce etymological discussions even with young learners to deepen their understanding of word meanings and spellings.
- Encourage the use of resources like thesauruses to expand vocabulary from an early age.
- Don't shy away from introducing complex linguistic concepts—students often rise to the challenge when given the opportunity.

The case study of Edie's writing sample serves as a powerful testament to the potential that lies within young learners when they are provided with rich, comprehensive language instruction from an early age. It underscores the importance of explicitly teaching the distinction between voiced and unvoiced consonants, particularly in pairs like /k/ and /g/, /t/ and /d/, and /f/ and /v/. By addressing these subtle phoneme differences, you can help students like Edie refine their pronunciation and, consequently, their spelling accuracy. As renowned literacy expert Dr Louisa Moats observes, "Children's brains are remarkably plastic. When we provide rich, comprehensive language instruction early on, we're not just teaching reading and writing—we're literally shaping neural pathways that will benefit students throughout their lives".

9. How many syllables?

Remember how we talked about vowels being the heart of each syllable? Well, we're going to see that in action now.

First, let's do something fun. We're going to clap out the syllables in our word "conscience". Ready? Let's do it together!

CON (clap) SCIENCE (clap).

Did you hear that? Two claps! That means our word has two syllables.

Now, I'm going to mark where we break these syllables with a black dot.

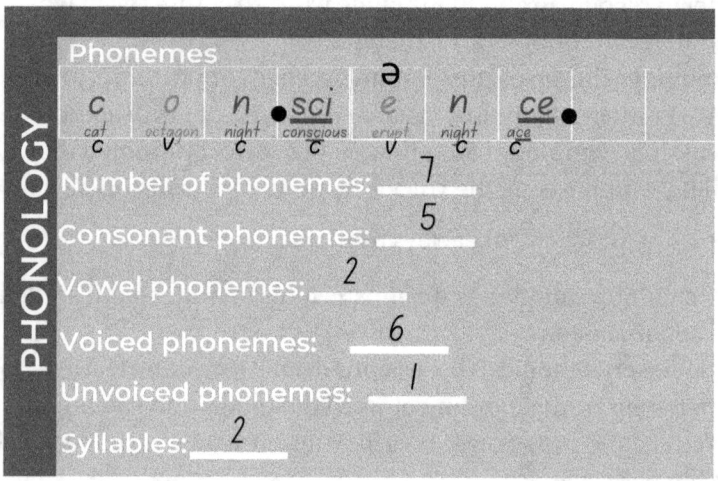

Can you see how each syllable has a vowel sound? In <con> we have the /ɒ/ sound and in "science" we have the /ə/ sound. It's like each syllable has its own vowel heartbeat!

This is really important. Every syllable in every word *must* have a vowel sound. Without it, our words would sound like a jumble of consonants. Isn't it amazing? Even in the shortest words, there's always at least one vowel sound. It's like the glue that holds our words together.

Sometimes, even language experts disagree about how many syllables a word has or where to break them. That's because when we speak, we might stress different parts of words, which can change how we hear the syllables. This is why, when we're learning to spell or read new words, we need to pay extra attention to these vowel sounds and syllables. So, next time a student is struggling to read a big word, encourage them to try breaking it into syllables and listen for those vowel sounds—they'll guide the student through the word like little language lighthouses!

10. Can you think of rhyming words?

When we rhyme, we're playing with the sounds in words. It's like we're creating little word songs in our heads. And guess what? This helps us remember words better.

Now, let's focus on our word "conscience". We're going to explore its sound structure.

The word "conscience" ends with the combination of sounds /əns/. For perfect rhymes, we need words whose stressed syllables share identical sounds, as do all sounds that follow the stressed syllable.

Now for the fun part: what are some other words that rhyme with "conscience"?

- Sentence
- Patience
- Presence.

These words share the same ending sound /əns/, which includes the vowel and the following consonants.

When we rhyme like this, we're actually training our ears to hear the smaller sounds in words. And here's a fun fact: the words "rhythm" and "rhyme" actually come from the same root word in history. It's like they're word cousins.

Next time you're reading a poem or singing a song, pay attention to the rhymes. You'll start noticing these sound patterns everywhere.

11. Can you identify an NPS (non-phonographic spelling)?

Let's break down the concept of NPS in a friendly way! Imagine you're saying a word, and there's a sneaky sound hiding in there that doesn't show up in the spelling. That's what we call an NPS, or non-phonographic spelling. It's like a game of hide-and-seek between sounds and letters!

The word "phonographic" is made up of <phono->, the sound (phoneme) you hear, and <-graphic>, the letter (grapheme) you see. Sometimes, you'll hear a sound when you say a word, but when you look at the spelling, there's no letter to represent it. Tricky, right? Don't worry if you get stuck on any fancy terms. Remember, your Teacher's Toolkit is always there at the beginning of each chapter, ready to help you out.

Let's look at two interesting words: "chasm" and "enthusiasm". At first glance, these words might seem a bit odd. Where's the vowel in the last syllable? But here's where we put on our detective hats and use the IPA—our secret code that shows us exactly how words sound.

Let's look at "chasm" first. In IPA, it's written as /kæz.əm/. Do you see that little upside-down "e"? There's a schwa in this word that's not present in the orthography. Now for "enthusiasm". In IPA, it's /ɪnθu:zi:æzəm/. Look at that—there's our friend the schwa again. So, even though our eyes might not see a vowel grapheme at the end of these words, our ears can hear that sneaky schwa.

The schwa sound is like the ninja of vowels. It's everywhere—in fact, it's the most common vowel sound in modern English—but it's often hard to spot in spelling. This is why it's so important for us as teachers to have tools like the IPA. It helps us uncover the hidden sounds in words and explain why English spelling can sometimes seem tricky.

Remember, every syllable needs a vowel phoneme, even if we can't always see a vowel grapheme. Next time you come across a word that seems to be missing a vowel, remember our friend the schwa. It might just be playing hide and seek!

Consonant phonemes can also be hiding in words. For example, let's break down "newspaper" using the IPA:

n j u: z. p eɪ. p ə.
n ew s. p a. p er.

Notice the /j/ sound highlighted in the image that isn't represented by a specific letter in the spelling. This "invisible sound" often leads to spelling errors as students attempt to represent every sound they hear, especially in the earlier years of schooling!

12. Read and record the IPA

If you look up the word "conscience" in the dictionary, you'll see some unusual symbols. These are the IPA symbols that represent the exact pronunciation of the word.

The IPA transcription of "conscience" is /ˈkɒn.ʃəns/. Each of these symbols represents a specific sound in English. By learning these symbols, we can accurately pronounce any word, even if we've never heard it before.

Now, let's record this on our LLGO. Above each letter, or grapheme, we'll write the corresponding IPA symbol. This helps us see how the written letters relate to the actual sounds.

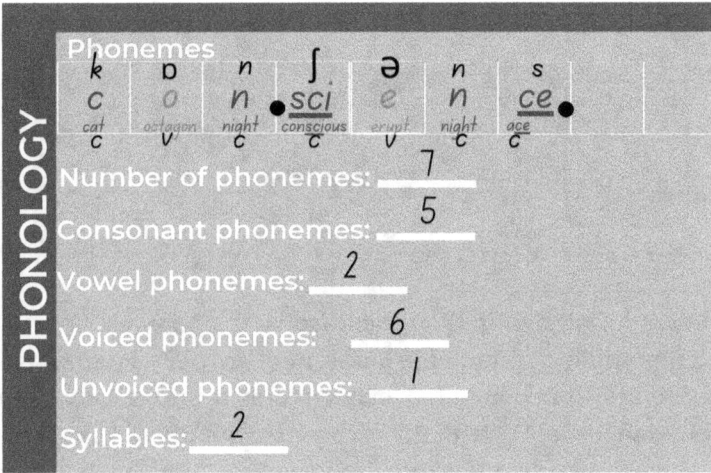

Let's take a closer look at how we've recorded the IPA symbols. Pay close attention to the alignment between the graphemes and phonemes.

See the letters <sci>? Even though there are three letters, they're represented by just one IPA symbol: /ʃ/. So, together they're a trigraph. This is important to understand. It shows us that sometimes multiple letters work together to create a single sound.

This is why it's so important to carefully place each IPA symbol in the correct position above the graphemes. It helps us visualise how letters combine to form sounds, which isn't always a one-to-one relationship in English.

By using the IPA, students can break down any word into its sound components. This is incredibly useful for improving their pronunciation and understanding the relationship between spelling and sound in English. Remember, this tool is always available to help them with pronunciation.

Case study: the power of IPA in upper primary and secondary classrooms

This case study explores how the IPA can be leveraged as a powerful tool in upper primary and secondary classrooms, fostering student agency.

Amid the usual hum of activity in my Year 4 classroom, nine-year-old Tessa is hunched over her work, scribbling intently in the margin. When approached, she reveals a strategy that would impress even seasoned linguists: unable to spell "consciousness", she's transcribing it into IPA symbols.

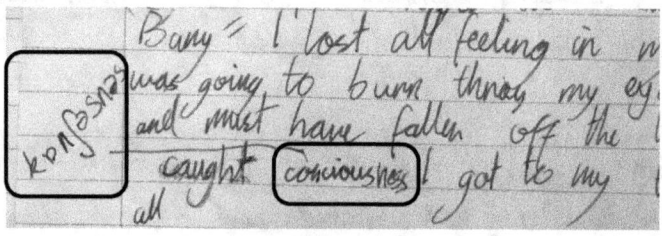

This moment of student-led problem-solving opens a window to the untapped potential of phoneme awareness in our classrooms. Tessa's approach demonstrates how IPA can serve as a bridge between spoken and written language, particularly for words with challenging phoneme–grapheme correspondences, and empower students to tackle spelling challenges independently. Her ability to identify sounds correctly indicates strong phonemic skills.

English, with its 44 sounds represented by over 200 possible graphemes, presents unique challenges for learners. The IPA serves as a universal code, allowing students to visualise sounds consistently, irrespective of spelling variations.

Case study: "Wednesday" in Year 4

To further illustrate the practical application of IPA, let's examine a lesson on spelling "Wednesday" with Year 4 students:

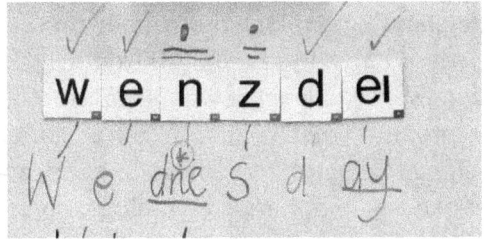

IPA Tiles © The THRASS Institute Australasia & Canada

I used IPA tiles to display the phonetic transcription /wɛnzdeɪ/. We identified the "easier" parts of the word, ticking which parts the students felt confident with, and recognised that the "tricky" part of the word was the <dne> trigraph representing the /n/ phoneme. This allowed students to focus without being overwhelmed by the entire word. This approach aligns with research on working memory capacity in different age groups (Neer, 2015), ensuring that information is presented in manageable chunks.

Case study: decoding spelling errors

Consider another Year 4 student's attempt at spelling "exist" as "igseist".

Traditional approaches might simply correct the error. However, a more informative analysis reveals:

- contextual understanding (the student used the word correctly in a sentence)
- phoneme accuracy (all sounds were correctly identified; you can hear the Aussie pronunciation!)
- plausible grapheme choices (the spelling shows logical sound-symbol correspondence).

Here are some instructional strategies to use in this situation:

- **Validate phoneme awareness:** Acknowledge the student's accurate sound identification.
- **Introduce IPA transcription:** Show the student the IPA spelling /ɪgzɪst/ to bridge pronunciation and orthography, and explain why they may have made their spelling choices. Notice that the spelling error wasn't too far off the IPA transcription!

- **Encourage etymological exploration:** Discuss any root word.
- **Analyse the morphological family:** Explore related words, such as "exist" and "existence" to reinforce spelling patterns.

This approach not only corrects the immediate error but also builds a framework for understanding similar words, enhancing long-term retention and linguistic awareness. Begin by gradually introducing IPA symbols, using them as a tool to demystify challenging words and sounds. This foundation will allow you to promote metacognition by encouraging students to articulate their spelling strategies, thereby fostering deeper metalinguistic awareness. Simultaneously, emphasise etymology, connecting spelling to word origins to make orthographic choices more logical and memorable for your students. Leverage IPA to differentiate instruction, addressing individual student needs, particularly for those grappling with phoneme-grapheme correspondences. This integrated approach represents a paradigm shift in spelling instruction, providing students with powerful tools to decode the complexities of English orthography. As Tessa's case demonstrates, when students understand the logic behind how words are spelled, they're better equipped to tackle unfamiliar words independently.

13. Is there a schwa?

Remember how we talked about the schwa being like a ninja vowel? Well, it's also kind of like the lazy cousin of vowels: it doesn't like to put in too much effort!

The schwa often appears in unstressed syllables and is often referred to as the "neutral" vowel. That means it doesn't get a lot of emphasis when we say it. It's like it's trying to hide in the word.

Let's focus on our word "conscience" again. Can you hear the schwa in there? It's in the last syllable.

Say it with me: "CON-science". Do you hear that "uh" sound near the end? That's our schwa! Here's a fun way to remember it: imagine someone jabs you in the ribs and you go "uh!" That's the sound of the schwa!

Now, here's something cool. In "conscience", the schwa sound is represented by the letter <e>. But remember, the schwa can be represented by a range of graphemes. For example, in the word "about", the <a> also makes a schwa sound, or in the word "measure", the trigraph <ure> represents a schwa sound. This is why English spelling can sometimes feel like a puzzle. The same sound can be spelled in different ways, and the same letter can make different sounds.

Now that you know about the schwa, when you're reading or spelling and you come across an unstressed vowel sound, think, "Could this be a schwa?"

14. Is there a diphone?

Sometimes one letter can make multiple sounds. We call this a "diphone". Think of a diphone like a letter that's really good at multitasking: it's doing two jobs at once.

Let's look at some examples. The word "emu" might look simple, but it's hiding a secret. That <u> at the end? It's actually making two sounds: /j/ (like the <y> in "yawn") and /uː/ (like the <oo> in "moon"). So "emu" actually has four sounds: /iː/, /m/, /j/ and /uː/. It's like the <u> is a magician pulling two sounds out of its hat!

This happens in other words too, like "music" and "ambulance". Listen carefully—can you hear how the <u> is doing double duty?

Now, let's talk about another example: the letter <x>. In words like "ox" and "box", <x> is also a diphone. It's not making one sound but two: /k/ and /s/. So "ox" actually has three sounds: /ɒ/, /k/ and /s/. In some words, <x> changes completely: in "exam", it's a diphone representing /g/ and /z/.

And here's one more mind-bender: in the word "once", the <o> is also a diphone. It's making the /w/ sound and /ʌ/ sound. So "once" has four sounds too: /w/, /ʌ/, /n/ and /s/.

This is why this knowledge is important right from the beginning of schooling. These are not advanced words or concepts! The fact is, more often than not, the sounds we hear don't match up one-to-one with the letters we see.

Case study: "rivulets"

In this case study, Year 6 students are engrossed in *Chinese Cinderella* by Adeline Yen Mah, their current novel study, when a seemingly simple sentence sparks a linguistic journey that will challenge their understanding of phonology and orthography: "Rivulets of water dripped from my hair."

As the class encounters this vivid description, a hand shoots up. "How do you pronounce 'rivulets'?" The question hangs in the air, a perfect opportunity to delve into the intricacies of English pronunciation and spelling.

To address the query, I write the IPA transcription on the board: /rɪvjuːləts/. "Look closely at the <u> in 'rivulets'," I prompt. "In the IPA, it's represented by /juː/. This is what we call a diphone—one letter making two sounds."

A student's eyes light up. "That's like 'futilely' from last week!" Indeed, we had explored this word the previous week, noting its similar phonetic structure.

This observation leads us to a thought-provoking discussion. "If the <u> makes two sounds, /j/ and /uː/, is it a consonant or a vowel?" The class buzzes with debate, challenging the conventional notion of vowels being limited to <a>, <e>, <i>, <o>, <u> and sometimes <y>.

We dissect "rivulets" further:

- Phonemes: 9 (/r/, /ɪ/, /v/, /j/, /uː/, /l/, /ə/, /t/, /s/)
- Syllables: 3 (ri-vu-lets)
- Vowel phonemes: 3 (/ɪ/, /uː/, /ə/).

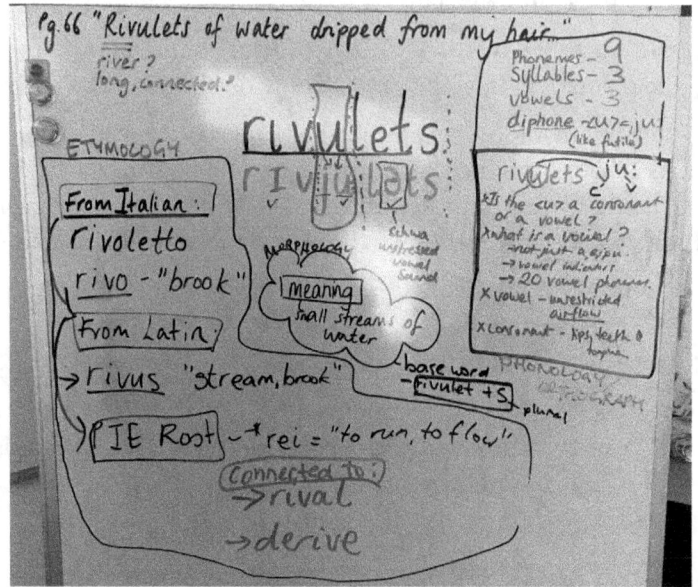

As we focus on the vowel phonemes, I answer the question: "In this word, the grapheme <u> is represented by two phonemes (sounds), a consonant and vowel phoneme. We can hear the vowel phoneme as we clap the syllable 'riv-u-lets'. This is called a "diphone"—one letter making two sounds." If I were to write this down in my LLGO, I could use either a black pen with a dotted line down the middle and then write the corresponding IPA symbol on each side, or I could write the letter in half red and half blue. This colour-coding indicates that this letter represents two sounds, both a consonant and a vowel—it's a diphone!

This case study demonstrates the power of integrating advanced linguistic concepts into everyday literacy instruction. By drawing upon our confidence in teaching linguistic metalanguage and terminology to embrace these teachable moments, we transform routine novel study lessons into vibrant linguistic investigations. Understanding diphones and the fluid nature of consonants and vowels in English helps students approach unfamiliar words with greater confidence and phonological sensitivity.

Teaching Tip!
- **IPA word wall:** Create a display of challenging words from your novel studies, complete with IPA transcriptions. Encourage students to add to it as they encounter new words.
- **Diphone detective:** Challenge students to find other words with diphones in their reading, fostering ongoing awareness of this linguistic feature.
- **Etymology exploration:** Extend the discussion by exploring the origins of words like "rivulet" (from Latin <rivulus>, diminutive of <rivus>, meaning "stream"), connecting pronunciation to word history.

15. Break it into onset and rime

Some syllables in some words are like a little word sandwich; they have two parts—the onset and the rime:

- The **onset** is like the entrée of the syllable. It's the consonant sound or sounds that come before the vowel.
- The **rime** is like the main course of the syllable. It includes the vowel and any consonants that come after it.

Now, let's look at our word "conscience". How many syllables does it have? That's right, two!

In the first syllable, <con>, we hear /kɒn/. Let's break it down:

- The onset is /k/. It's the entrée, the starting sound.
- The rime is /ɒn/. It's the main course, the vowel and what follows.

Now for the second syllable, "science", we hear /ʃəns/. Let's break that down too:

- The onset is /ʃ/. It's that <sh> sound at the beginning.
- The rime is /əns/. It's the rest of the syllable, including our lazy friend the schwa!

Tracking and Monitoring Student Progress in Phonology

Monitoring the progress of phonological skills in upper primary students involves ongoing assessment and observation to track their growth. Following are examples of progress-monitoring activities for older students, which will provide you with valuable insights into your students' phonological skill development and help guide instructional decisions to support their continued growth.

1. **Observation and anecdotal records:**
   - Observe students during phonological sensitivity and phoneme awareness activities, and record anecdotal notes on their progress. Document their ability to blend, segment and manipulate sounds during class activities, small group sessions or independent work.
   - While students are segmenting words into individual phonemes, document observations of their proficiency. Record specific examples of students accurately segmenting words as well as instances when they struggle.
   - Observe how students identify and generate rhyming words. Note students' ability to recognise rhyming patterns and produce rhyming words independently.
   - Observe students' application of phonological skills during reading and writing tasks. Note how students use their phonological knowledge to decode unfamiliar words, spell challenging words and apply phoneme–grapheme correspondence strategies in their writing.

2. **Progress checks during reading and writing tasks:**
   - Monitor students' progress in applying phonological skills during reading and writing tasks. Observe their ability to decode and spell multisyllabic words, identify patterns and use phonological strategies to tackle challenging vocabulary.
   - Assess students' reading fluency by asking them to read a passage aloud for one minute while you record the number of words read correctly. Use this data to track students' fluency progress over time.
   - Analyse students' writing for common errors in spelling, grammar, punctuation and sentence structure. Use this analysis to provide targeted feedback and guide instruction in areas of need.

3. **Formative assessments:**
   - Use formative assessments, such as exit slips (brief assessments that gauge student understanding and retention of the day's

key concepts), quizzes or oral assessments to gauge students' understanding of phonological concepts and their ability to apply phoneme awareness skills in various contexts.
- At the beginning of class, ask questions about the previous day's lesson while students are getting settled. At the end of the lesson, use tools like Padlet or Poll Everywhere for exit slips to measure progress towards learning objectives.
- Create polls and quizzes with tools like Socrative, Quizlet, Kahoot, or Quizalize to gauge students' understanding. Assign low point values to quizzes to ensure students make an effort without putting excessive pressure on grades.
- Use the Phonology Lens Skills Teacher Checklist to assess student proficiency in each area:

The Phonology Lens Skills Teacher Checklist	
Key Features	**Skills Checklist**
Phonological Sensitivity	☐ Manipulates phonemes ☐ Recognises onset and rime ☐ Claps out syllables ☐ Identifies rhymes
Phoneme Awareness	☐ Segments and blends phonemes ☐ Distinguishes between consonants and vowels ☐ Differentiates voiced and unvoiced phonemes ☐ Understands non-phonographic spellings ☐ Recognises diphones
Phonetics	☐ Masters pronunciation and articulation ☐ Understands the physical aspects of speech production ☐ Decodes and uses the International Phonetic Alphabet (IPA) ☐ Recognises the schwa sound in unstressed syllables

Student self-assessment

Implement self-assessment tools for students to reflect on their own phonological awareness skills, set goals and track their progress over time. This encourages metacognition and self-regulation, and empowers students to take ownership over their phonological skill development.

1. Have students maintain personal Phonology Lens Journals where they record examples of words they find challenging to pronounce, segment or spell. Encourage them to reflect on their progress and note any strategies they use to improve their phonological skills.
2. Provide students with open-ended reflection prompts related to phonological skills, such as "What phonological skill do you feel most confident in? Why?" or "What strategies can you use to improve your phoneme awareness?" This encourages students to think critically about their phonological abilities.
3. Provide your students with a checklist of phonological sensitivity and phoneme awareness skills (see following) and ask them to self-assess their proficiency in each area. This allows students to reflect on their phonological abilities and identify areas for improvement.

The Phoneme Phenomenon Self-Assessment Tool for Students: Decoding your linguistic DNA

This self-assessment checklist is designed to help you explore and evaluate your phonological sensitivity and phoneme awareness skills. These abilities form the foundation of your linguistic capabilities, much like DNA forms the blueprint of life. As you work through this checklist, you'll have the opportunity to reflect on various aspects of language sound patterns, from rhyming and syllable awareness to phoneme manipulation and non-phonographic spelling. By rating your proficiency in each area, you'll gain insights into your strengths and areas for growth in language processing.

Remember, this is not a test but a tool for self-discovery. Be honest in your evaluations and use this checklist to:

1. *recognise your linguistic strengths*
2. *identify areas where you can improve*
3. *set personal goals for enhancing your language skills*
4. *track your progress over time.*

As you decode your "linguistic DNA", you may uncover abilities you didn't know you had or find new areas of interest to explore. This self-assessment is your first step in understanding the complex and fascinating world of language sounds that you navigate every day.

Rate your proficiency in each skill area:

The Phonology Lens Student Self-Assessment

Phonological Sensitivity

Rhyming	☐ I can identify rhyming words. ☐ I can generate rhyming words for a given word. ☐ I can distinguish between words that rhyme and those that don't.
Phoneme Manipulation	☐ I can add phonemes to words (e.g. "at" → "cat"). ☐ I can delete phonemes from words (e.g. "stop" → "top"). ☐ I can substitute phonemes in words (e.g. "cat" → "cot").
Syllable Awareness	☐ I can count the number of syllables in words. ☐ I can identify the stressed syllable in multisyllabic words. ☐ I can manipulate (add, delete or substitute) syllables in words.
Alliteration	☐ I can recognise words that start with the same sound. ☐ I can generate words that start with a given sound.

Phoneme Awareness

Blending	☐ I can blend individual sounds to form words. ☐ I can blend onset and rime to form words.
Segmenting	☐ I can break words into individual sounds. ☐ I can separate words into onset and rime.
Consonant and Vowel Phoneme Identification	☐ I can identify initial consonant sounds in words. ☐ I can identify final consonant sounds in words. ☐ I can identify medial vowel sounds in words. ☐ I can distinguish between short and long vowel sounds.
Diphones	☐ I can identify diphones.
NPS	☐ I can recognise non-phonographic spelling (NPS) in a word. ☐ I can explain why some words are spelled differently to how they sound.

Phonetics

The Schwa	☐ I can recognise the stressed and unstressed syllables in a word. ☐ I can find schwas in different word parts. ☐ I can hear the reduced 'uh' sound in unstressed syllables.

The IPA	☐ I can recognise common IPA symbols for English sounds. ☐ I can use the IPA symbols to break down and pronounce unfamiliar words.
My Reflection	
Which skills do you feel most confident about?	
Which skills do you think you need to improve?	
What strategies could help you with achieving that?	

Remember, this self-assessment is a tool for your own growth. Be honest in your evaluation and use it to set goals for improving your phonological sensitivity and phoneme awareness skills.

From Contemplation to Classroom Innovation

You can revisit this chapter to find guidance on:

- using The Phonology Lens to break down complex vocabulary across subject areas
- incorporating Phoneme Awareness activities into reading and writing instruction
- applying phonological principles to support clear communication and presentation skills
- implementing orthographic mapping techniques to improve spelling and word recognition. (More on this in the next chapter!)

Following the theoretical discussion, this chapter concludes with a series of practical activities designed to help you implement this knowledge in your school or classroom. These practical exercises aim to bridge the gap between theory and practice, offering you concrete tools to enhance your students' phonological skills now that you understand the key components of the Phonology Lens. These activities would be perfect to run in staff meetings or collaborative team planning sessions after reading each chapter.

Contemplate and Consider!

You've been locked in the Phonology Lab and the only way out is to solve a series of puzzles using your knowledge of the Phonology Lens. Work together, think critically and unlock the secrets of language to escape!

Form small groups of three or four teachers. Each group will work through the challenges below. The first group to complete all challenges correctly "escapes" the room!

Materials:

- Large sheets of paper or whiteboard
- Pens
- Sticky notes
- Timer (set for 30 minutes).

Challenge 1—The Component Cipher (5 minutes): On the wall, you see a jumbled list of terms:

- Awareness
- Phoneme
- Phonological
- Sensitivity
- Phonetics.

Your task is to identify the three Key Features of the Phonology Lens and arrange them from broadest to most specific.

Challenge 2—Sensitivity Sorting (7 minutes): You find a box labelled "Phonological Sensitivity Features". Inside are various linguistic elements written on sticky notes:

- Clapping and counting the number of syllables
- Identifying the first sound in a word
- Rhyming words
- Blending phonemes
- Segmenting words into phonemes
- Recognising words with the same beginning sound
- Identifying words in a group that don't rhyme.

Sort these elements into categories that represent the features of Phonological Sensitivity. Hint: look for patterns related to size of sound units and types of sound manipulation.

Challenge 3—The Awareness Analyser (5 minutes): To unlock the next clue, you must explain the difference between Phonological Sensitivity and Phoneme Awareness. Write your explanation on the whiteboard. Hint: think about the scope and specificity of each term.

Challenge 4—Toolbox Treasure Hunt (8 minutes): Scattered around the room are various tools and resources:

- IPA chart
- Dictionary
- Abacus
- Xylophone
- QR code for a voice recording app
- Phoneme cards.

Your task is to identify which ones are useful for unpacking phonetics and explain how each could be used.

Challenge 5—Synthesis Cipher (5 minutes): To escape the room, each group must create a brief, engaging explanation of how all these elements work together in the Phonology Lens. Be prepared to present your explanation to the whole group.

Debrief: After the activity, discuss the following questions as a whole group:

- What new connections did you make between these concepts?
- How might this deeper understanding impact your teaching?
- What strategies from this activity could you adapt for your students?

Answer Key

- **Challenge 1:** Phonological Sensitivity (larger sound units); Phoneme Awareness (manipulating individual sound units); Phonetics (producing individual sounds).
- **Challenge 2:** Syllable Level: Clapping syllables; Counting syllables. Onset–Rime Level: Rhyming Words; Identifying words in a group that don't rhyme; Recognising words with the same beginning sound. Manipulating Phonemes Level: Identifying the first sound in a word; Blending phonemes; Segmenting words into phonemes. (This sorting is based on the size of sound units—from larger to smaller—and types of sound manipulation.)
- **Challenge 3:** The key difference is that Phonological Sensitivity is a broader skill that includes awareness of various sound units, while Phoneme Awareness specifically focuses on the smallest units of sound (phonemes) in spoken language.

- **Challenge 4:** IPA chart (provides a standardised set of symbols for representing speech sounds, which is helpful for transcribing and analysing speech across languages); dictionary (offers pronunciation guides and phonetic transcriptions, which assist in understanding standard pronunciations and phonetic variations); voice recording app (captures and plays back speech samples, enabling repeated listening and analysis of speech sounds); phoneme cards (provide visual and tactile representations of individual phonemes, aiding in teaching and learning phoneme awareness and manipulation). The items not directly useful to phonetics are the abacus (more related to mathematics, although it could be used as an analogy or to represent individual sounds!) and the xylophone (while it produces sounds, it's not specifically designed for speech sound analysis).

Implement and Innovate!

Materials:

- Whiteboard and pens
- Sticky notes
- Timer
- Handouts with the Guiding Questions from this chapter and assessment templates
- Role-play props (e.g. name tags, simple costumes).

Activity 1: Word Wizards (30 minutes): Everyone pairs up with another teaching partner. Each pair chooses a subject area (e.g. novel studies, science, mathematics) and selects a challenging vocabulary word from that context. They write their chosen word on a sticky note and place it on the designated area of the whiteboard.

Each pair writes their chosen word on their handout, and then takes turns with their partner asking and answering each Guiding Question about their word. Be as detailed as possible!

After 15 minutes, have a quick share-out: each pair presents their word and the most interesting phonological feature they discovered.

Activity 2: Assessment Architects (30 minutes): Form groups of four or five teachers. Each group designs a brief, engaging phonological skills assessment for upper primary or secondary students. The assessment should include:

- at least one task for each major area of the Phonology Lens
- a mix of oral and written components
- a creative element (e.g. a game, digital tool, or hands-on activity).

Also, brainstorm ideas for progress monitoring. How can you track student growth over time?

After 20 minutes, each group presents their assessment idea to the whole workshop to vote on the most creative and effective design!

Activity 3: Conference Roleplay (30 minutes): Stay in your groups from Activity 2. Each person will take on a role:

- Teacher
- Student
- Observers.

Using the provided template as a starting point, conduct a mock teacher–student conference about phonological progress, covering:

- the student's phonological strengths
- areas for growth
- the student's self-assessment
- teacher feedback
- goals.

Rotate roles so everyone gets a chance to be the teacher.

Observers should note:

- effective questioning techniques
- how well the teacher explains the components of the Phonology Lens
- the quality of personalised feedback.

After each roleplay, take two minutes for the observers to provide constructive feedback.

Wrap-up (10 minutes): Discuss these reflection questions:

1. How has this workshop changed your approach to teaching phonology?
2. What's one strategy you're excited to implement in your classroom?
3. What challenges do you anticipate, and how might you overcome them?

Share your reflections on sticky notes and post them on an "Implementation Ideas" board. (You could set this up in your staff room!)

Remember, the key to mastering these skills is practice and adaptation. Use these activities as a springboard for continuous improvement in your phonological instruction.

CHAPTER 4

Your Guide to the Orthography Lens

"People put their faith in simple spelling 'rules', learned in isolation, but these always fail to work, partly because there are too many exceptions and partly because the explanation necessarily involves other aspects of language."
~ David Crystal

By the end of this chapter, you will have fresh insights that will transform how you approach teaching word recognition and spelling:

1. **Rethink word recognition:** Forget the old idea that we memorise words just by seeing them. Your students' brains are not just cameras taking snapshots—they're linguistic supercomputers processing language in incredible ways. Discover why relying solely on "learning words by sight" might not be as effective as we once thought.
2. **Explore the logic of English orthography:** Ever feel like English spelling is a mystery? Fear not! The study of English orthography offers a consistent and logical framework that can help you and your students make sense of written language.
3. **Embrace patterns over rules:** Let's face it: spelling "rules" can be a bit rigid and often don't hold up because of all the exceptions in English. Instead, let's focus on patterns. Patterns are predictable and make learning easier by helping students spot recurring sequences and conventions of letters and sounds.

4. **The alphabetic principle:** Understand how letters (graphemes) represent sounds (phonemes) in words, while recognising that English is a morphophonemic language where spelling often reflects both sound and meaning. This understanding lays the foundation for orthographic mapping and efficient word recognition.
5. **Bring words to life:** By teaching spelling in context, you're showing students that spelling isn't just about memorising a list of words—it's about understanding how words work in real-life communication.
6. **Deliver clear and explicit instruction:** While context is super important, there's also a lot of value in being clear and direct. Explicit instruction means having the knowledge to guide your students through specific spelling patterns as they read and write.

Introducing The Orthography Lens

At the heart of every written word lies a hidden world of intricate patterns and predictable sequences—a world governed by the principles of the Orthography Lens, unveiling the power that letters hold within the words they form. By examining graphemes (letters) and their positions, combinations and sequences, the Orthography Lens reveals an entirely new layer of logic, order and understanding in written language.

The Orthography Lens is an invaluable tool for all teachers, as it enables a deeper exploration and understanding of the alphabetic principle, orthographic knowledge and the conventions that govern letter patterns within words. This Lens isn't just a theoretical concept—it's a vital component of linguistic instruction, with research consistently showing that strong orthographic knowledge supports spelling proficiency, reading comprehension and written expression (Daffern et al., 2024; Adoniou, 2022). For upper primary and secondary students, mastering orthographic principles becomes critical as they encounter more complex texts and vocabulary.

The Orthography Lens promises to transform your understanding of written language. It offers more than just a new perspective—it provides a comprehensive framework for decoding the complexities of English orthography.

Ultimately, this deep understanding of orthography leads to the development of orthographic mapping—the mental process that allows readers to form lasting connections between the written form, pronunciation and meaning of words. As students master the intricacies revealed by the Orthography Lens, they develop this fundamental skill that supports their journey toward fluent reading and writing. Orthographic mapping is the end result of this exploration, enabling students to instantly recognise familiar words and efficiently decode new ones, marking a significant milestone in their literacy development.

The front of the Orthography Lens serves as our entry point into this specialised field of study. Here, we encounter the etymological roots that define our focus: <ortho-> meaning "correct" and <-graphy> meaning "writing", encapsulating the essence of our inquiry—the study of correct writing systems.

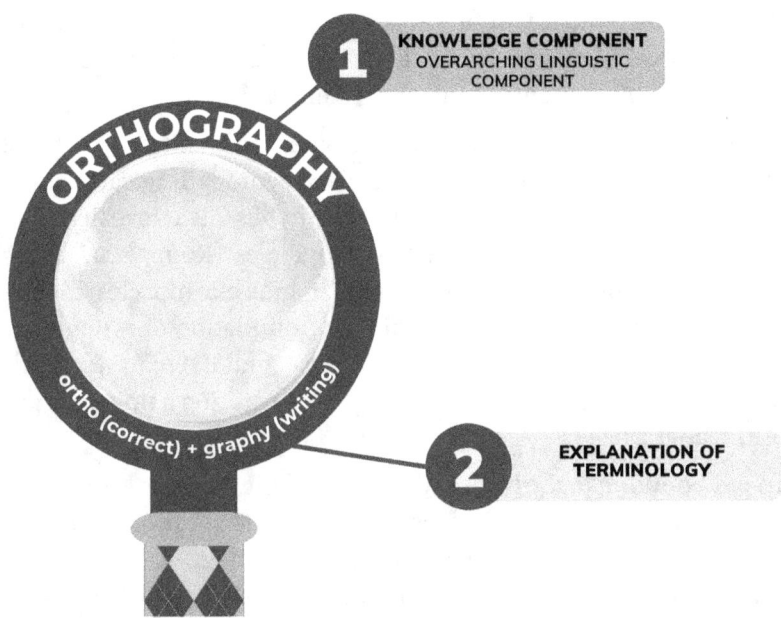

Orthography, in its broadest sense, encompasses the standardised writing system of a language. It includes the conventions for spelling, punctuation and capitalisation—elements that are key for effective written communication. However, our exploration goes beyond mere conventions. Recent research has challenged traditional notions of word recognition, revealing that the storage and retrieval of words is not primarily a function of the visual system (Carreiras et al., 2014). This insight renders strategies like "learning words by sight" for spelling tests once a week less effective than previously thought.

Instead, a thorough study of English orthography provides us with a consistent and logical framework for understanding written language. By mastering these orthographic principles, we enhance our ability to communicate clearly and accurately in writing.

As students progress through their school journey, strong orthographic knowledge becomes increasingly important. Research has consistently shown that a solid grasp of orthographic principles underpins the development of literacy skills (Apel, 2011). At the heart of this lies the process of orthographic mapping—the cognitive alchemy that transforms letters into meaning. This remarkable mental feat allows students to connect the visual patterns of letters with their corresponding sounds and meanings, storing words in their long-term memory for instant retrieval (Kilpatrick, 2016). As students refine this skill, they develop a vast high-frequency word vocabulary (see how I didn't use the terms "sight words" or "heart words"!), enabling them to read with fluency.

But here's where it gets truly exciting: orthographic mapping isn't just for early readers. Even older students struggling with reading can benefit from explicit instruction in this area. Research has also revealed that orthographic skills are transferable across languages (Koda, 2007). This means that as students strengthen their orthographic muscles in one language, they're simultaneously building a foundation for linguistic success in others. For both native speakers and second language learners, developing strong orthographic knowledge is like acquiring a universal key to the world's languages.

As we turn our attention to the back of the Orthography Lens, we encounter a set of **Key Features**. These serve as critical signposts in our journey through word study, highlighting essential terminology and concepts. To facilitate a comprehensive understanding, these features have been translated into a carefully curated series of **Guiding Questions**.

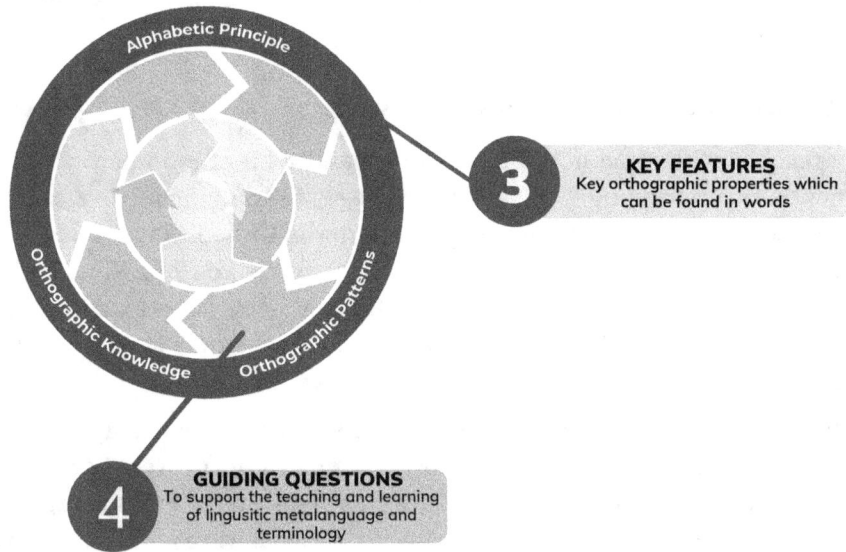

Sound and script: the power of complementary Lenses

The Phonology and Orthography Lenses offer unique perspectives on language, working together to provide a comprehensive understanding of words. The Phonology Lens focuses on the sound system, allowing analysis of individual phonemes, while the Orthography Lens examines the written representation of language.

These Lenses are most effective when used complementarily, incorporating the processes of encoding (phoneme-grapheme correspondence) and decoding (grapheme-phoneme correspondence). When encoding, we start with the Phonology Lens to explore sounds, then transition to the Orthography Lens to analyse how these sounds are represented in writing. Conversely, when decoding, we begin with the Orthography Lens to examine written symbols, then use the Phonology Lens to determine their corresponding sounds.

This approach leverages the close relationship between speech and writing, offering deeper insights into language structure. For instance, when examining the word "night", the Phonology Lens reveals the sounds /n/, /aɪ/ and /t/, while the Orthography Lens highlights the spelling and introduces terms like "trigraph". The encoding process shows how these sounds are represented in writing, while the decoding process demonstrates how readers interpret these written symbols to produce the correct sounds.

Remember, these Lenses can be used in isolation or as part of a repertoire of strategies.

Key Features of the Orthography Lens

As a teacher with a passion for linguistics, and a bit of a nomad when it comes to my upbringing, I've had the privilege of experiencing diverse city layouts across the globe. My journey began in the United Kingdom, where I was born, and has allowed me to live in and experience Hong Kong, India and America before I finally settled in Australia. Each of these locations has offered me unique insights into the parallels between urban design and language structure.

Consider, for instance, the stark contrast between the organically evolved streets of London and the meticulously planned grid of New York City. London's winding roads, shaped by centuries of history, mirror the organic evolution of the English language, with its irregular verbs and borrowed words. New York's grid system, on the other hand, reflects a more structured approach, akin to the rules of grammar that provide a framework for language use.

The layout of Washington, D.C., particularly fascinates me. Its radial avenues overlaid onto a grid system create a unique pattern that reminds me of the interplay between phonology and orthography in literacy instruction. Just as French-American architect and civil engineer Pierre Charles L'Enfant's plan for Washington combines different design elements, effective reading instruction integrates various approaches to language learning.

Mumbai in India showcases a complex blend of planned and unplanned development, mirroring the diverse linguistic landscape of our classrooms. Just as Mumbai's urban fabric interweaves modern skyscrapers with historic neighbourhoods and informal settlements, our students bring rich language experiences. This urban mosaic reflects the layered nature of language learning, where structured teaching in the classroom intertwines with natural language exposure at home and cultural influences from the community.

Hong Kong's dense urban landscape, with its mix of colonial and modern architecture, parallels the way different linguistic influences have shaped English over time. It's a vivid reminder of how language, like cities, adapts and evolves with cultural interactions.

Finally, Sydney, with its mix of grid patterns in the CBD and more organic layouts in older suburbs, reflects a balance between structure and adaptability. This balance is essential in literacy learning, where we strive to teach conventions and patterns of orthography while also fostering creativity and flexibility in language use. I have found my more recent home of Adelaide, with its planned city centre surrounded by parklands, offers another perspective on how clear boundaries and open spaces can coexist, much like how we define orthographic patterns and conventions while allowing for creative expression.

As teachers, we can draw inspiration from these urban planning concepts to enhance our language instruction. Just as city planners create navigable spaces, we can structure our lessons to guide students through the complexities of language, creating clear pathways for learning while allowing room for exploration and discovery.

Imagine orthography, the spelling system of our language, as a bustling, well-planned city. This city represents the intricate world of written language, with each word symbolising a building. Discover the city's design through these Key Features:

1. **Alphabetic Principle:** Think of this as the foundational blueprint of the city. It's the understanding that spoken words are made up of individual sounds (phonemes) and that these sounds are represented by letters or letter combinations (graphemes) in written language. Just as city planners use a blueprint to guide the layout of streets and buildings, readers and writers use the alphabetic principle to decode and encode words. The alphabetic principle can be viewed in two ways:
   - **Phoneme–Grapheme Correspondence (PGC)** is like knowing how to construct buildings using the city's approved materials. It helps writers choose the right letters to represent sounds when spelling words.
   - **Grapheme–Phoneme Correspondence (GPC)** is like knowing how to interpret the city's architectural plans. It helps readers associate written symbols with their corresponding sounds when reading words.
2. **Orthographic Knowledge:** This is akin to the diverse architectural styles that characterise different parts of the city. Just as architects use various design elements to create distinct building styles, readers and writers use orthographic knowledge to recognise and construct words with different letter combinations, allowing them to navigate the city of words with confidence.

3. **Orthographic Patterns:** Just as cities have comprehensive planning schemes and building regulations that govern construction across different suburbs, written language has patterns that appear across various words. Once you're familiar with these regulations, you can easily understand how different "structures" are put together and navigate even the most complex areas of the language landscape. These patterns serve as the underlying conventions (often called "rules") helping readers and writers construct and interpret words correctly throughout the linguistic cityscape.

In this orthographic city, your students start as tourists, gradually becoming skilled urban explorers, then architects and eventually master city planners themselves. Through this journey, they develop orthographic mapping skills that allow them to construct and navigate written language with expertise and ease, effortlessly recognising and producing words.

Let's dive into the components which make up each Key Feature.

Components of the Alphabetic Principle: The Teachers' Toolkit

The alphabetic principle forms the bedrock of literacy development.

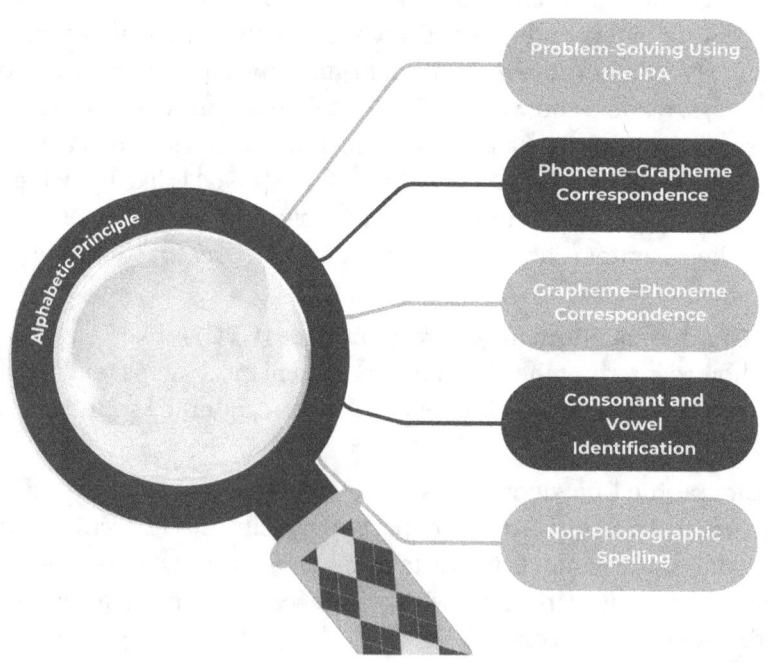

1. **Problem-Solving Using the IPA** is an effective strategy when your students can read a word but don't know how to pronounce it. English, like many languages, has numerous orthographic inconsistencies. Words with similar spellings may have different pronunciations (such as "cough" versus "bough") and words with different spellings may sound the same (such as "there" versus "their"). IPA transcriptions cut through these inconsistencies, providing a clear guide to pronunciation regardless of spelling. Understanding the relationship between IPA symbols and written letters can help your students make more informed guesses about the pronunciation of unfamiliar words based on their spelling. While learning the entire IPA system can be challenging, even a basic understanding of key symbols can significantly enhance your students' ability to decode and pronounce unfamiliar words.

2. **Phoneme–Grapheme Correspondence** involves connecting the sounds in spoken words (phonemes) to the letters or letter combinations that represent those sounds in written words (graphemes). Be sure to emphasise that there often isn't a one-to-one correspondence between sounds and letters! Each phoneme in the English language can be represented by one or more graphemes. Think *from sound to symbol* (spelling and writing).

3. **Grapheme–Phoneme Correspondence** refers to the relationship between written symbols (graphemes) and the sounds (phonemes) they represent in spoken language. Think from *symbol to sound* (reading). Think of PGC and GPC as two different perspectives on the same relationship—like looking at a coin from both sides.

4. **Consonant and Vowel Identification** and their roles in words is a precursor to understanding grapheme–phoneme correspondence, hence the inclusion of this knowledge in the Phonology Lens too. Revisiting this knowledge helps in understanding word stress and pronunciation patterns, as consonants and vowels are crucial for identifying syllables. The arrangement of consonants and vowels in a word also provides important cues for pronunciation. Many common orthographic patterns in English are based on the relationships between consonants and vowels, such as a digraph after a single vowel—compare "running" and "ruling". This pattern helps indicate the pronunciation of the preceding vowel, with the digraph often signalling a short monophthong (a single vowel phoneme in which the tongue remains in the same position) and the graph frequently indicating a long monophthong.

5. **Non-Phonographic Spelling** refers to words that don't follow typical sound-to-letter correspondences, often due to historical, etymological or morphological reasons. Non-phonographic spellings will challenge your students to move beyond simple phoneme–grapheme correspondences, encouraging them to develop a more sophisticated understanding of the English writing system. Encountering non-phonographic spellings will encourage your students to develop and use multiple strategies for spelling. Exploring why words are spelled in certain ways, especially when they don't match their pronunciation, will encourage your students to make connections between related words and spelling patterns, think about language more analytically and develop their metalinguistic awareness.

Components of Orthographic Knowledge: The Teachers' Toolkit

There's an essential characteristic of the English writing system we need to address: the fact that it's *morphophonemic*, a fancy term that means it represents both sound (phonemes) and meaning (morphemes). As a result, one letter doesn't always stand for one sound, which can make English spelling seem like a puzzle. This is where orthographic knowledge comes to the rescue:

1. **Spelling It Out** aloud forces students to think about each letter and letter combination consciously. This process helps cement the connection between sounds and their written representations. For example, let's take the word <knight>: k–n–i–g–h–t. By spelling it out, students become aware of the digraph <kn> making one sound /n/ and the trigraph <igh> making one sound /aɪ/, and how these elements come together to form the word. This exercise highlights the morphophonemic nature of English, showing how spelling preserves meaning (the <k> links "knight") even when pronunciation has changed over time.

2. **Graphs** are the fundamental units of our linguistic city. Graphs are single letters representing individual sounds, like individual plots of land that have the potential to support distinct structures. For example, the <c> in "cat" is like a single-family home—simple, recognisable and capable of producing a clear result when developed.

3. **Digraphs** are two letters that support each other to produce a unique sound. Just like in urban planning, some structures work better when combined. The <sh> in "ship" is akin to a well-designed duplex where

both units complement each other; in "beach" the <ea> and the <ch> resemble harmonious mixed-use buildings with residential and commercial spaces.

4. **Trigraphs** are three letters coming together to create a single, complex sound. The <igh> in "high" is like a skyscraper, producing an elegant and distinctive addition to the skyline.

5. **Quadgraphs**, uncommon but striking, are the iconic landmarks of our linguistic cityscape. They combine four letters to produce one sophisticated sound, much like how a complex architectural structure results in a single, breathtaking edifice. The <eigh> in "eight" is comparable to a unique piece of urban architecture that stands out because of its specific design considerations.

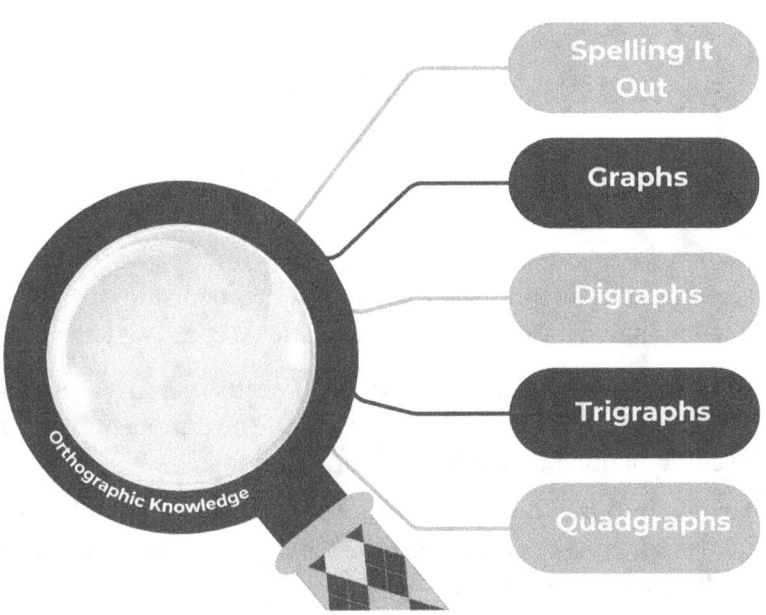

Components of Orthographic Patterns: The Teachers' Toolkit

Orthographic patterns are the predictable conventions of English spelling. Understanding these patterns can boost students' confidence and proficiency in language, specifically helping to answer the question, "How do I know which spelling to choose?"

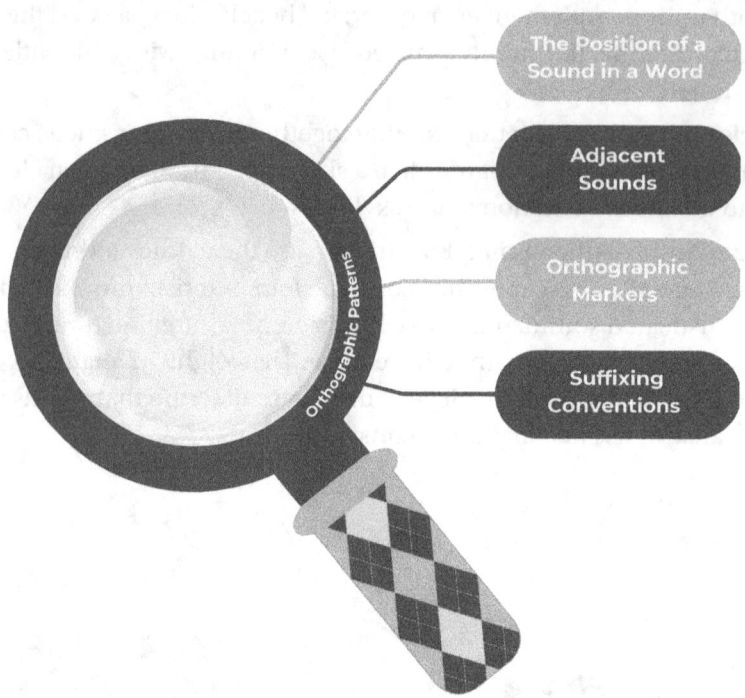

Understanding orthographic patterns involves recognising various factors that influence spelling. Here's how these elements come together:

1. **The Position of a Sound in a Word** can affect its spelling, such as with the /k/ sound at the end of "back" versus the beginning of "kite." The <ck> combination often follows a monophthong.

2. **Adjacent Sounds**—the sounds before or after a given sound—can influence spelling. For example, the /t/ in "stretch" is influenced by the preceding "s", creating a "blend".

3. **Orthographic Markers** are letters and combinations of letters that do not themselves correspond to phonemes. They serve a number of functions (Scibetta Hegland, 2021). To illustrate this, let's look at the final single non-syllabic <e> that comes at the end of many English words. This marker can signal pronunciation, changing the preceding vowel from a monophthong to a diphthong, such as in words like "cake" and "time". Unfortunately, over time, this "single function" has developed into a rule and been given the title of the "silent" or "bossy" <e> pattern. This rule does not work for many words ending

in <e>, encountered at the beginning of literacy learning, for example, "have", "come", "here", "there", "love" and so on, confusing many learners. When teaching language for the purpose of understanding the structure and meaning connections in words—not just focusing on the phonological perspective—I want you to shift the focus from memorising a rule about vowel sounds to understanding the word's structure and its relationship to other words. By investigating words with final <e> through word sums and matrices, your students can see that the <e> is an integral part of the base element, not just a silent letter added to change pronunciation. This understanding can help your students spell related words, such as caking (<cake> plus <-ing>, where the <e> is replaced by the suffix <-ing>) or timed (<time> plus <-ed>, where the <e> remains as part of the suffix <-ed>). However, this final, single, non-syllabic <e> marker is also found in words that are not pronounced with a long monophthong—it can also support recognition of morphemic structures in words such as "laps" and "lapse", "teas" and "tease", "brows" and "browse", and "pleas" and "please" (Scibetta Hegland, 2021). Without the <e>, these words would be spelled exactly the same! This <e> flags to the reader that one is a base word and the second is the plural form of a different word. Also, the word-final <e> is not the only type of orthographic marker—another type is the etymological marker, which is when the spelling of a word results from its history. So many students are taught that these are silent letters—just think of the <w> in "answer" and "two". Etymology impacts the modern spelling of words. For example, the <gh> in "night" reflects its historical pronunciation—it was once pronounced with a guttural sound—and the <ph> in "phone" represents the /f/ sound because of the word's Greek origin. Many of these graphemes are historical remnants and have nothing to do with the word's pronunciation today.

4. **Suffixing Conventions** include replacing or changing letters, such as changing "happy" to "happier" by replacing the final <y> with <i>, or recognising that "happy" becomes "happiness" by adding the suffix <-ness>, changing the adjective to a noun.

By understanding these factors, you can help your students navigate the complexities of English spelling and add another tool to their linguistic toolbox.

Teaching Tip!

A monophthong is a single, pure vowel sound that doesn't change quality during pronunciation. Derived from Greek, <mono-> means "single" or "one" and <-phthong> means "sound" or "voice". So, a monophthong is literally a "single sound" vowel. Monophthongs can be long or short. Using the correct terminology in your teaching matters because:

- it's more precise than "short vowel sound"
- it focuses on the sound's quality, not its length
- it contrasts with diphthongs—<di-> comes from the Greek for "two", and diphthongs represent vowel sounds that change during pronunciation.

Here are some examples of monophthongs in Australian English:

- /iː/ as in "see" or "bee"
- /ɪ/ as in "sit" or "pin"
- /e/ as in "bed" or "pet"
- /æ/ as in "cat" or "hat"
- /ʌ/ as in "cut" or "but"
- /ɑː/ as in "car" or "far"
- /ɒ/ as in "hot" or "pot"
- /ɔː/ as in "saw" or "door"
- /ʊ/ as in "put" or "foot"
- /uː/ as in "blue" or "two"

Exploring "Conscience" Through the Orthography Lens

After examining the word "conscience" through the Phonology Lens, we're now shifting our focus to the Orthography Lens to understand its spelling and structure.

Project the LLGO digital template onto your interactive whiteboard and place the Orthography Lens magnet next to the Orthography section.

In the centre of the LLGO, write "conscience". Let's use the Guiding Questions to explore how the word's structure relates to its meaning, paying special attention to the spelling.

Embarking on the Orthography Expedition: A journey through 11 Guiding Questions

Imagine these questions as your trusty compass on a grand expedition through the vast landscape of English spelling. Just as a compass provides direction, these questions offer a structured approach to help you navigate the foundational pathways of the alphabetic principle, the avenues of orthographic knowledge and the intersections of orthographic patterns.

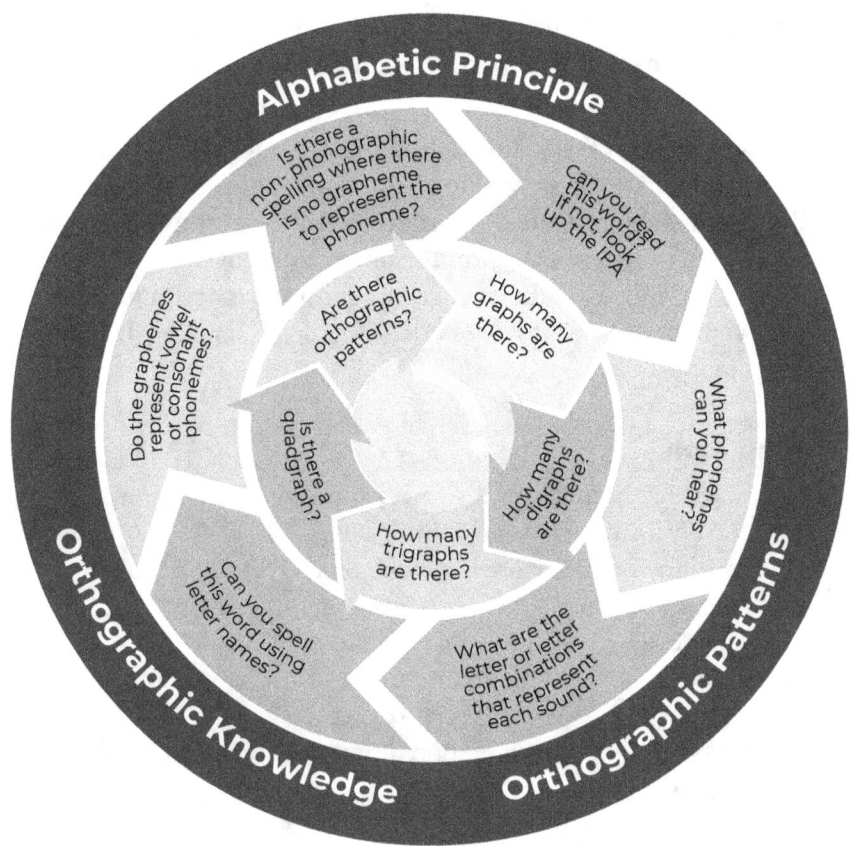

1. Can you read this word? If not, look up the IPA.

Imagine asking a student to read the word "conscience" but instead they pronounce it "conscious". They do sound very similar, don't they?

Let's break this down using the IPA symbols to see where the confusion might arise from. "Conscience" is pronounced /kɒn.ʃəns/, while "conscious" is pronounced /kɒn.ʃəs/. Notice the difference? The ending sounds are slightly different: there is an extra phoneme in the word "conscience", the /n/ sound.

Write down the IPA transcription for both words to show the difference.

Using the IPA to problem-solve unfamiliar words is a highly effective strategy for both teachers and language learners. The IPA's strength lies in its universal representation of sounds across all spoken languages, providing a standardised system that transcends the inconsistencies of traditional spelling. This allows your students to pinpoint exact pronunciations, especially for words they've never encountered before or do not know how to pronounce.

If your students can't say the word, there is absolutely no point in even worrying about the spelling! For languages with orthographic irregularities, like English, the IPA serves as a bridge, cutting across spelling inconsistencies to reveal true pronunciation. Moreover, its multisensory nature—visual symbols, auditory associations and kinaesthetic practice of mouth movements—caters to diverse learning styles, making it an inclusive educational tool.

Teaching Tip!
- Introduce IPA gradually, starting with common symbols and progressively introduce more complex ones.
- When introducing new words, include their IPA transcriptions.
- Design games or exercises that involve matching IPA symbols to sounds or words.
- Teach students how to find and interpret IPA transcriptions in dictionaries.
- Use IPA to highlight pronunciation differences between similar words or across dialects.

Case study: blending sounds, decoding minds—IPA settles the "cerebral" debate

In a highly able Year 6 classroom, during a reading of Sharon Draper's *Out of My Mind*, a seemingly simple pronunciation debate sparked an unforgettable learning moment. The protagonist, Melody, was described as having cerebral palsy, igniting a passionate discussion among the students.

Isabelle, a confident 12-year-old, asserted it was pronounced "cerebal" /serəbəl/, citing her mother as the authority. Another student countered with /səriːbəl/, creating a perfect teachable moment.

Instead of immediately settling the debate, I decided to seize this opportunity to demonstrate the power of collaborative learning and linguistic exploration. I wrote the central question, "How do we say it?" on the LLGO, noting the students' suggested pronunciations in IPA with question marks.

When asked about potential resources to find the correct IPA, the class suggested the online *Cambridge Dictionary*. As I transcribed the correct IPA, I guided the students through a mini-lesson on phonetics. They counted syllables, marked with dots and highlighted the schwa sounds. A key discovery was the <br> consonant blend in "cerebral", which students identified as "two or more consonants in the same syllable set".

This lesson revealed a surprising truth: many adults might struggle with the correct pronunciation of "cerebral". The beauty of this moment lay not in correction but in empowering these bright young minds to uncover the answer themselves. For me, this case study beautifully illustrates what our role is as teachers: we are facilitators of learning, not authority figures. By guiding our students to use linguistic tools and critical thinking, I was able to transform a potential (albeit light-hearted) conflict into an engaging, collaborative learning experience. The use of IPA and the LLGO turned a simple pronunciation question into a rich exploration of phonetics.

Building on the previous day's insights, we delved deeper into "cerebral palsy", focusing on etymology. The exploration of "palsy" led to a fascinating discovery: its Greek root <paralysis>. Students quickly identified this as a cognate, prompting me to record their definition: "a word taken from another language that has not been modified".

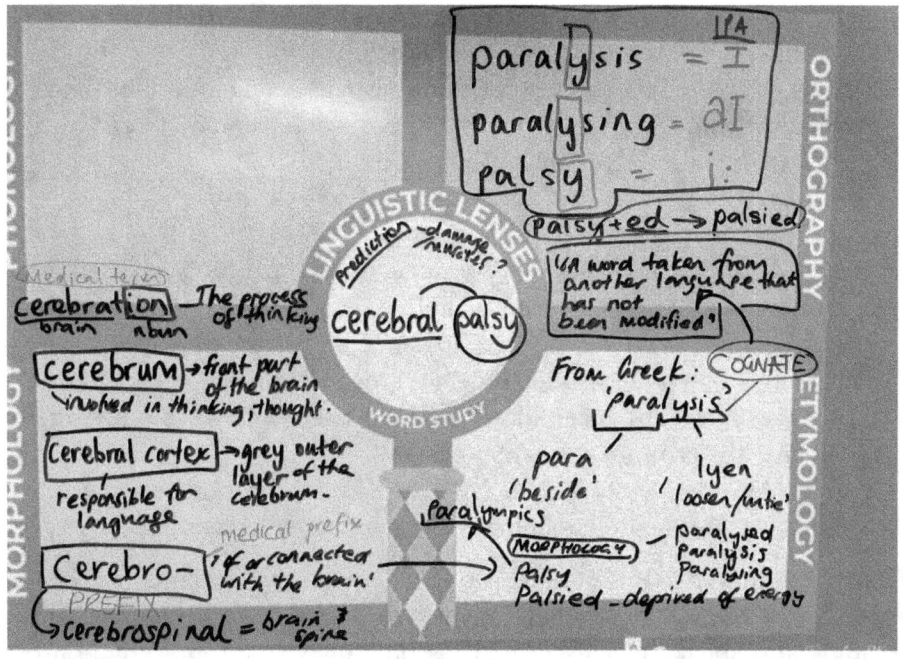

Your Guide to the Orthography Lens

This revelation opened doors to a network of etymological relatives:

- paralysis
- paralysing
- Paralympics.

Of course, we had to embark on an intriguing discussion about the chameleon-like nature of the letter <y> in these words. Using a red pen, I highlighted the <y> in each word (see the Orthography box), demonstrating its varied pronunciations through IPA symbols:

1. paralysis /pərælɪsɪs/
2. paralysing /pærəlaɪzɪŋ/
3. palsy /pɔːlziː/

The pronunciation shifts in "paralysis", "paralysing" and "palsy" are fascinating examples of how the letter <y> can represent different sounds in English. Here's how I broke down each case:

1. **paralysis /pərælɪsɪs/:** Here, the <y> is pronounced as a monophthong sound /ɪ/. This is common when <y> appears at the end of a multisyllable word.
2. **paralysing /pærəlaɪzɪŋ/:** In this case, the <y> is pronounced as a diphthong sound /aɪ/. This shift occurs because the <y> is followed by a suffix, <-ing>, which often triggers a change in pronunciation to maintain the base word's stress pattern.
3. **palsy /pɔːlziː/:** The <y> here is pronounced as a long monophthong sound /iː/. This is typical when <y> appears at the end of a short word or in an unstressed final syllable.

These shifts occur due to several linguistic factors:

- **Syllable position:** The <y> sound can change depending on whether it's in a stressed or unstressed syllable.
- **Word length:** Shorter words like "palsy" tend to have different pronunciation patterns than longer words.
- **Morphological changes:** Adding suffixes, like <-ing> in "paralysing", can alter the pronunciation of the base.
- **Historical sound changes:** As languages evolve, pronunciation can shift over time, leading to differences even in related words.

Understanding these shifts no doubt helped my students recognise patterns in English pronunciation, which I could see enhancing their reading and speaking skills in that lesson. This visual representation on the LLGO illuminated how a single letter can produce distinct sounds in related words, deepening students' understanding of phonetic principles and etymological connections.

CASE STUDY: Using the IPA to pronounce "obsequious"

Picture this: you're in a Year 6 classroom, your students engrossed in the novel *Chinese Cinderella* by Adeline Yen Mah, when suddenly a student stumbles upon the word "obsequious" and looks up, bewildered.

"She is so slimy and ob… obse… obseq… How do I say it?"

"Excellent question! What do we usually do when we encounter a tricky word?"

"Skip it!" the students cry in unison.

"Skip it?" you reply. "Oh no! Everyone, allow me to introduce our secret weapon: the International Phonetic Alphabet, or IPA for short! The IPA is like a universal translator for sounds. It doesn't care about tricky spellings; it just tells us exactly how to pronounce words. Let's see it in action!"

You type "obsequious" into the online *Cambridge Dictionary*.

"Behold! The IPA says it's /əbsiːkwɪəs/. Now, who wants to be our IPA detective?"

A student says, "I see a funny upside-down <e> at the beginning. What's that?"

"Ah, the infamous 'schwa'! It's like the ninja of vowel sounds—sneaky and often unnoticed. It's the 'uh' sound in 'about.'"

"There's a colon after the <i>. Does that mean we stretch it out?"

"Exactly! It's like the 'ee' in 'see.'"

The students take turns identifying sounds, clapping syllables and finally pronouncing the word together.

"Now that we can say it, let's figure out what it means." You type the word into the Online Etymology Dictionary (etymonline.com). "According to our linguistic time machine, 'obsequious' comes from Latin: <ob> means 'after' and <sequi> means 'to follow'. So, it literally means…"

"To follow after someone?"

"But not just follow—to follow eagerly, almost too eagerly. Like a puppy following its owner, but in a slimy way!"

You write a "How-to guide" next to the word web so that the students can remember for next time:

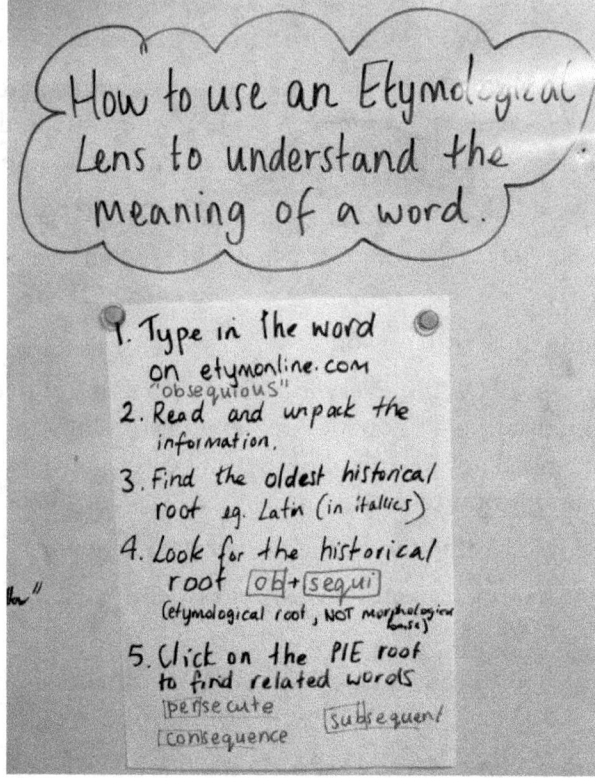

You continue, "Let's explore some related words. Can anyone identify words that might share this etymological root?"

A student pipes up: "Would 'sequence' be related? It seems to have the <sequi> part."

"Excellent connection. Yes, 'sequence' relates to following in order. Any others?"

"How about 'consequence'? That also seems to follow from something."

"Very astute. These words all share the Latin root <sequi>. Understanding these connections can significantly enhance your vocabulary and comprehension.

"Now, let's put it all together. In our story, when it says, 'She is so slimy and obsequious,' what do you think it means?"

"Oh! She's like… super eager to please someone, but in a fake way?"

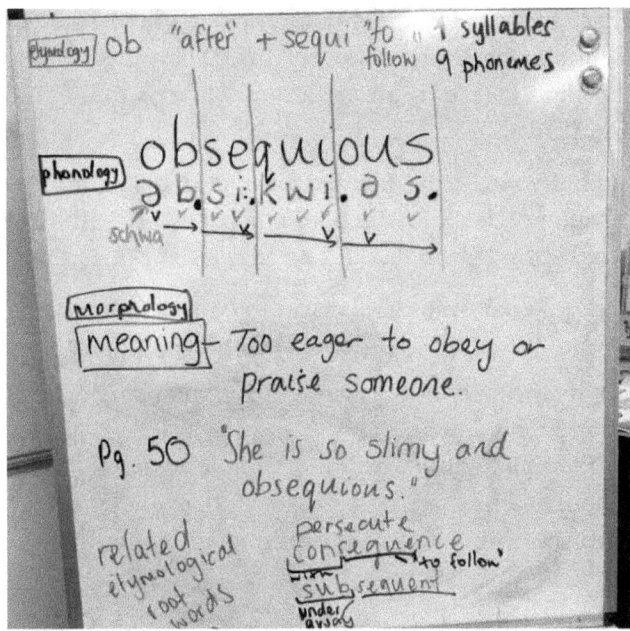

Remember that every unfamiliar word is an opportunity for a mini linguistic adventure. By combining phonology, orthography, morphology and etymology in engaging ways, you're not just teaching vocabulary—you're cultivating word detectives who will never look at language the same way again! So, the next time a student stumbles on a word, don't let them skip it. Instead, grab your linguistic magnifying glass and say, "We have a mystery to solve!"

Contemplate and Consider!

Here's a set of prompts, reflection questions and activities to help you and your colleagues or teaching teams understand and apply the IPA in your classrooms. If you work in content-specific or subject-specialist teaching teams, I suggest breaking into those groups for the following activities:

1. **Recognising the IPA's value in decoding words:** Imagine you're a student encountering the word "pneumonia" for the first time in writing. How might the IPA help?

- How does the IPA bridge the gap between spelling and pronunciation?
- In what ways might the IPA be particularly useful for English as an Additional Language or Dialect (EALD) learners?
- How could the IPA support students with dyslexia or other reading difficulties?

Create a simple "decoder ring" using common English graphemes and their IPA equivalents. Use it to "decode" a list of words with irregular spellings. Discuss how this tool could be adapted for classroom use.

2. **Analysing the "obsequious" classroom conversation:** Let's break down how the IPA helped students tackle "obsequious":
    - What specific IPA symbols were most crucial in helping students pronounce this word?
    - How did breaking the word into syllables using IPA aid comprehension?
    - What misconceptions about pronunciation did the IPA help clarify?

    In small groups, role-play the classroom conversation, taking turns being the teacher and students. Afterwards, discuss how you might improve or expand on the original approach.

3. **Appreciating phoneme–grapheme correspondences:** Consider the words "thought", "through" and "bough". How does the IPA illuminate their pronunciation differences?
    - How does understanding phoneme–grapheme correspondences support reading fluency?
    - In what ways might this knowledge aid spelling instruction?
    - How could awareness of these correspondences benefit students' writing skills?

    Create a visual map showing all the possible graphemes for a single phoneme (e.g. /f/ as in <f>, <ph>, <gh>). Then, do the reverse, mapping all possible phonemes for a single grapheme (e.g. <ough>). Discuss the implications for teaching and learning.

4. **Exploring IPA-based teaching strategies:** Let's design an engaging IPA-based activity for a specific lesson in your subject area:
    - How can the IPA be integrated into your existing curriculum?

- What potential challenges might you face when introducing the IPA, and how could you address them?
- How might you differentiate IPA instruction for diverse learners?

Design a subject-specific "escape room" activity where students must use their IPA knowledge to solve puzzles and escape. Share ideas and collaborate on creating interdisciplinary connections.

Challenge activity—"IPA in action": Create a short video (2-3 minutes) demonstrating how you would introduce and use the IPA in your classroom. Include at least one interactive element and explain how it supports your lesson's learning objectives.

After watching each other's videos, discuss:

- What creative approaches did you observe?
- How did different subject areas adapt the IPA to their needs?
- What new ideas have you gained for your own teaching practice?

Answer Key

1. The IPA transcription of "pneumonia" is /njuːməʊnɪə/. This shows the exact sounds in the word, revealing the <pn> digraph at the beginning and the schwa at the end. By providing this detailed phonetic information, students can say "pneumonia" correctly despite its challenging orthography.

   - The IPA provides a consistent, one-to-one correspondence between symbols and sounds, unlike English spelling. It accurately represents all sounds in a word, including those not reflected in the spelling (i.e. non-phonographic spellings), helping learners understand how to say words that don't follow typical spelling patterns or conventions.
   - The IPA helps learners pronounce unfamiliar words correctly without relying on inconsistent English spelling rules. It provides a universal system for representing sounds across different languages, assisting in identifying and producing sounds that may not exist in students' native languages. It also supports self-study and independent learning of pronunciation.
   - The IPA's consistent system for decoding words reduces confusion caused by irregular spellings. It helps break down words into individual sounds, supporting phonological awareness. It provides a visual representation of sounds, which can aid in processing

and memory. It can be used to create personalised strategies for tackling challenging words.

2. The IPA transcription for "obsequious" is /əbsiːkwɪəs/.
   - The following IPA symbols were most crucial in helping students pronounce this word:
     - /ə/ shows the unstressed first syllable
     - /b/ clarifies the <b> sound, which might be unclear from spelling alone
     - /iː/ represents the long monophthong <e>
     - /k/ and /w/ show <q> and <u> pronounced as two separate sounds
     - /ə/ indicates the unstressed vowel sound in the final syllable.
   - The syllable breakdown of "obsequious" is ob-se-qui-ous. This reveals the word's four-syllable structure and shows the clear separation between 'se' and 'qui'. It demonstrates how each syllable contributes to the overall pronunciation. It also helps students tackle the word part by part, making it less intimidating
   - The IPA helped to clarify the following pronunciation misconceptions:
     - The first <o> is pronounced as a schwa (/ə/); there's no /ɒ/ sound, as the spelling might suggest.
     - The stress is on the second syllable, not the first or third.
     - The 'qui' is pronounced as /kwɪ/, not /kɪ/ or /kwiː/.
     - The final 'ous' is pronounced /əs/, not /ʊs/ or /aʊs/.

3. The IPA transcriptions for "thought", "through" and "bough" are /θɔːt/, /θruː/ and /baʊ/. The IPA illuminates the pronunciation differences by showing that all three words have different vowel sounds despite sharing the same <-ough> spelling.
   - Understanding phoneme–grapheme correspondences supports reading fluency by
     - enhancing word recognition speed by associating grapheme patterns with phonemes
     - improving decoding skills for unfamiliar words
     - helping readers anticipate pronunciation based on spelling patterns
     - reducing cognitive load, allowing more focus on comprehension
     - supporting automatic word reading, a key component of fluency.

- This knowledge aids spelling instruction by:
    - helping students understand the logic behind spelling patterns
    - supporting teaching of orthographic patterns and conventions in spelling
    - helping to break words into phonemes for accurate spelling
    - enhancing students' ability to self-correct spelling errors
    - supporting the development of strategies for spelling unfamiliar words.
- Awareness of these correspondences can benefit students' writing skills by:
    - improving spelling accuracy in written work
    - enhancing confidence in using a wider vocabulary in writing
    - supporting more efficient proofreading and editing skills
    - helping students make informed choices about word selection based on sound patterns
    - facilitating the understanding and use of homophones and homographs
    - improving students' ability to create rhymes and play with language in creative writing
    - supporting better understanding of pronunciation guides in dictionaries, aiding independent vocabulary expansion.

2. What phonemes can you hear?

Now that we've practiced the pronunciation, let's take it a step further. What phonemes can you hear in the word "conscience"? Remember to count the phonemes in the word first. There are seven sounds: /k/, /ɒ/, /n/, /ʃ/, /ə/, /n/ and /s/.

This strategy is important when you're trying to spell a word. By segmenting each phoneme, you make sure to record every sound.

Understanding both phoneme–grapheme correspondences (PGCs) and grapheme–phoneme correspondences (GPCs) is crucial for students to develop orthographic knowledge, which is essential for proficient reading, writing and spelling. Here's why:

- **Reading skills:** GPCs are fundamental for decoding unfamiliar words. When students encounter a new word, they use their knowledge of GPCs to sound it out. As students become more proficient, they develop

orthographic mapping skills, which allow them to instantly recognise familiar words without sounding them out (building sight vocabulary).
- **Writing and spelling skills:** PGCs are essential for encoding sounds into written words. When students write or spell, they rely on their knowledge of PGCs to represent the sounds they hear. Strong orthographic knowledge helps students choose the correct spelling patterns, especially for words with multiple possible representations, such as "rain" and "reign".

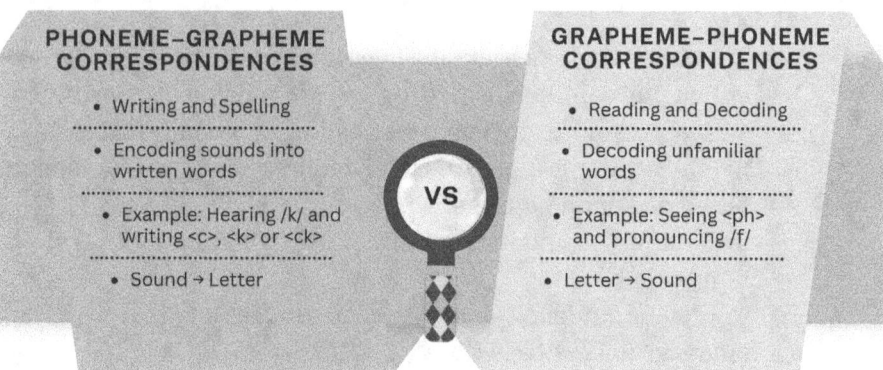

- **Building vocabulary:** Understanding both PGCs and GPCs helps students make connections between spoken and written forms of words, facilitating vocabulary acquisition and retention. Once students can hear the phonemes, they can move on to the graphemes which represent them.

3. What are the letter or letter combinations that represent each sound?

Now that we've identified the phonemes, let's look at the spelling. What are the letter or letter combinations for each sound in "conscience"? Let's break it down together:

/k/ = <c>
/ɒ/ = <o>
/n/ = <n>
/ʃ/ = <sci>
/ə/ = <e>
/n/ = <n>
/s/ = <ce>.

Contemplate and Consider!

As teachers, we often find ourselves at the crossroads of various teaching approaches, especially when it comes to foundational literacy skills. This became starkly apparent during my recent tour of preschools for my four-year-old daughter. At each preschool, I was met with this surprising directive: "You don't need to teach letter names. Children only need to know their sounds now." The educators insisted that teaching letter names would confuse young learners, presenting this approach as current best practice. As both a parent and a teacher, I found this stance not only alarming but also contradictory to my professional understanding of early literacy development. This experience highlights a significant shift in early childhood education philosophy that warrants careful examination and discussion among educators and parents alike. In light of this emerging trend, it's vital to critically evaluate the potential impacts of omitting letter-name instruction and consider whether this approach truly serves our young learners' best interests. Let's contemplate and consider this.

Have you ever wondered why some children seem to grasp reading more quickly than others? The answer might lie in their alphabet knowledge. Research suggests that a child's ability to recognise letter names is a strong predictor of future reading success. But why?

Consider this: letter names are like anchors in the sea of literacy. They provide stability in a language where sounds can be represented by multiple letters. Think about the word "phone". How would you explain its spelling to a child who only knows letter sounds?

In your experience, have you noticed a correlation between students' letter-name knowledge and their reading progress? Share an anecdote that supports or challenges this idea.

Handwriting also plays a role in literacy. Imagine teaching a child to ride a bike without letting them touch the handlebars. Sounds counterintuitive, right? Similarly, teaching literacy without emphasising handwriting ignores a crucial piece of the puzzle. When children form letters by hand, they're not just improving their penmanship—they're creating neural pathways that enhance letter recognition, phonemic awareness and even spelling skills. It's a multisensory approach that engages visual, kinaesthetic and auditory learning simultaneously.

In your next staff meeting, have colleagues write a short sentence with their non-dominant hand. Discuss how this experience might relate to a child's early writing attempts and the cognitive processes involved.

Here's a thought-provoking question: could handwriting be the missing link between letter-name knowledge and phonics instruction? Consider a typical lesson where you teach the letter <b>. Introduce the letter name: "This is the letter <b>." Then, demonstrate its formation: "Let's write <b> together. Start at the top, straight line down...". Finally, connect it to its sound: "<b> represents /b/ as in 'ball'." This integrated approach allows children to connect the letter's name, shape and sound in one cohesive experience.

How might this integrated approach impact your instruction? What challenges or benefits do you foresee in implementing this approach?

Think about how often we use letter names in daily life:

- Spelling out our names over the phone
- Organising files alphabetically
- Using acronyms like "ASAP" or "NASA".

By teaching letter names, we're not just preparing children for reading—we're equipping them with a vital communication tool.

With your colleagues, list five everyday situations in which knowing letter names is important. How can you incorporate these real-world applications into your literacy instruction?

As we navigate the complex world of literacy instruction, perhaps the key lies not in choosing between letter names and sounds but in finding a harmonious balance. By integrating handwriting, letter-name knowledge and phonics instruction, we create a robust foundation for literacy development.

How will this discussion influence your approach to early literacy instruction? What small change could you implement tomorrow to enhance your students' alphabet knowledge?

Case study: a "sighn" of something greater—why morphological relationships often trump phonological ones

This case study, drawn from students in their first year of formal schooling in Australia, illustrates how a seemingly simple spelling mistake can open doors to rich, multifaceted learning opportunities that span the Phonology, Orthography, Morphology and Etymology Lenses. During an independent writing exercise following a class excursion to a wildlife park, a gifted six-year-old student produced the spelling "sighn" for the word "sign".

This error, far from being a mere mistake to be corrected, presented an invaluable opportunity to explore the complexities of English orthography and challenge students' thinking about word structure and meaning.

The student's spelling choice revealed sophisticated phoneme–grapheme awareness:

1. /s/ is represented by <s>
2. /aɪ/ is represented by <igh>
3. /n/ is represented by <n>.

The student correctly identified the three phonemes in 'sign' and chose plausible phoneme–grapheme correspondences for each. This level of phoneme awareness is commendable, particularly for a six-year-old! The choice of <igh> for the /aɪ/ phoneme shows an understanding of complex graphemes, as this trigraph does indeed represent this phoneme in words like "light", "night" and "high". This insight is necessary for teachers to recognise the reasoning behind students' spelling choices rather than dismissing them as mere errors.

Rather than simply marking the spelling as incorrect, this error was leveraged as "My Favourite No"—a pedagogical approach that uses errors as springboards for deeper learning. This strategy is beneficial for several reasons:

1. It fosters a growth mindset by reframing mistakes as learning opportunities.
2. It encourages critical thinking and metalinguistic awareness.
3. It allows for differentiation and extension of learning for gifted students.

More on this later!

I gathered a small group of students, including the original writer, for an extension activity where I presented them with a collection of words including morphological relatives of "sign"—"signal", "significant", "assign", "design", "resign" and "signature"—alongside "sigh" and "sighing":

I then tasked them with sorting these words into two morphological families. This activity served multiple purposes:

- It introduced the concept of morphological families.
- It challenged the students to look beyond surface-level orthography to consider deeper structural and semantic relationships between words.

- It provided an opportunity to discuss the sometimes counterintuitive nature of English orthography, where words that sound different (like "sign" and "signal") can be closely related in meaning and spelling.

Following the sorting activity, I introduced a "word web" to visually represent the morphological relationships between the words:

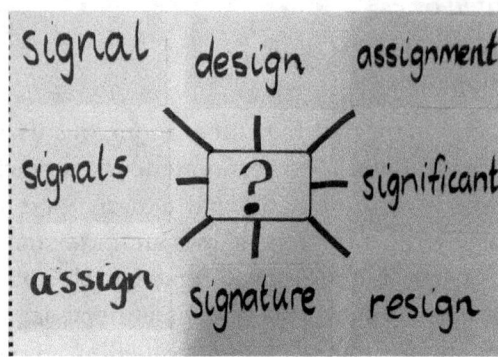

This led to a discussion about the shared base word and an exploration of the etymological roots of these words. I explained the Latin root <signare>, demonstrating how understanding word origins can illuminate seemingly difficult spellings. As we know, etymological insight is crucial for several reasons:

- It helps students understand that English spelling is not arbitrary but often reflects historical and linguistic factors.
- It introduces students to the concept of word roots, which can aid in vocabulary development and reading comprehension.
- It fosters an appreciation for the richness and complexity of language.

The difference in pronunciation between "sign" and "signal" was used to highlight a key point: in English, morphological relationships often trump phonological ones. This understanding is fundamental for several reasons:

- It helps students move beyond an overreliance on phonic spelling and reading strategies.
- It introduces the concept of consistent spelling patterns across word families, which can aid in both spelling and vocabulary development.
- It prepares students for the more advanced linguistic concepts they will encounter in later years.

To build on the student's initial choice of <igh> for the /aɪ/ phoneme, I added a follow-up activity so that the students could explore various graphemes representing this sound. I wrote words such as "aisle", "height", "either", "buy" and "tiger" on strips of paper. I used a red pen to signal the vowel graphemes and blue to identify the consonant graphemes.

The students sorted these words based on the position of the /aɪ/ phoneme within each word. This activity:

- demonstrated the versatility of English orthography
- enhanced the students' awareness of positional constraints on certain graphemes
- reinforced the understanding that the same phoneme can be represented by different graphemes.

I guided the students' learning as we investigated the positional orthographic conventions and patterns of certain graphemes, such as whether <igh> ever appears at the beginning of words or if <y> only appears at the end. I created another poster with columns for "initial", "medial" and "final", representing the position of the /aɪ/ phoneme within each word. I explicitly guided this study, and we placed the words accordingly:

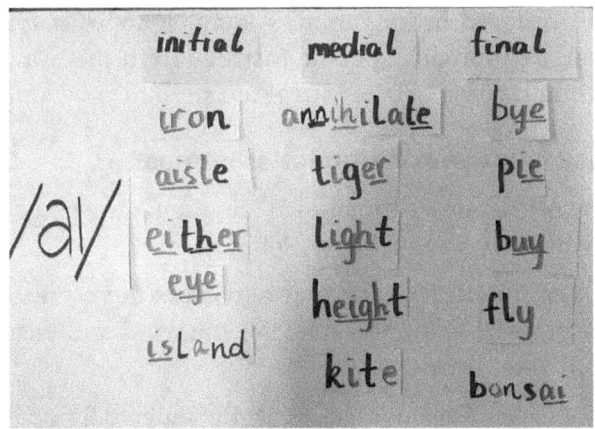

We ended with an in-depth exploration of the <igh> grapheme, inspired by the student's original spelling choice. Students collaboratively generated a list of words containing <igh>, including "light", "might", "high", "fight", "sigh" and "knight". This exercise naturally progressed to discussions about suffixes and compound words, such as "highway" and "tightrope". The inclusion of "knight" and "night" provided a springboard for examining how spelling preserves etymological information despite evolving pronunciations, while also illustrating how orthography aids in distinguishing homophones and enhancing reading comprehension.

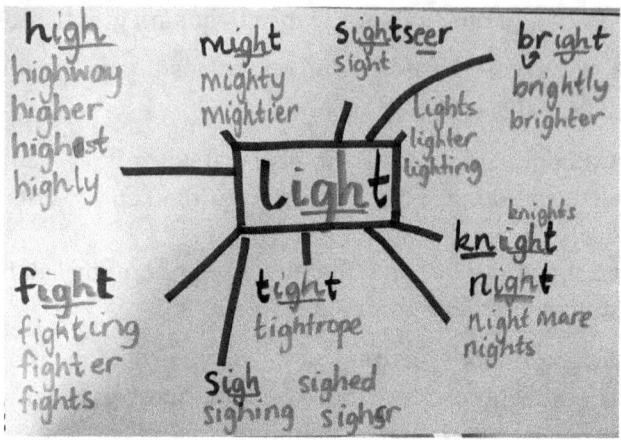

What I love about this case study is that it shows how metalinguistic instruction goes beyond teaching correct spelling—it equips students with the tools to analyse, understand and appreciate the English language's organised and ordered orthographic system. I hope that this example encourages you to approach spelling instruction in this way, even in the first year of school and especially with gifted students in your class!

4. Can you spell this word using letter names?

Now that we've broken down the sounds and their letter combinations, can you spell the word "conscience" using letter names?

Spelling aloud is important because it reinforces the correct sequence of letters in your mind. It helps you visualise the word and ensures that you remember each letter correctly.

Repetition is another effective strategy. By repeatedly spelling a word aloud, you strengthen your memory of its structure and spelling, making it easier to recall when needed.

Ask your students to spell the word "conscience" three times, and tick a "Spell it" box on the LLGO each time.

Teaching Tip!

Repetition is useful for:

- **Reinforcing memory:** Repetition strengthens memory retention, making it easier for students to recall the correct spelling of words.
- **Correcting errors:** Regular practice with immediate feedback helps students identify and correct errors, leading to improved spelling accuracy.
- **Building confidence:** As students become more familiar with spelling patterns through repetition, their confidence in spelling new words increases.

Case study: My Favourite No

As I watched my Year 5 students file back into the classroom after their NAPLAN Language Conventions assessment, I could feel the tension in the air. Slumped shoulders, furrowed brows and audible sighs filled the room. "It was so hard," one student mumbled, while another chimed in, "I'm not sure I did well". I knew I had to act fast to turn this mood around and make the most of our learning time.

That's when I decided to introduce the "My Favourite No" activity. It's a fantastic tool I've used before to foster a growth mindset, and I thought it would be perfect for this situation. I explained to the students that we'd be looking at common errors from the test—not to criticise but to learn and grow. You should have seen how their eyes lit up when I told them we'd be celebrating mistakes!

Here's how it works. Students anonymously submit answers to a question on small slips of paper. I sort them into correct and incorrect piles, then choose "my favourite no"—an answer that shows a common misunderstanding or gives us a great teaching opportunity. We then discuss it as a class, identifying what was done right and where we can improve.

One of the first examples we looked at was the spelling of "nutritious". It was a goldmine for morphology discussion. I asked the class, "What's the base in this word?" and a student quickly replied, "<nutri->!" We then talked about what happens when we add the suffix <-tious>. It was wonderful to see them grasp how it changes the word into an adjective, describing something that's full of nourishment.

We explored the spelling of the word, and I brought up the word "nutrient". The students quickly made the connection between "nutritious" and "nutrient", noting how they both share the same bound base but have different suffixes. It was a great opportunity to compare and contrast word formation, deepening their understanding of bound bases and suffixes. I decided to break down the process step-by-step, knowing that this level of detail would really cement their understanding.

"Let's look at these words more closely," I said, writing them on the board. "What is the bound base here? Remember, a bound base is a root that cannot stand alone and must be combined with affixes to form words."

"<Nutri->!" one student called out.

"Excellent!" I praised. "Now, watch what happens when we add suffixes to this bound base."

I wrote out the words, clearly separating the bound base from the suffix:

<nutri-> + <-ent> = *nutrient*
<nutri-> + <-tious> = *nutritious*

"Notice anything interesting about how the words change?" I prompted.

There was a moment of silence as the students studied the board. Then, a hand shot up. "The endings are different, but they both relate to nourishment!"

"Spot on!" I beamed. "In fact, both words come from the Latin word <nutrire> which means 'to nourish.'"

I then explained how in "nutritious", we use the suffix <-tious> which means "full of" or "having the quality of", while in "nutrient", we use <-ent> which forms a noun or adjective meaning "serving to" or "producing". To drive the point home, I had the students practice pronouncing the words, emphasising the different endings:

nutritious /njuːtrɪʃəs/
nutrient /njuːtriənt/

The class echoed the pronunciations, and I could see the lightbulbs turning on as they made the connection between the stem and the different suffixes.

"Can you think of other words that use the bound base <nutri->?" I challenged them.

Hands shot up across the room. "Nutrition!" one student offered. "Nutritionist!" said another.

"Brilliant examples!" I encouraged. "Now, let's compare 'nutritious' with another interesting word: 'magician,'" I said, writing both words on the board. "What do you notice about these words?"

A student raised her hand. "They both have a <sh> sound in them!"

"Excellent observation!" I praised. "In linguistics, we use a special symbol for this sound. It's written like this: /ʃ/. Can anyone tell me where you hear this /ʃ/ sound in these words?"

"In 'nutritious,' it's in the middle," one student offered. "And in 'magician,' it's near the end," added another.

"Let's break these down," I said, writing on the board:

nutritious /nju:trɪʃəs/
magician /məʒɪʃən/

"See how in both words, the /ʃ/ sound comes before the last syllable? But look at how they're spelled differently. In "nutritious", we use <ti> to make the /ʃ/ sound, while in "magician", we use <ci>. Isn't it fascinating how English can use different letter combinations to create the same sound?" I paused, letting the information sink in. "Now, why do you think this happens?"

A student raised her hand. "Is it because English is weird?"

The class chuckled and I smiled. "Well, there's a bit more to it than that. It's actually due to something called 'historical sound changes'. You see, these words come from Latin, and over time, their pronunciation changed, but the spelling stayed the same."

I wrote on the board:

nutritious (from Latin <nutricius>)
magician (from Latin <magicus>)

"In Latin, these were pronounced differently. But in English, when <ti> and <ci> are followed by another vowel sound, especially in unstressed syllables, they often change to the /ʃ/ sound. Can anyone think of other words where this happens?" I asked.

Hands shot up across the room.

"How about 'special'?"

"Partial!" called out another student.

"Notice how in both "special" and "partial", the /ʃ/ sound is spelled differently but sounds the same."

I then wrote a few more examples:

    social   confidential
    essential   artificial

"Look at these words. Can you see the pattern? In all of these, the <ci> or <ti> comes before the last syllable and makes the /ʃ/ sound. Understanding these patterns can really help with both pronunciation and spelling. It's like unlocking a secret code in English!"

As we moved on to the word "realistically", I saw another golden opportunity to deepen the students' understanding of morphology and phonology. The misspelling "realisticly" was a perfect springboard for our discussion.

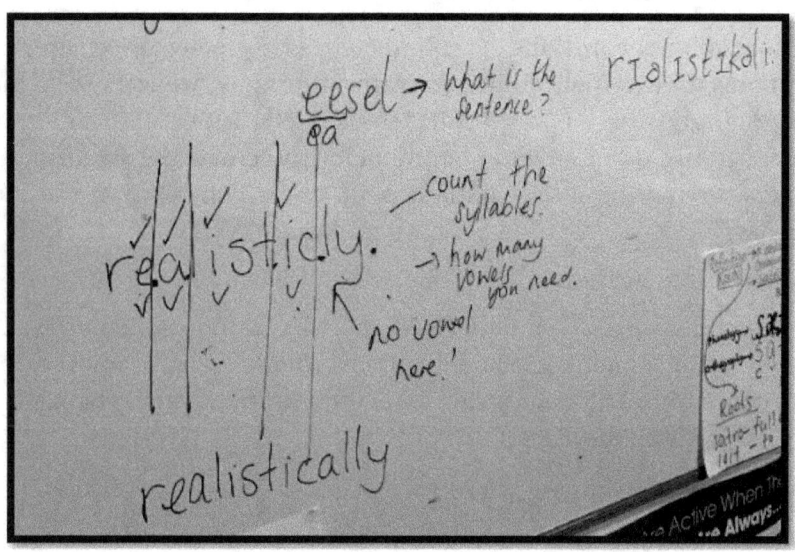

"Let's break this word down," I said, writing the spelling error "realisticly" on the board. "First, let's clap out the syllables together."

The class joined in, clapping rhythmically: "Re–a–lis–tic–a–lly." Six distinct claps rang out.

"Great! Now, how many vowel sounds did you hear?" I asked.

"Six!" they chorused, their eyes lighting up at the realisation.

118   Using Linguistic Lenses to Journey into Words

"Exactly! And in our misspelling, 'realisticly', how many vowels do we see?"

There was a moment of quiet as they counted. "Only five!" a student exclaimed.

"So, what's missing?" I prompted.

"The second <a>!" several voices called out.

"Spot on! But here's where it gets interesting," I said, lowering my voice conspiratorially. "That second <a> makes a very special sound. We call it the 'schwa' sound. It's like a quick /uh/ sound that often happens in unstressed syllables."

I wrote the phonetic symbol for schwa on the board: /ə/.

"In 'realistically', each letter <a> is representing the schwa sound: /ri:əlɪstɪkəli:/. It's why the second schwa is easy to miss when spelling.

The students' faces showed a mix of surprise and intrigue. They were discovering that English pronunciation often doesn't match its spelling in predictable ways.

"Now, let's break this word down morphologically," I began. "The word 'realistically' is composed of several meaningful parts. Can anyone identify the base word?"

After a moment, a hand went up. "Is it 'real'?"

"Excellent!" I smiled. "You're absolutely correct. 'Real' is our base word here. Now, let's look at how we build upon this base to create related words."

I wrote on the board:

<real> + <-ist> = *realist*
<real> + <-ist> + <-ic> = *realistic*
<real> + <-ist> + <-ic> + <-al> + <-ly> = *realistically*

"Let's break down each part and understand its meaning," I continued:

1. "**<real>** is our base word, meaning 'actually existing or occurring'.
2. "**<-ist>** is a suffix meaning 'one who practices or is concerned with something, or holds certain principles'.
3. "**<-ic>** is an adjective-forming suffix meaning 'having the nature of, relating to'.
4. "**<-al>** is another adjective-forming suffix, often used to create adjectives from nouns.
5. "**<-ly>** is an adverb-forming suffix meaning 'in a (specified) manner'.

"So, when we combine these morphemes, we get:

- "**realist:** a person who accepts or deals with things as they really are
- "**realistic:** representing things in a way that is accurate and true to life
- "**realistically:** in a way that shows a practical and sensible idea of what can be achieved or expected.

"Now, you might notice something interesting when we add <-ly> to 'realistic,'" I pointed out. "We don't just add <-ly> but <-ally>. Why is that?"

I wrote on the board:

<basic> + <-ly> = basically
<tragic> + <-ly> = tragically
<realistic> + <-ly> = realistically

"This is due to a spelling convention in English. When we add <-ly> to words ending in <-ic>, we insert <-al> before adding <-ly>. This helps maintain the correct pronunciation and stress pattern of the word. Let's look at a few more examples of how we add the suffix <-ly> to different bases:

- When a base ends with a consonant, we add <-ly>, resulting in no change to the base: <careful> + <-ly> = <carefully>.
- When a base ends with a <y> preceded by a consonant, we apply the <y>-to-<i> convention: <happy> + <-ly> = <happily>.
- When a base ends with <-le> we replace the <e> with <y>: <gentle> + <-ly> = <gently>.
- When a base ends with <-ic> we add <-al>: <basic> + <-ly> = <basically>.
- When a base ends with <-e> (except <-le>), we keep the <e> and add <-ly>: <absolute> + <-ly> = <absolutely>.

"This exploration of 'realistically' has taken us on a journey through morphemes, suffixes and spelling conventions. It shows us how words are built from meaningful parts and how these parts combine to create meaning. Understanding these patterns can help us decode unfamiliar words and appreciate the logic behind English word formation."

I concluded, "Remember, in morphology, we always start with the base word and add affixes to create new words with related meanings. This systematic approach helps us understand the relationships between words and their meanings".

As we wrapped up this part of the lesson, I reflected on how these seemingly small details—a schwa sound here, a digraph there—were actually huge stepping stones in the students' path to understanding. By breaking down words in this way, we weren't just improving spelling—we were developing a deeper understanding of how English works, fostering skills that would serve them well in reading, writing and even learning other languages.

What struck me most about this lesson was how quickly the mood in the classroom shifted. We went from post-test anxiety to engaged, collaborative learning in a matter of minutes. By openly discussing mistakes, we took away the stigma associated with errors. Students were receiving immediate feedback on concepts they'd just grappled with in the test, and they were learning from each other's insights. By the end of the lesson, the change in the students was tangible. Their shoulders were straighter, conversations were animated, and several students told me how excited they were to apply their new understanding to future writing tasks. It was a powerful reminder of how we can turn challenging moments into valuable learning opportunities.

The day after this discussion, the students sat the NAPLAN writing test, and after the test I could sense a mix of relief and anticipation in the classroom. As we settled into our reflection session, I was eager to hear about the sophisticated vocabulary choices my students had made in their writing. One of my highly gifted Year 5 students, her eyes shining with pride, raised her hand. "I used the word '**unfathomable**' in my writing!" she announced. I was impressed—it was certainly a sophisticated word choice for an 11-year-old:

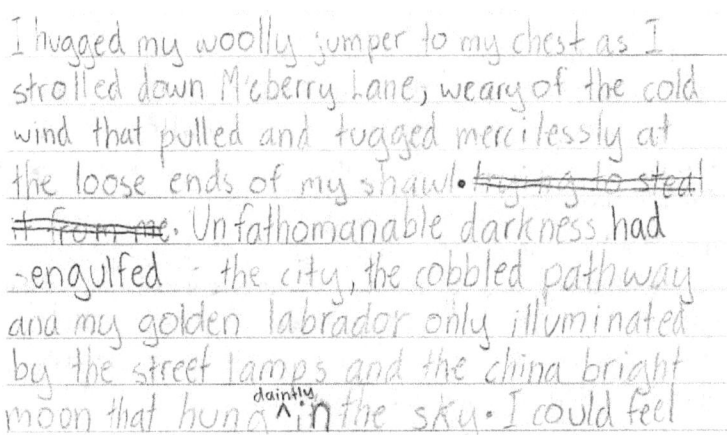

"That's fantastic!" I praised. However, I realised she had actually said "unfathomanable". But before I jumped in to correct her, I saw an opportunity for a valuable learning moment.

"Could you explain what the word means and how it's built?" I asked, picking up a pen and moving towards the whiteboard.

She nodded enthusiastically. "Well, 'fathom' is the base word," she began confidently. "It means 'to understand or comprehend something.'"

I wrote "fathom" on the board as she continued. "Then there's the prefix <un->, which means 'not,'" she explained. I added "un" to the board. "And finally, we add the suffix <-able>, which means 'capable of,'" she finished.

As I wrote "able" on the board, I could see her eyes widen slightly. She looked at the word on the board, then back at me. "Oh," she said softly, a mix of realisation and uncertainty in her voice. "I think... I have been adding an extra <-an> when I say it."

I smiled encouragingly. "You've done an excellent job breaking down the word. Let's look at it together." We examined the word on the board.

"You're absolutely right about the structure," I affirmed. "And you've just discovered something important about pronunciation and spelling. Sometimes, the way we hear or say a word might not match exactly how it's spelled."

I could see a flicker of disappointment cross her face, but it was quickly replaced by curiosity. "The most important thing," I continued, addressing the whole class now, "is that you're stretching yourselves, trying out new vocabulary and thinking deeply about how words are constructed. That's what real learning looks like."

I turned back to the student. "You should be incredibly proud. Not only did you use a sophisticated word in your writing, but you've also shown us all how to analyse word structure. And most importantly, you've demonstrated something even more valuable—the ability to recognise and learn from mistakes."

This moment highlighted something significant about teaching gifted students: often, these high-achieving learners can struggle most with accepting mistakes. They're used to getting things right, and the fear of being wrong can sometimes hold them back from taking risks or fully engaging with challenging material.

"Remember," I said to the class, "our goal isn't perfection. It's learning. Every mistake is an opportunity to understand something better." I could see nods around the room, and the gifted student's posture relaxed, a small smile returning to her face. "Now," I continued, "let's think about other words that use 'fathom' as a base. Any ideas?"

Hands shot up around the room and soon we were exploring a whole morphological family of words: fathomless, unfathomably, fathoming. The energy in the room was clear as students discovered connections and patterns they hadn't noticed before. As the lesson wound down, I reflected on how this moment, sparked by a simple mispronunciation, had turned into a rich exploration of language and, more importantly, of the learning process itself. It reinforced for me the importance of creating a classroom environment where mistakes are not just accepted but celebrated as learning opportunities.

For gifted students especially, these moments can be transformative. By embracing the process of learning, including the missteps along the way, they can develop resilience, curiosity and a growth mindset that will serve them well beyond their school years. As teachers, our role is not just to impart knowledge but to foster this love of learning and discovery. When we can turn a potential moment of embarrassment into one of insight and growth, we're truly fulfilling that role.

5. Do the graphemes represent vowel or consonant phonemes?

Now that we've spelled out "conscience" and practiced it through repetition, let's take a closer look at the graphemes and syllables. Do the graphemes in "conscience" represent vowel or consonant phonemes? And how many syllables does the word have?

Let's break it down together. Remember, we're revisiting the phoneme-grapheme correspondences to help with our spelling. This can be done orally, reflecting back to the phonology section on our LLGO. "Conscience" has two syllables—'con' and 'science':

- <c> represents the consonant phoneme /k/
- <o> represents the vowel phoneme /ɒ/
- <n> represents the consonant phoneme /n/
- <sci> is a trigraph that represents the consonant phoneme /ʃ/
- <e> represents the vowel phoneme /ə/, the schwa
- <n> represents the consonant phoneme /n/
- <ce> is a digraph that represents the consonant phoneme /s/.

By orally practicing these phoneme-grapheme correspondences and understanding how they fit into the syllables, we can improve our spelling accuracy. Reflecting on this helps us see the structure of words more clearly.

6. Is there a non-phonographic spelling where there is no grapheme to represent the phoneme?

Now, let's consider another aspect of spelling. In "conscience," all the phonemes are represented using our knowledge of graphemes, graphs, digraphs and trigraphs. This means there isn't a non-phonographic spelling in this word. Each sound we hear has a corresponding letter or combination of letters.

An example of a non-phonographic spelling would be if there was a phoneme we heard but didn't have a letter to record it with, like in the words "newspaper" or "enthusiasm", where certain sounds aren't directly mapped by a specific grapheme or graphemes: /njuːzpeɪpə/ and /ɪnθuːziːæzəm/.

Teaching Tip!
Collect orthographic word families: group words with similar non-phonographic spellings so your students can recognise patterns.

7. How many graphs are there?

Now, let's identify how many graphs are in this word. But first, let's clarify what a graph is: a graph is one single letter that represents one sound or phoneme.

Let's count the graphs in "conscience":

- <c> represents /k/
- <o> represents /ɒ/
- <n> represents /n/
- <e> represents /ə/
- <n> represents /n/.

So, in "conscience", we have five graphs: <c>, <o>, <n>, <e> and <n>, as each of these letters represents one sound.

8. How many digraphs are there?

Now that we've identified the graphs in "conscience", let's move on to digraphs. Digraphs are two letters that come together to make one sound. The prefix <di–> means "two", and <graph> means "letter".

In "conscience", we have the digraph <ce>, which represents the /s/ sound. This is a great example of how two letters can work together to produce a single phoneme.

Let's look at some other words where <di-> means two: "dioxide" refers to a compound with two oxygen atoms, and "dialogue" refers to a conversation between two people.

9. How many trigraphs are there?

Now, let's explore trigraphs. Trigraphs are combinations of three letters that come together to make one sound. The prefix <tri-> means "three", and <graph> means "letter".

In "conscience", we have the trigraph <sci>, which represents the /ʃ/ sound.

Other examples of trigraphs include <igh> in "light", which represents the /aɪ/ sound, and <tch> in "watch", which represents the /tʃ/ sound.

Case study: the silent knight of spelling

Let's take a closer look at the word "knight". Traditionally, many of us were taught that the <k> and <gh> in "knight" are "silent letters". However, this explanation falls short and can actually hinder students' understanding of English orthography. Instead, let's apply more accurate and helpful terminology.

Rather than calling <k> a silent letter, we should recognise <kn> as a digraph. In Old English, both the <k> and the <n> were pronounced. Over time, the pronunciation changed, but the spelling preserved the word's history. This digraph appears in several words with a shared etymological root, such as "knit", "knot" and "knead".

Instead of labelling <gh> as silent, we recognise <igh> as a trigraph representing the /aɪ/ phoneme (the diphthong sound of "eye"). This trigraph appears in many words, including "high", "sigh" and "thigh".

A diphthong is a single-syllable sound that consists of a movement or glide from one position to another. In essence, it's a glide between two vowel positions. The term comes from the Greek <di-> meaning "two" and <phthongos> meaning "sound" or "tone".

In Standard Australian English there are eight diphthongs (see page 43).

Teaching Tip!

In the IPA, diphthongs are represented by two symbols, reflecting the two sound positions that make up the diphthong. This dual representation is helpful for understanding and teaching diphthongs. The two symbols show the starting point and the direction of movement of the tongue during pronunciation. Unlike some other phonetic features, diphthongs don't require special additional markers in IPA.

When introducing diphthongs to students, emphasise the movement from one vowel position to another. You can use hand gestures or visual aids to demonstrate this gliding motion. For instance, draw an arrow from the first vowel symbol to the second to illustrate the sound change. Remember, the ability to recognise and produce diphthongs correctly is important for accurate pronunciation in many languages, especially English. Highlighting the two-symbol nature of diphthongs in IPA can help your students better understand and reproduce these sounds.

Redefining "silent letters" as part of digraphs and trigraphs fosters a robust, accurate and professional dialogue that extends beyond the classroom. By eschewing simplistic explanations such as "silent letters" or playful but misleading phrases like "the letters are in jail", you pave the way for sustainable learning that grows with your students. Take a look at one of the classroom conversations I encountered during the research phase of my doctoral study:

> *Teacher:* "Yesterday we were talking about how some boys have been taught 'silent letters' in the past if they have joined us from other schools."
>
> *Student:* "I was taught that silent letters were 'in jail.'"
>
> *Teacher:* "Why were they in jail?"
>
> *Student:* "Because they are silent."
>
> *Teacher:* "We had a little laugh about that, didn't we?"

Using accurate terms provides a logical framework that prevents the formation of hard-to-shake misconceptions later in your students' educational journey. Moreover, this logic transforms spelling from a set of arbitrary rules to be memorised into a fascinating exploration of language evolution. For instance, explaining the historical significance of spellings like <kn> offers students a window into the rich tapestry of linguistic history. This approach also enhances pattern recognition skills, enabling students to draw connections between words, thereby improving both their spelling and reading abilities. By using accurate terminology, you demonstrate respect for your students' intellectual capabilities, preparing them for advanced language study regardless of their current level. Finally, this logic facilitates cross-linguistic connections, allowing students to draw parallels with other languages, such as recognising that the <k> in "knight" is still pronounced in related German words like "knecht".

Teaching Tip!

When teaching words like "knight", try this approach:

1. Introduce <kn> as a digraph that represents the /n/ sound in modern English but historically represented both the /k/ and /n/ sounds.
2. Explain <igh> as a trigraph representing the diphthong /aɪ/.
3. Discuss how these spellings preserve the word's history and connect it to related words.
4. Encourage students to find other words with these digraphs and trigraphs.

Remember, our goal is to equip students with tools for understanding language, not just memorising spellings. By using precise, scientific terminology and explaining the logic behind spellings, we're helping students on a sustainable learning journey!

10. Is there a quadgraph?

Now, let's consider whether there's a quadgraph in "conscience". A quadgraph is a combination of four letters that make one sound. The prefix <quad-> means four.

Before we dive into examples, let's think of other words with <quad>. For instance, "quadrilateral" refers to a shape with four sides, and "quadruple" means four times as much.

In the word "conscience", there isn't a quadgraph, as no four-letter combination represents a single sound.

Quadgraphs are less common but can be found in words like "eight" and "drought".

11. Are there orthographic patterns?

Orthographic patterns are the regularities and conventions in the spelling of words within a language. These patterns help us understand how sounds are represented by letters and letter combinations in written language. They are crucial for developing reading and spelling skills as they provide a framework for predicting how words are spelled.

Traditionally, spelling "rules" have been taught as absolute guidelines for spelling words correctly. However, these rules can often be seen as rigid and unsustainable for learners due to the numerous exceptions in the English language. For example, the rule "<i> before <e> except after <c>" has many exceptions, such as "weird" and "seize". In contrast, using the term "patterns" is more effective because patterns are more predictable and plausible, allowing your students to recognise recurring sequences of letters and sounds. Patterns offer a more flexible approach, accommodating exceptions and variations more naturally. Understanding orthographic patterns not only helps us with spelling but deepens our appreciation for the intricacies of the English language.

Here's an example of how you could explore this in your classroom:

Teacher (You): "Let's start with the letter <c> in 'conscience'. Here, <c> represents the /k/ sound, a common pattern when <c> is followed by the letters <a>, <o> or <u>. Can anyone share examples of <c> making the /k/ sound?"

Student: "Cat! Cold! Cup!"

Teacher: "Exactly! In 'cat', 'cold' and 'cup', <c> makes the /k/ sound. However, when <c> is followed by <e>, <i> or <y>, it usually makes the /s/ sound, as in 'cent', 'city' and 'cycle'. This contrast is a great example of how context changes pronunciation. Now, let's examine the trigraph <sci> in 'conscience'. This combination represents the /ʃ/ sound. Can anyone think of another word with <sci>?"

Student: "Conscious!"

Teacher: "Perfect; <sci> gives us the /ʃ/ sound in 'conscious' too. Another example is in the word 'omniscience', which means 'all-knowing', but here it is pronounced differently. This pattern often appears in words with Latin roots, showing its historical influence on English: here, <sci–> is derived from Latin <scire>, meaning 'to know'. It often appears in words related to knowledge and awareness."

Student: "What about <-ence>? Is it a suffix in 'conscience'?"

Teacher: *"Typically, <-ence> turns verbs or adjectives into nouns, indicating a state or condition. It's a common ending in English. For example, 'presence' means 'the state of being present.' Can anyone name another word with <-ence>?"*

Student: *"Absence!"*

Teacher: *"Exactly! 'Absence' is 'the state of being absent.' However, in 'conscience,' <-ence> isn't functioning as a typical suffix. Instead, it's part of the root word derived from Latin <scientia>, meaning 'knowledge.' This highlights the importance of understanding word etymology."*

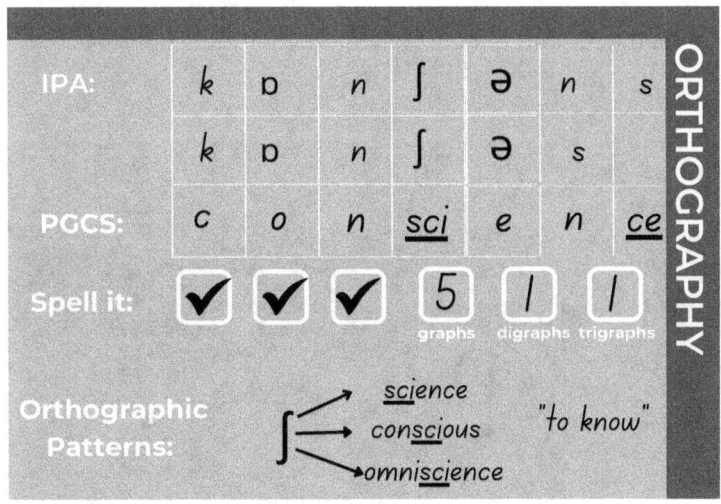

Case study: exploring orthographic patterns through Out of My Mind

This case study delves into a word study based on Sharon Draper's acclaimed novel *Out of My Mind*, focusing on the word "iridescent" using the LLGO. I have included this example to highlight how you can enhance your students' morphological and orthographic awareness.

The word "iridescent" captures the vibrant play of colours, akin to those seen in a soap bubble. By analysing this word through each Linguistic Lens, students gained a comprehensive understanding of its structure and usage. Over the page, you can see a completed LLGO, after we had worked through the Guiding Questions of each Lens.

For this example, we will home in on the key learning when we used our Orthography Lens.

When examining the word using the Orthography Lens, the focus shifted to identifying orthographic patterns. The transformation of "iridescent" into "iridescence" offers a perfect example. Replacing the suffix <-ent> with <-ence> is a morphological shift that changes an adjective into a noun. This is not an isolated phenomenon but rather a common orthographic pattern in English, as seen in transformations like "silent" into "silence", "absent" into "absence" and "patient" into "patience". The day following the word study, students revisited the concept of orthographic patterns. Encouraged to brainstorm additional examples, they identified "present" into "presence" and "independent" into "independence". This exercise not only reinforced their understanding but also empowered them to apply their knowledge independently.

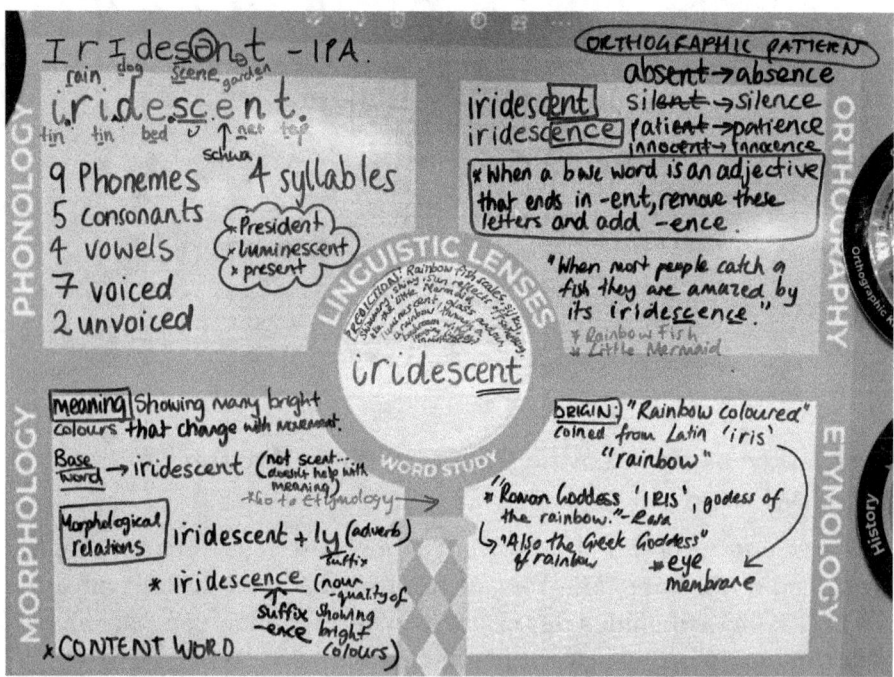

This pattern is a convention of English spelling. It is essential to clarify for students that while these patterns are prevalent, they are not rigid rules. English is a language known for its exceptions.

Teaching Tip!

When discussing orthographic patterns, emphasise the importance of using the term "patterns" rather than "rules". This approach encourages a more flexible understanding of English spelling, fostering a learning environment that is both sustainable and truthful. Engaging students in identifying these patterns cultivates their ability to predict similar morphological changes, enhancing their spelling and vocabulary skills.

Contemplate and Consider!

This exercise is designed to help you and your colleagues reflect on your understanding of orthographic patterns and consider how these insights can be applied to your classrooms:

- Take a moment to write down your initial thoughts on orthographic patterns. How has your understanding evolved after engaging with this case study?
- Reflect on your current teaching practices. How can your understanding of orthographic patterns influence and improve these practices?
- Consider how a deeper focus on orthographic patterns might impact your students' learning outcomes. What changes do you anticipate?

Implement and Innovate!

Be empowered to bring the principles of orthographic patterns into your classrooms creatively and effectively by trying the following activities. Work in teaching teams, grade partners or small groups to complete the following:

- Develop a lesson plan that incorporates orthographic pattern exercises. In small groups, brainstorm different ways to integrate these exercises into existing curriculum topics. Consider how to adapt activities for various age groups and learning levels. Each group will present a draft lesson plan, highlighting key activities and objectives.
- Develop a method for gathering and utilising student feedback. Design a feedback form or survey that students can fill out after participating in orthographic pattern activities. Discuss how this feedback can inform future lesson planning and teaching methods.

Tracking and Monitoring Student Progress in Orthography

Effective tracking and monitoring of student progress in orthography is fundamental for developing strong spelling and writing skills. Here are some practical strategies and tools you can use to assess and enhance your students' orthographic abilities, focusing on three key areas: correct spelling of grapheme-phoneme correspondences, understanding of orthographic terms and application of spelling patterns.

1. **Correct spelling of phoneme-grapheme correspondences:**
   - Use activities that require students to break down words into individual sounds and match them with corresponding graphemes.
   - Implement word sorting activities where students categorise words based on their grapheme-phoneme correspondences.
2. **Understanding of orthographic terms:**
   - Teach orthographic terms such as "graph", "digraph" and "trigraph" through explicit and direct instruction. Use visual aids and examples to clarify these concepts.
   - Have students create interactive examples where they define and illustrate each orthographic term. This can be a reference tool for future learning.
   - Use tools like Kahoot to create quizzes that focus on identifying and using orthographic terms correctly. This reinforces learning in a fun and engaging way.
3. **Application of spelling patterns:** Provide writing prompts or dictations that encourage the use of specific spelling patterns. Review students' writing to assess their application of these patterns.

The Orthography Lens Rubric

By utilising this tool, you can effectively assess students' current orthographic understanding, identify areas needing focused instruction, monitor progress and customise your teaching approaches to meet your individual student requirements. This tool also serves as a valuable resource for both anecdotal and summative assessments, offering a clear pathway for students to develop their understanding of English orthography. Each category is assessed across three levels of proficiency:

1. **Glimpser:** The initial stage, where students are beginning to recognise basic orthographic concepts

2. **Observer:** An intermediate level, where students can apply common conventions and recognise more complex patterns
3. **Analyst:** The advanced level, where students can analyse, explain and apply sophisticated orthographic principles.

The Orthography Lens Rubric

Key Feature	Glimpser	Observer	Analyst
Phoneme–Grapheme Correspondence (Encoding sounds)	Can identify simple phoneme–grapheme correspondences	Can recognise most phoneme–grapheme correspondences	Can analyse most phoneme–grapheme and non-phonographic correspondences
Orthographic Knowledge (Encoding sounds into written words)	Can identify common graphs and digraphs (e.g. <sh> and <ch>) and spell simple words using this spelling knowledge	Can recognise and use trigraphs (e.g. <tch>) and quadgraphs in various word positions and mostly spell with accuracy	Can analyse and use various letter combinations, including etymology-based spellings (e.g. <ph> in "phone") to spell with accuracy
Orthographic Patterns (Drawing on morphological and etymological spelling strategies)	Can identify basic spelling patterns based on sound position (e.g. /k/ in "**k**ite" vs "ba**ck**")	Can recognise and apply common suffixing conventions (e.g. "happy" to "happier") and use some spelling strategies, including morphological knowledge and common etymological patterns to spell	Can analyse and explain complex orthographic patterns, including adjacent sound influences, etymology-based spellings and advanced suffixing conventions, justifying the most appropriate spelling strategies for complex or unfamiliar words

Your Guide to the Orthography Lens

Regular assessment, coupled with engaging activities and feedback, can help your students develop a strong understanding of spelling patterns and orthographic terms.

From Contemplation to Classroom Innovation

At its core, the Orthography Lens is a powerful tool that reveals the order and understanding embedded in the seemingly simple letters of our alphabet. The Orthography Lens is not merely a theoretical construct—it is an essential component of effective linguistic instruction. By examining graphemes and their positions, combinations and sequences, you can illuminate the grapheme-phoneme correspondences and orthographic knowledge that are crucial for your students to master spelling, reading comprehension and written expression.

Research consistently highlights the importance of strong orthographic knowledge in supporting literacy skills. For upper primary and secondary students, understanding orthographic principles becomes vital as they navigate increasingly complex texts and vocabulary. By supporting your students to understand the intricacies of orthographic mapping—the mental process that connects visual letters to their corresponding sounds—you help them gain a deeper appreciation for how this fundamental skill supports their journey towards fluent reading and writing.

To conclude this chapter, I invite you to embrace the Orthography Lens as a pathway to classroom innovation, transforming contemplation into actionable strategies that enrich the learning experience. Have fun!

Contemplate and Consider!

Explore the intricacies of orthographic mapping and discover innovative ways to apply it in the classroom:

1. **Word Treasure Hunt:** Organise your fellow teachers into small groups. Provide each group with LLGOs (focusing on the Phonology and Orthography boxes) featuring different complex words such as "photosynthesis", "quixotic" and "anachronism". Encourage groups to dive into the exploration of these words.
2. **Decode and Visualise:** Challenge each group to decode the grapheme-phoneme correspondences of their assigned words. Using colourful pens or digital tools, each group creates a visual

representation of their orthographic discoveries. Encourage creativity and clarity in their visualisations.
3. **Speed Sharing Session:** Organise a "speed sharing" session where groups rotate around the room to present their orthographic maps to others. Facilitate discussions on how these insights can enhance spelling and reading instruction in the classroom.

By participating in this activity, you and your colleagues will gain a deeper understanding of orthographic mapping and how it can be used to improve literacy instruction. I am sure that the collaborative and creative nature of the activity will inspire you all to think critically about your teaching practices and explore new strategies for enhancing student learning!

Answer Key

Photosynthesis /fəʊ.təʊ.sɪn.θə.sɪs/:
- The <ph> digraph represents the /f/ sound, a common Greek-origin spelling.
- <o> in the first syllable is pronounced as a diphthong /əʊ/.
- <t> is a graph making the sound /t/ as in "tap".
- The second <o> is also the diphthong /əʊ/ in an unstressed position.
- <syn> comes from Greek, meaning "together", and is pronounced /sɪn/.
- <th> represents the voiceless fricative /θ/.
- The final <e> represents the schwa /ə/ like in "garden".
- The final syllable includes /s/ as in "sun", /ɪ/ as in "tin" and /s/ as in "sun".
- <photo> is from the Greek "phōs" meaning "light" and <thesis> comes from Greek "tithenai" meaning "to place" or "put". Together the meaning can be deduced as "putting together with light".

Quixotic /kwɪk.sɒt.ɪk/:
- <q> and <u> represent two separate sounds: /k/ and /w/. This can often be confused as one sound on older phonic charts.
- <i> is pronounced as a short monophthong /ɪ/.
- <x> is a diphone representing two sounds: /k/ and /s/.
- <o> is pronounced as a short monophthong /ɒ/.
- <t> is a graph pronounced /t/ as in "tap".
- <ic> is a common adjectival ending, pronounced /ɪ/ and /k/.
- This word is an eponym—more on this in the Etymology Lens!

Anachronism /ənæk.rə.nɪ.zəm/:
- The initial <a> is reduced to a schwa /ə/ in unstressed position.
- <n> is pronounced /n/ as in "net".
- The letter <a> is pronounced as the short monopthong /æ/.
- The <ch> digraph represents the /k/ sound as in "school".
- The graph <r> is pronounced with the /r/ phoneme as in "rain".
- <o> is reduced to a schwa /ə/ in unstressed position.
- <n> is pronounced /n/ as in "net".
- <ism> is a common noun-forming suffix, pronounced /ɪzəm/.
- The grapheme <chron> connects to words around time like "chronological" or "chronic". The etymological root <ana> means "against". Therefore, we can deduce the meaning "against time", with the suffix indicating that this is a noun, therefore it is a "thing". So, an anachronism is "a thing that is chronologically out of place" or "an error in computing time".

All three words have Greek or Latin origins, which explains some of their unique spelling patterns. Also, the orthography doesn't always directly correspond to the phonology, showcasing the complexity of English spelling–sound relationships—and the need to move on to the Morphology and Etymology Lens to understand the meaning of the word!

Implement and Innovate!

Develop engaging lesson plans that incorporate the Orthography Lens to enhance your students' learning:

1. Invite your fellow teachers to select a text or a set of vocabulary words that align with their current unit or theme, ensuring it resonates with students' interests and year levels.
2. Design a lesson plan that incorporates orthographic principles, thinking creatively about how to make phoneme–grapheme correspondences engaging and interactive for your students.
3. Suggest using multimedia tools, games or hands-on activities to bring orthographic concepts to life.
4. Organise a "lesson swap" where you exchange your lesson plans with your colleagues. Provide constructive feedback on each other's plans, or if you are brave enough, take part in peer observation using the observation tool in Chapter 8! Encourage everyone to share insights

on what worked well and how they might adapt ideas for their own classrooms.

Through this activity, you and your colleagues will gain practical experience in designing lessons that effectively integrate orthographic principles. The collaborative nature of the lesson swap and feedback session will foster a supportive learning community, supporting you all to refine your instructional strategies and inspire each other with innovative ideas. This approach not only enhances your fellow teachers' pedagogical skills but also enriches students' learning experiences by making orthography an engaging and integral part of the curriculum.

Implement and Innovate!

Encourage personal reflection and professional growth through thoughtful journalling:

- Provide everyone with handouts featuring engaging prompts, such as, "How can the Orthography Lens enhance my teaching practice?" Use prompts that encourage all teachers to think deeply about their teaching approach and potential innovations.
- Give teachers dedicated time to engage in introspective journalling, allowing them to explore their thoughts and consider practical classroom applications of the Orthography Lens. Play calming music to create a reflective atmosphere.
- Organise a "reflection circle" where colleagues can share their insights and experiences with the group (if they want to!). Set up a space in your staff room where everyone can post their thoughts and reflections, enabling colleagues to draw inspiration from each other's ideas and experiences.

This activity fosters a reflective practice among you and your colleagues, encouraging everyone to consider how the Orthography Lens can be integrated into their teaching. By sharing insights and displaying reflections, I know that you can inspire each other and cultivate a collaborative learning environment. This reflective journalling journey not only promotes personal and professional growth but also enhances the overall teaching and learning experience by encouraging innovative approaches to orthography.

CHAPTER 5

Your Guide to the Morphology Lens

"We know of no studies showing that teaching beginning readers about morphology results in weaker outcomes than phonology-first instruction. Therefore, there is no evidence-based reason to exclude morphology from early literacy instruction. In fact, the evidence supports the opposite conclusion."

~ *Anderson et al.*

By the end of this chapter, you will have the following key knowledge to help you revolutionise your approach to teaching word structure, meaning and spelling:

1. **Morphological awareness:** Dive deep into morphology, the study of word structure and formation, uncovering the building blocks that form the foundation of our language.
2. **Word relationships:** Master the art of identifying and grouping words based on shared morphemes and exploring how morphologically related words share meaning and often spelling patterns.
3. **Prefixes, suffixes and base words:** Sharpen your skills in analysing words by breaking them into constituent parts and discovering how affixes modify word meaning and function, enhancing vocabulary instruction.
4. **The morphology versus phonology spelling paradigm shift:** Recognise the supremacy of morphological relationships over phonological ones in English spelling and understand how this principle ensures consistent spelling across morphological relations.

5. **Vocabulary expansion:** Harness morphological knowledge to infer meanings of unfamiliar words, and build robust vocabularies by understanding word formation from known morphemes.
6. **Reading comprehension:** Apply morphological analysis to break down challenging words in texts and enhance students' reading comprehension through improved word attack skills.
7. **Spelling strategies beyond phonic foundations:** Develop advanced spelling strategies rooted in morphological patterns and transition from basic phonic spelling to sophisticated orthographic knowledge.

Introducing the Morphology Lens

Meet the Morphology Lens! In this chapter, we dive into the world of morphology, where words are constructed like intricate LEGO creations. Each morpheme, whether a prefix, suffix, base, or affix, acts as a building block that significantly impacts word class, grammatical form and function. Morphology is the crucial linguistic feature that connects directly to patterns, pronunciations and meanings, much like how LEGO pieces fit together to create a cohesive model. This journey will showcase how these elements work in harmony to shape language, providing a comprehensive understanding of word construction.

Each Linguistic Lens has its own distinct features, and the Morphology Lens is no different. At the top of the Lens is the core focus of this area of linguistic knowledge. At the bottom, there's a straightforward explanation: <morph-> means change, like in "metamorphosis", and <-ology> means "the study of". So, morphology is the study of how words change.

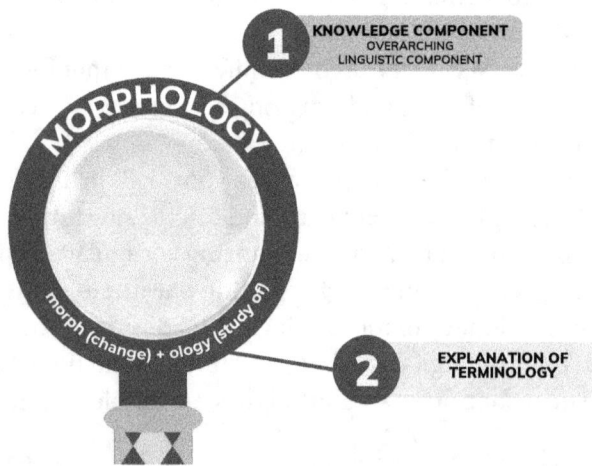

The back of the Morphology Lens spotlights essential morphological **Key Features** for your word study. These elements have been carefully transformed into a series of **Guiding Questions**, creating a comprehensive framework to support continuous learning and understanding of the English language. This setup offers clear and accessible metalanguage to help you delve into the dynamic process of language exploration.

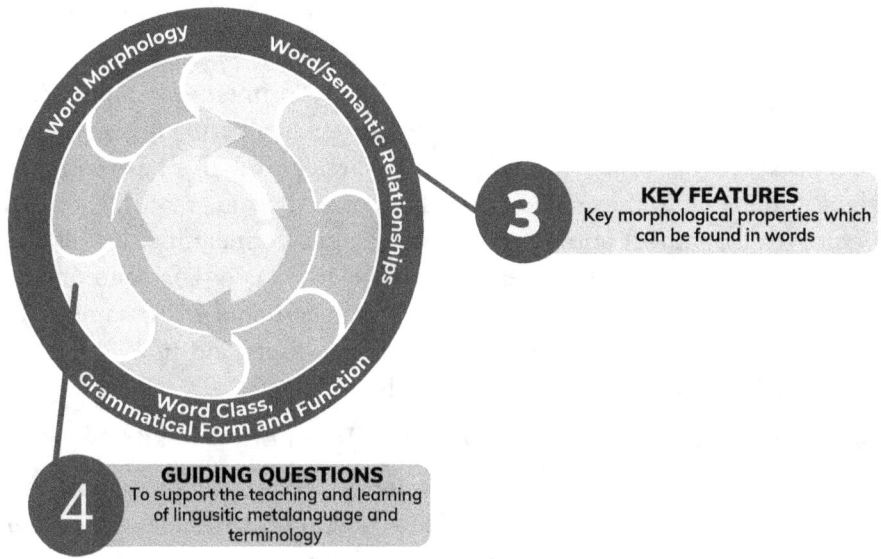

Key Features of the Morphology Lens

Morphology is the art of word construction. It's the study of the smallest units of meaning, known as morphemes. Think of morphemes as the building blocks of language. Just as you can combine LEGO bricks to create anything from a simple house to a complex spaceship, morphemes come together to form new words or modify existing ones, adding layers of meaning and complexity. Understanding morphology using the Morphology Lens involves exploring the following Key Features, which are located on the back outer ring of the Lens:

1. **Word Morphology:** Morphology examines how words are formed by combining morphemes. For example, the word "unhappiness" is built from the morphemes <un-> (a prefix meaning "not"), "happy" (a base word) and <-ness> (a suffix indicating a state or quality).

2. **Word/Semantic Relationships:** Morphology helps us understand how words relate to each other in meaning. It reveals how words can be transformed to express different ideas, like turning "teach" into "teacher" to indicate someone who performs the action.
3. **Word Class, Grammatical Form and Function:** Affixes (prefixes and suffixes) are the magic tools that alter a word's class, grammatical form and function. They can turn a verb into a noun, an adjective into an adverb, and much more. For instance, adding <-ly> to "quick" transforms it into "quickly", changing its role in a sentence.

Imagine language as a giant jigsaw puzzle. Each morpheme is a piece with a unique shape and meaning. Some pieces are small but crucial, like prefixes and suffixes, while others are larger and more central, like base words or stems. When you fit these pieces together correctly, you create a complete picture (or a complex one)—a word with a specific meaning. Just as in a puzzle, the arrangement matters—a misplaced puzzle piece can change the entire image, and a misplaced morpheme can alter the meaning of a word. Morphology is the guide that helps us understand how to put the pieces together to communicate effectively.

Components of Word Morphology: The Teachers' Toolkit

By exploring word morphology, you (alongside your students) can gain insights into how language is built and how meanings are conveyed through word formation. Here is a visual snapshot of the components which make up word morphology:

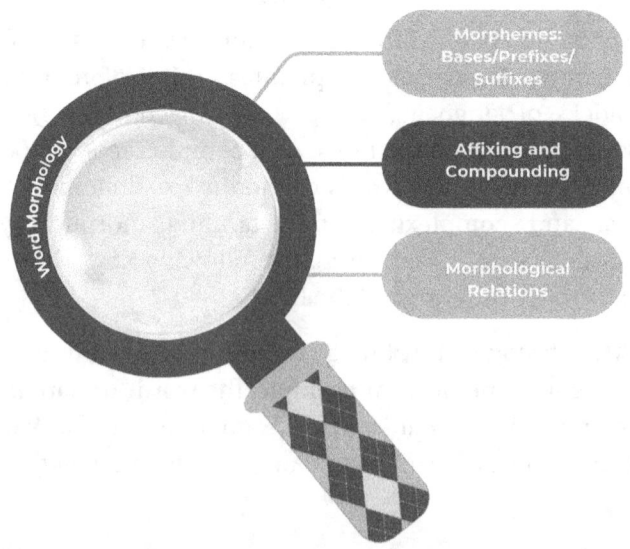

1. **Morphemes** are the LEGO pieces of language. They come in types:
   - **Bases** are the core parts of words that carry the primary meaning. For example, in "unhappiness", "happy" is the base word. A base word can be free or bound: free bases can stand alone, like "teach", but bound bases cannot, like <struct> in "construction", "instructor" and "structure".
   - **Prefixes** are like add-ons at the start of words that tweak its meaning. In "unhappiness", <un-> flips "happy" on its head.
   - **Suffixes** go at the end of words to change how they work or what they mean. The <-ness> in "unhappiness" turns "happy" into a "thing".
2. **Affixing and Compounding** are the two main ways words get built:
   - **Affixing:** Slap on a prefix or suffix and you've got a new word. Like magic, "happy" becomes "unhappiness" with a few tweaks. Next time you see a word, ask yourself, "What does that suffix mean?" or "How does this prefix change things up?"
   - **Compounding:** Mix two words together and voilà! You've got something new, like "rainbow", "lightbulb" or "highway".
3. **Morphological Relations:** Words are connected, like family members. Take "pleasing", "pleasure", "pleasantly", "unpleasantness" and "displease"—they all share the base word "please". Spotting these connections helps you see patterns and understand language better. By incorporating these concepts into your teaching, you can help students develop a deeper understanding of language structure, enhancing their vocabulary and comprehension skills. This approach not only makes language learning more engaging but also equips students with tools to decode and construct words effectively.

Components of Word/Semantic Relationships: The Teachers' Toolkit

Semantic relationships are how words are connected in meaning. Just as a spider web connects points to form a pattern, each word is a node linked to others through similarities or differences. Recognising these patterns and connections will allow your students to use what they already know to understand new words.

By analysing word and semantic relationships through the Morphology Lens, you will be able to support your students to uncover patterns and connections between related words. This approach will not only build their vocabulary but also enhance their understanding of language, impacting their reading comprehension and their choice of words when writing. Here's how it works:

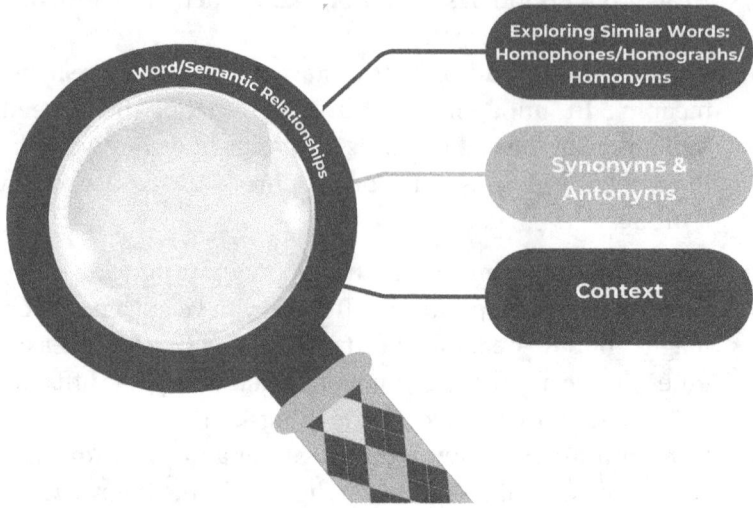

1. **Exploring Similar Words:**
   - **Homophones** are words that sound the same but have different meanings and spellings, like "pair" and "pear". Understanding homophones helps students recognise that pronunciation doesn't always determine meaning. Think <homo> = "same", <phone> = "sound"!
   - **Homographs** are words that are spelled the same but have different meanings and/or pronunciations, such as "lead" (to guide) and "lead" (a type of metal). Recognising homographs teaches students that context is key to understanding. This is why words cannot be taught in isolation! Think <homo> = "same", <graph> = "letter"!
   - **Homonyms** are both homophones and homographs, like "bat" (an animal) and "bat" (a piece of sports equipment). Exploring homonyms helps students appreciate the richness of language.
2. **Synonyms and Antonyms:** Synonyms are words with similar meanings, like "happy" and "joyful", while antonyms are words with opposite meanings, like "hot" and "cold". Learning these helps students expand their vocabulary by understanding different ways

to express ideas. Encouraging students to list words with similar or opposite meanings helps them build a network of related words, making it easier to remember and use them.

3. **Context:** Writing words in sentences shows students how the meaning of a word can change depending on how it's used. For instance, see how context affects the meaning of "light" in "a light breeze" as opposed to "turn on the light".

Components of Word Class, Grammatical Form and Function: The Teachers' Toolkit

Understanding the intricacies of word morphology is essential for understanding the depth of English spelling, particularly in terms of word class, grammatical form and function. By exploring bases and stems, and affixes and their roles as inflectional and derivational morphemes, we can see how words are modified to convey different meanings and how this changes their grammatical form. This foundational knowledge not only enriches vocabulary but also enhances comprehension of English as a morphophonemic language, where spelling reflects both sound and meaning.

Word classes, also known as parts of speech, are essential categories that describe the function of words within sentences, helping us understand and construct language effectively. Nouns name people, places, things or ideas, serving as subjects or objects, while verbs describe actions, states or occurrences, forming the core of predicates. Adjectives modify nouns by providing additional details, and adverbs modify verbs, adjectives or other adverbs to indicate how, when, where or to what extent actions occur. Pronouns replace nouns to avoid repetition, and prepositions show relationships between nouns and other words, often indicating direction, location or time. Conjunctions connect words, phrases or clauses, building complex sentences; they can be coordinating, like "and" or "but", and subordinating, like "because" or "although". Lastly, interjections express strong emotion or surprise, often standing alone, such as "wow" or "ouch".

By explicitly teaching affixes and their relationship to word classes, you provide your students with a framework for analysing and constructing sentences.

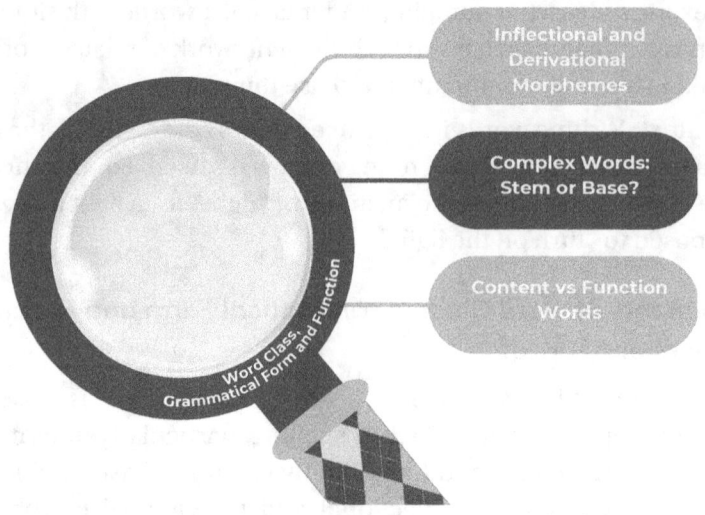

1. **Inflectional and Derivational Morphemes:**
    - **Inflectional Morphemes** modify a word to express different grammatical categories without changing its core meaning or word class. They include endings like <-s>, <-ed>, <-ing>, <-er> and <-est>. Inflectional morphemes convey grammatical information such as tense, number and degree. For example, the adjectives "low," "lower" and "lowest" illustrate how the inflectional endings <-er> and <-est> modify the adjective to express comparative and superlative forms while keeping it an adjective.
    - **Derivational Morphemes** create new words and can change the word class. They include prefixes like <un-> and suffixes like <-ful>. Unlike inflectional morphemes, derivational morphemes can change a word's grammatical category, creating entirely new words. For example, the verb "support" becomes the noun "supporter" with the addition of the suffix <-er>. However, derivational morphemes do not always change a word's grammatical category. For example, by adding the prefix <un->, "supported" transforms into "unsupported", altering its meaning while maintaining its word class as an adjective.
2. **Complex Words: Stem or Base?**
    - A **Complex Word** is a base word combined with a derivational element, such as an affix or a suffix. For example, <live> plus <-ly> equals "lively", and <im-> plus <possible> equals "impossible".

- What is a **Base**? Let's look at the word "interaction". If you ask your students what the base word is in "interaction", some might say <interact>, whilst others might say <act>. However, we cannot refer to <interact> as a base, because it is a complex word with a base and a prefix: <inter-> plus <act> equals "interact". Dr Peter Bowers refers to the word "stem" as a needed morphological term in which I can apply to this example. I can call "interact" the stem of the word "interaction", but it is not the base.
- A **Stem** is the form of a word to which affixes are added. It can be a base word or a modified form that serves as the foundation for further morphological changes. For example, while "interact" is not a base, it is a stem because further affixes can be added to it, such as <-ion> to make "interaction". For another example, "joy" is a base word and "enjoy" is not, but "enjoy" acts as a stem for further derivation, such as "enjoyment".

3. **Content vs Function Words:** We can categorise words into two main types—content words and function words:
    - **Content Words** carry the main meaning in a sentence. They are the words that give us the most information and are often the focus of communication. They include nouns (words that name people, places, things or ideas, such as "dog", "city" and "happiness"), verbs (words that describe actions or states, such as "run", "think" and "exist"), adjectives (words that describe or modify nouns, such as "happy", "blue" and "large") and adverbs (words that modify verbs, adjectives or other adverbs, such as "quickly", "very" and "well"). Content words are usually open class, meaning new words can be added to these categories as language evolves (such as "blog" and "selfie").
    - **Function Words**, on the other hand, have little lexical meaning on their own but are crucial for the grammatical structure of a sentence. They help to connect content words and clarify relationships between them. They include prepositions (words that show relationships in time or space, such as "in", "on" and "at"), conjunctions (words that connect clauses or sentences, such as "and", "but" and "because"), articles (words that define a noun as specific or unspecific, such as "the", "a" or "an"), pronouns (words that replace nouns, such as "he", "she" and "they") and auxiliary verbs (helping verbs that add grammatical meaning, such

as "is", "have" and "do"). Function words are typically closed class, meaning new words are rarely added to these categories.

Exploring "Conscience" Through the Morphology Lens

Now, let's step back into the classroom, where I can show you how to use the Morphology Lens to support your teaching.

Begin by explaining to the class that we've already explored how "conscience" sounds through the Phonology Lens and examined its spelling through the Orthography Lens, so now it is time to embark on a journey to understand its morphological structure and how that connects to its meaning. Project the LLGO digital template onto the interactive whiteboard and place the Morphology Lens magnet next to the Morphology section, saying to the class, "Using the LLGO, we'll break down 'conscience' even further. This will help us understand its components and reinforce its meaning".

In the centre of the LLGO, write "conscience" and say to the students, "Let's continue to fill this out together, focusing on its morphological structure. Let's use the Guiding Questions to explore how the word's parts relate to its meaning. Pay special attention to bases, affixes and stems!"

Through this exploration, students will gain a deeper understanding of "conscience", not just as a word but as a concept intricately tied to its morphological components. By revisiting "conscience" through multiple Lenses, we ensure that students not only memorise the word but also grasp its full significance.

Setting off on a Morphological Adventure: Navigating the 12 Guiding Questions

You can now consider yourself as a seasoned traveller, having already set out and uncovered the phonological and orthographic features hidden within the linguistic landscape. Moving on to the Morphology Lens, your map is a series of 12 Guiding Questions, each designed to help you and your students delve into the features of a word's morphology.

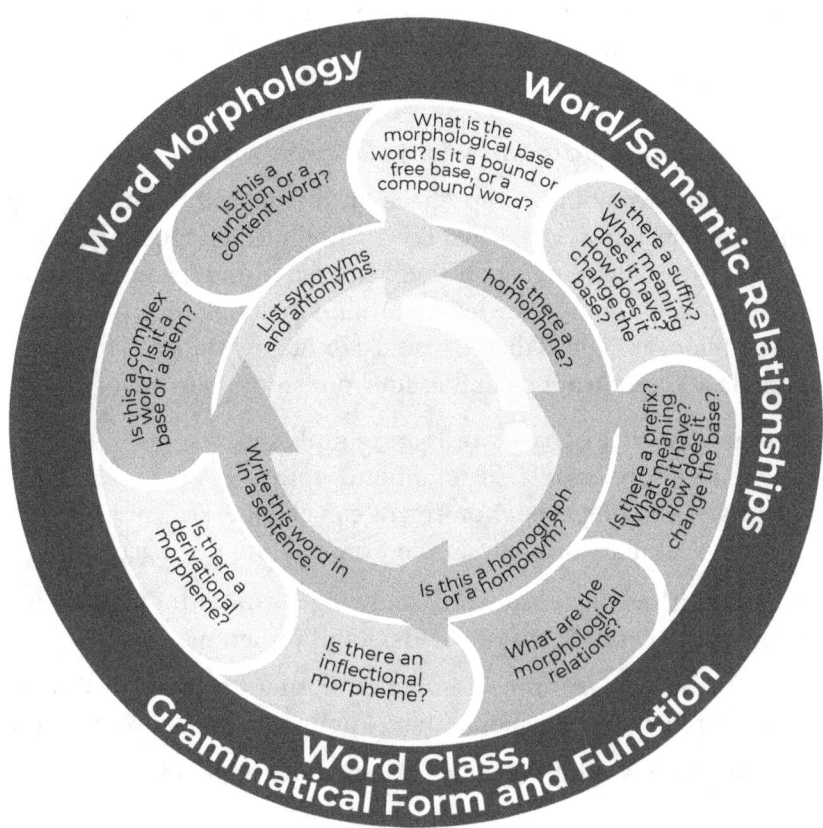

1. What is the morphological base word? Is it a bound or free base, or a compound word?

Let's start by identifying the morphological base word of "conscience": it is "science". "Science" comes from the Latin word <scientia>, which means "knowledge". So, in "conscience", the base word "science" refers to knowledge. This base gives us a clue about the meaning of "conscience", which involves knowledge of right and wrong.

Now that we know <science> is the base element of "conscience", let's discuss whether it's a bound or free base in this word. A free base can stand alone as a word, but a bound base can't. So, in the word "conscience", <science> is free because it can be used on its own—right? Actually, while <science> is indeed a free base when it stands alone, in "conscience" it functions as a bound base. This is because we can't separate <con> and <science> in "conscience" and have them keep the same meaning. It's bound to the prefix <con-> to create a new meaning. This shows us how a typically free base like <science> can become bound in certain words. Understanding this helps us see how "conscience" is built from elements that work together to create its unique meaning.

Case study: dare to "dream" with your lower primary students

When teaching a reading comprehension lesson with a small group of students aged six and seven, I had the goal of introducing morphology in an engaging way, building upon their emerging understanding of word structure. I chose to centre the lesson around the book *In Your Dreams* by Dawn McMillan, as I felt its theme would capture my student's imagination and provide accessible opportunities for word study. I aimed to:

- introduce the idea of base words and simple suffixes
- explore a few dream-related compound words
- encourage thinking about how words can change
- expand vocabulary through simple word-building exercises.

I chose "dream" as our base word, knowing it would be familiar to the children and offer several easy-to-understand variations.

We began by reading *In Your Dreams* aloud. After finishing, I asked a few simple comprehension questions. Then, I pointed to the title of the book.

"What's the main word in this title?" I asked. A couple of hands went up hesitantly.

"Dream!" one student exclaimed after I called on them.

"Excellent! Now, let's think about what words we can make using "dream" as our starting point."

My students thought for a moment before offering suggestions. I wrote each one on our poster:

- "Dreams"
- "Dreaming"
- "Dreamy"
- "Dreamily".

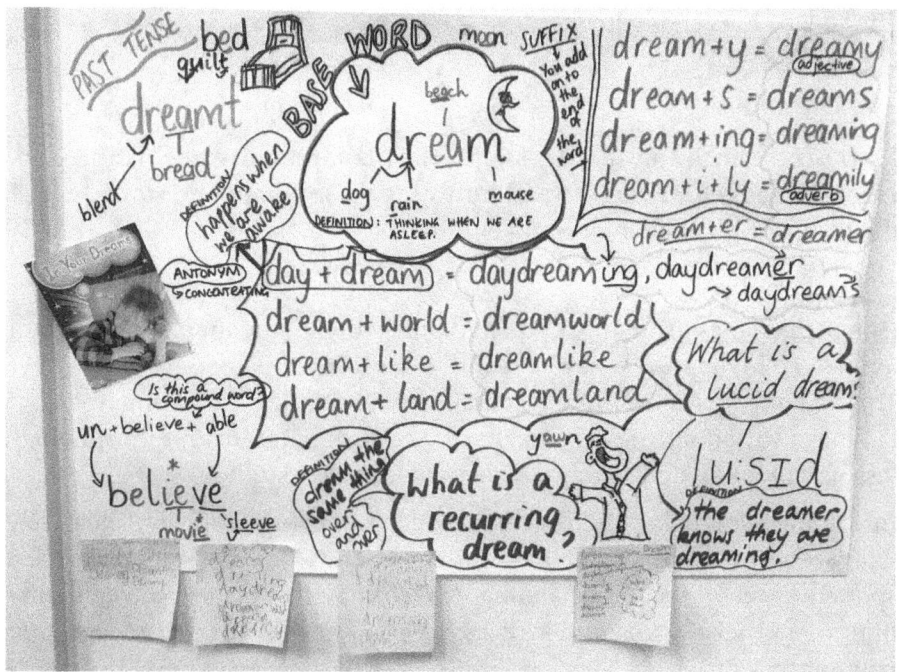

As I added each word, I made sure to point out the changes. "Look at how we've changed 'dream,'" I said. "What did we add to make 'dreams'?"

"An <s>!" one child called out.

"Great noticing! And what about 'dreaming'? What did we add there?"

Another student spelled out proudly, "<i-n-g>."

"And what did we add to make 'dreamy'?"

"We added a <y> at the end!"

"Excellent observation! This <y> is called a 'suffix'. It changes the meaning of our base word slightly. Can anyone tell me how 'dreamy' is different from 'dream'?"

One student explained, "Dreamy is like when something feels like a dream, but it's not actually a dream".

Building on their interest, I introduced compound words. "Now, let's think about words that have 'dream' as part of them, but combined with another word."

Your Guide to the Morphology Lens 151

The suggestions came quickly:

- "Dreamworld"
- "Dreamlike"
- "Dreamland"
- "Daydream".

I wrote these on the poster. "These are called 'compound words,'" I explained. I then guided the students to add suffixes to these compound words, which they found both challenging and exciting:

- "Daydreamer"
- "Daydreams".

One of the most surprising moments came when a student raised her hand and said, "My grandma says 'dreamt' instead of 'dreamed'. Is that right?" This led to an impromptu discussion on irregular verbs and regional language variations. It was amazing to see how naturally our morphology lesson had integrated so many aspects of language study.

In the days following the lesson, I noticed students applying their new knowledge to unfamiliar words in their reading, pointing out when they spotted an <-s> or <-ing> ending. My Year 1 students were confidently hunting for base words and suffixes, creating new words and recognising compound words.

Case study: a Year 2 class's journey through "convict" history

When I introduced a non-fiction text about convicts in Australian history to my Year 2 students, I was excited about the language learning opportunities it presented. Little did I know that we were about to embark on a journey that would teach us all—myself included—valuable lessons about the intricacies of word structure and the importance of careful investigation.

As we dove into the text, we encountered several challenging words:

- "corroboree"
- "escapes"
- "penal settlement"
- "apprentice"
- "customs"
- "European"
- "convict".

Each word became a mini adventure, a chance to dig deeper into the structure of language.

When we hit the word "convict", hands shot up immediately. "What's a convict?". This question led us down an unexpected path of discovery. Initially, I confidently broke it down as <con> and <vict>, explaining that it meant "people convicted of a crime". We even started to create a word web, connecting it to words like "convicted" and "conviction". However, as we dug deeper, I realised I had made a mistake. This became a powerful teachable moment. I told the class, "You know what? I think I've made an error here. Let's investigate this together."

We looked up the etymology of "convict" and discovered it comes from Latin: <con-> meaning "with" or "thoroughly" and <vincere> meaning "to conquer" or "to prove guilty".

I explained to the class, "Sometimes, parts of words that look like they might be base words aren't actually used on their own in English. We call these 'bound base elements.'"

This led to an exciting discussion about words which shared the same bound base element:

- "conviction"—<con-> + <vict> + <-ion>)
- "evict"—<e-> + <vict>
- "victor"—<vict> + <-or>
- "victory"—<vict> + <-or> + <-y>.

The students were fascinated by how these words all shared a common ancestor but had evolved different meanings.

One student raised their hand. "So, does this mean we have to be really careful when we're breaking down words?"

"Absolutely!" I replied. "This is why we need to be word detectives, always questioning and investigating."

We decided to start a "Word Mystery" board in our classroom where we could post words we were unsure about and investigate them together.

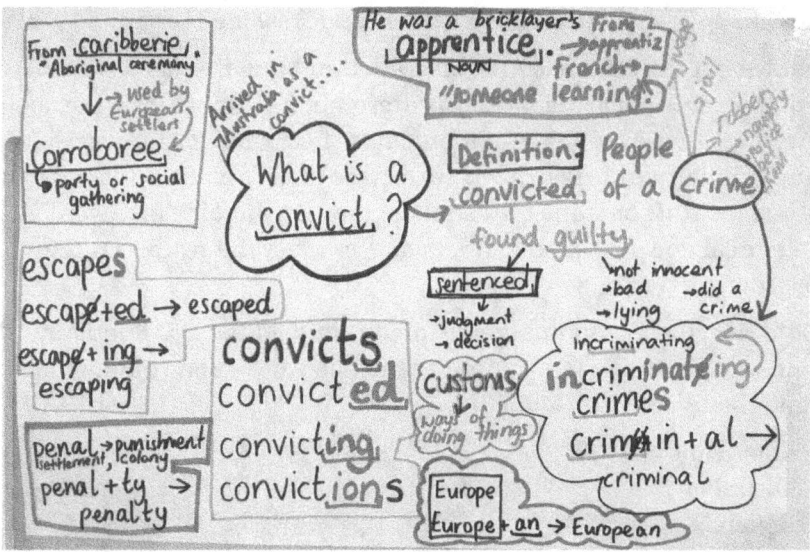

Your Guide to the Morphology Lens

When exploring orthographic patterns in English, one important concept to understand is how base words ending in a vowel interact with vowel suffixes. The pattern we observe is that when adding a vowel suffix to a base word ending in a vowel, we typically remove the vowel at the end of the base word. For example, let's consider the word "escape" we encountered:

- <escape> + <-ing> = "escaping"
- <escape> + <-ed> = <escaped>.

This orthographic pattern helps preserve the pronunciation of the word and prevents an awkward doubling of vowels that could lead to confusion in reading or speaking. The reasoning behind this pattern is rooted in the phonological structure of English. By removing the final vowel of the base word, we maintain a consistent syllable structure and avoid creating a sequence of two adjacent vowels that might alter the pronunciation of the word unpredictably.

As we have discussed throughout this book, it's really important to note that this is a pattern rather than an absolute rule. English, being a complex language with influences from many sources, does have exceptions—some words retain their final vowel for clarity or historical reasons, such as "shoeing" or "canoeing".

"Penal settlement" provided another rich exploration. We broke it down:

- "Penal" related to "punishment".
- "Settlement" is a place where people settle.

This led to a fantastic discussion about prefixes and suffixes. We discovered words like "penalty", "penalties", "settler", and "resettled".

When we got to "European", we had another breakthrough. We looked at the suffix <-an> which means "of" or "resembling". This suffix is particularly interesting when we look at nationalities. Take the word "Australian", for example. When we break it down, we can see that it's made up of <Australia> and <-an>. So, if someone is Australian, they are literally "of Australia". This simple breakdown helps us understand not just the word's structure but also its deeper meaning.

I could see the lightbulbs going off in students' eyes. Suddenly, they recognised the same <-an> suffix at work and were calling out nationalities left and right:

- "American!"
- "Australian!"
- "Italian!"

I said to the students, "This pattern provides a consistent way to form adjectives related to nationalities or places of origin. The <-an> suffix allows for the derivation of new words from existing nouns. Using the same suffix across many different base words—country names—creates a predictable structure that makes learning and using these words easier."

We made a list on poster paper, highlighting the meaning and function of the suffixes. We then created a word bank of meaningful words we had encountered from this lesson, which the students could revise and revisit for homework. These were not words for rote memorisation but words that had been explicitly taught.

Looking back on these lessons, I'm amazed at how a seemingly dry historical text became a gateway to language discovery. The "convict" mishap turned into one of our most valuable learning experiences, teaching us all about the importance of careful research and critical thinking in language study. What struck me most was how this approach levelled the playing field. Students who usually struggled with reading were excelling at spotting patterns and making connections. It wasn't just about memorising definitions anymore—it was about understanding how our language works and being open to new discoveries. The confidence I saw growing in my students was remarkable. They started approaching unfamiliar words with curiosity rather than apprehension. They became true word detectives, eager to crack the code of any new term they encountered and always ready to question and investigate further.

Contemplate and Consider!

When analysing the word "penal", it is crucial to distinguish between its morphological base in modern English and its etymological root. This distinction highlights the difference between synchronic (current) and diachronic (historical) linguistic analysis and the importance of having two different Lenses for Morphology and Etymology.

In modern English morphology, "penal" functions as the base for derived words such as "penalise" and "penally". As a morphological base, "penal" is a free morpheme (it can stand alone as a word) and is the simplest form of the word in current English usage, the form to which affixes can be added.

From a historical perspective, the etymological root of "penal" is the Latin <poena> meaning "punishment". This root is not a word in modern

English but rather the historical source of a modern English word. Etymological analysis reveals <poen-> or <pen-> as the root in Latin and <-al> as a suffix that was added to create the Latin <poenalis>, and the entire word <poenalis> was then borrowed into English and adapted as "penal". Other English words sharing this etymological root include "penalty", "punish" and 'impunity'.

Key Differences Between Morphological Bases and Etymological Roots

	Morphological base	Etymological root
Time frame	Current language use	Historical origin
Function in the language	Active part of word formation in modern English	Historical source, not necessarily productive in modern English
Visibility to speakers	Recognisable to most native speakers	Often only visible through etymological study

The distinction between the morphological base <penal> and its etymological root <poena> is crucial for accurate linguistic analysis, effective language teaching and understanding word relationships in both current usage and historical context. Recognising this difference helps in developing a sustainable and logical understanding of word structure and language change, which is valuable for both language learners and linguists.

2. Is there a suffix? What meaning does it have? How does it change the base?

We've talked about the base word, but does "conscience" have a suffix?

A suffix is a letter or group of letters added to the end of a word to change its meaning or function. In this case, "conscience" is formed with a prefix and a base word, but no suffix. Understanding what there isn't is just as important as knowing what is.

Case study: a Year 2 introduction to morphological and etymological instruction

In early literacy instruction, the importance of morphological and etymological instruction cannot be overstated. For Year 2 students, these approaches offer a powerful gateway to enhanced vocabulary development and reading comprehension. Morphemes, as the smallest units of meaning in language, can provide your young students with intrinsic clues to decipher unfamiliar words and make predictions about the story they are about to read.

This case study explores a series of Year 2 lessons that demonstrate how integrating morphological and etymological instruction can transform vocabulary learning from rote memorisation into an engaging, investigative process. By focusing on the meaningful parts of words, we empower students to become active participants in their language learning journey.

Before delving into specific lessons, it's important to understand that the various Linguistic Lenses—Phonology, Orthography, Morphology and Etymology—are deeply interrelated. This interconnectedness forms the foundation of what will become a comprehensive approach to language instruction in your very own classroom.

Morphology, the study of word structure and formation, is intimately linked with etymology, the study of word origins and historical development. Together, these Lenses provide a powerful toolkit for unpacking any vocabulary word you encounter. For instance, understanding the morphological structure of a word often leads to insights about its etymological roots, and vice versa.

Consider the word "bilingual" from a Year 6 lesson where it appeared in the sentence "bilingual store signs were common" in a novel and confused my students. By showing them the morphology and etymology of this word—neither of which could be done in isolation—they were able to comprehend this unfamiliar word:

- Morphologically, we can break it down into <bi-> (two) and <lingual> (relating to language). They were then able to connect this knowledge to words like "biennial", "combination", "biscuit" and "bicycle".
- Etymologically, we traced <bi-> to Latin, meaning "twice, double, twofold" and <lingual> from Latin <lingua> meaning "tongue, language".

This interplay between morphology and etymology enriched my students' understanding of the word, allowing them to conclude for themselves that the meaning was "speaking two languages", making this experience more memorable and connecting it to a broader network of related words.

My Year 2 lesson began with a seemingly simple yet effective approach: unpacking the title of a book to help make predictions about the text to come. This approach immediately engaged students, sparking curiosity and setting the stage for deeper linguistic exploration. When introducing the book *George Stephenson: The Train Man* by Sean Callery, we didn't just read the title—we dissected it. Students were encouraged to identify familiar word parts and discuss their meanings. This led to a rich conversation about the base word "train", where I asked the students what prefixes and suffixes they could add to the base. Words such as "retraining", "untrain", "overtraining", "trainload", "trainable", "housetrained", "trainer", "training", "trains" and "trainman" were all suggested.

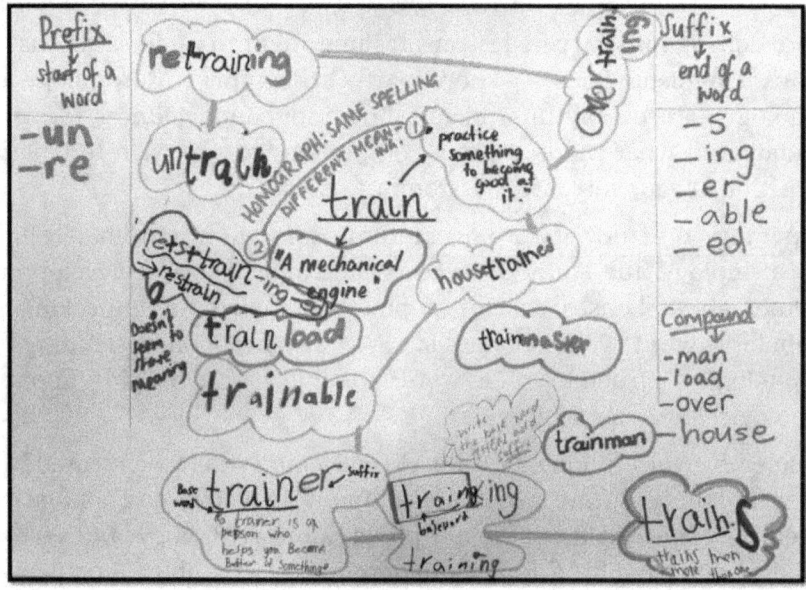

This authentic classroom conversation also led to discussing compound words. It provided opportunities to unpack "My Favourite No" when a student suggested "restraining" and, upon closer inspection, it was decided that this word didn't seem to share the same meaning with the other words.

Teaching Tip!

Predicting a text's content based on its title is a valuable strategy for readers of *all* ages, including older students. This example from my Year 5 classroom demonstrates how incorporating etymology can enhance this prediction process and deepen students' engagement with the material. When introducing a non-fiction text about melting glaciers in the Himalayas, I covered the entire page, including illustrations, just leaving the title:

Students identified "Himalayas" as a proper noun because of the capital letter and because it was a place name they had heard about. I recorded their thinking, but it wasn't until we used the Etymology Lens that they really started to understand the meaning. I broke down "Himalayas" into its Sanskrit roots: <Hima> meaning "snow" and <alaya> meaning "abode" or "home". Students used this etymological information to make informed predictions about the text's content, such as "snowy and cold", but when it came to the word "home", we needed to look at synonyms. We discussed words like "home", "place", "fief" and "domain". After this they were able to deduce the word's meaning as "the home of snow".

This brief etymology exploration at the beginning of the lesson prepared my students for reading with a deeper understanding of the text's context.

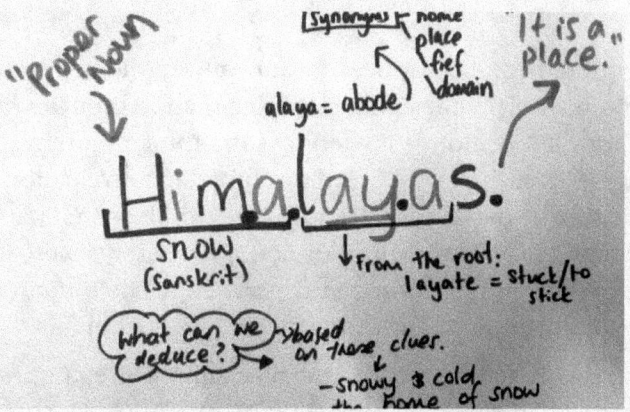

As we examined *George Stephenson: The Train Man*, I chose words I knew would act as springboards for interesting word study activities. For example, looking at "engineer" and "engine", we inquired whether "engine" was the base word and if <-er> was the suffix, exploring the word sum <engine> plus <-er>. We tested this thought by seeing if the suffix held meaning, and the students decided it meant "someone who...". They gave examples of "teacher", "dreamer", "dancer", "worker", "builder", "singer", "trainer" and "marker", and I posed the question, "Does the suffix <-er> carry meaning?" On Post-it notes, they wrote their response: "Yes, because it means someone who does something." In this example, we were not looking at the sounds in the word "engineer" but the morphology, because that was what was going to help us with reading comprehension!

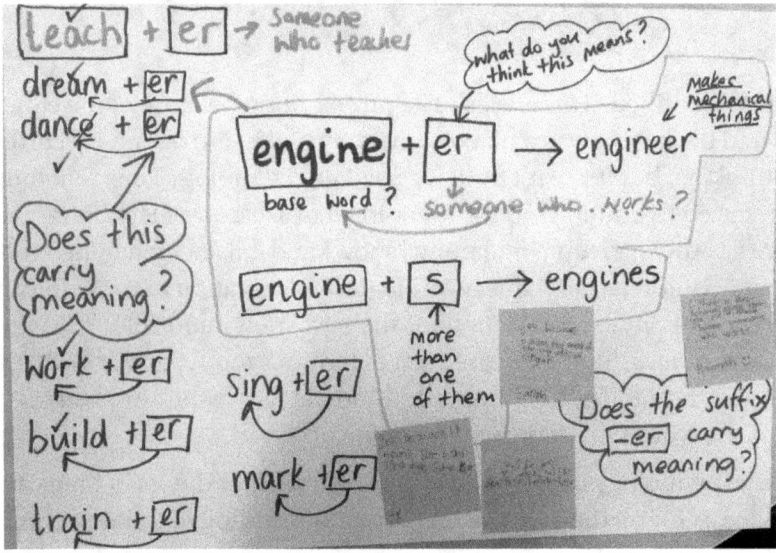

When encountering "locomotive" in our railway-themed book, we broke it down into its morphemes: <loco-> (place) and <motive> (moving). We discussed how a locomotive is literally something that moves from place to place. This simple breakdown led to a broader conversation about other words with similar parts, such as "localise" (to place in a particular area) and "motivate" (to cause to move or act). My students were fascinated to learn that understanding these word parts could help them decode and comprehend other unfamiliar words they might encounter.

To further enrich our vocabulary exploration, I prepared etymological investigations that sparked engagement and boosted comprehension.

We traced the origins of "locomotive" back to Latin, explaining how words evolve over time. I had prepared excerpts from the Online Etymology Dictionary (etymonline.com) so that I could also use this opportunity to show them how to conduct their own etymological exploration, teaching them explicitly how to search for the answers.

One of the highlights of this lesson was when the students uncovered that a locomotive engine without rails is called a "traction engine", which is where the word "tractor" comes from. It was this link and its connection to this student's prior knowledge which made this teaching moment so great.

With this knowledge on hand, we jointly constructed a simple timeline:

1. Latin <locus> (place) plus <motivus> (moving)
2. French "locomotif"
3. English "locomotive".

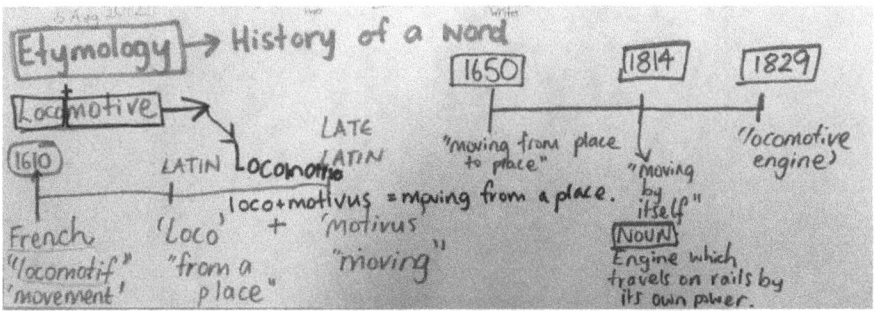

This historical journey captivated the students. One student remarked, "It's like the word travelled through time, just like a train travels across the country!" This analogy not only demonstrated understanding but also helped cement the word's meaning in the students' minds.

One of the most enlightening aspects of our lessons was the collection and analysis of suffixes. We focused particularly on collecting the suffixes we had encountered, such as <-er>, <-eer> and <-an>, exploring how these endings change word meanings and functions.

For <-eer>, we looked at the meaning and function of the suffix being "a person who deals with" and how its grammatical form and function maintains a noun as a noun. This led us to a discussion about <-er> versus <-eer>. We looked at examples of the latter, including "engineer", "volunteer" and "mountaineer". The students quickly grasped that this suffix often indicates a person who specialises in or is associated with something. One student excitedly pointed out, "So a puppeteer is someone who works with puppets!" "Puppet" is a noun and "puppeteer" is a noun. Another student commented, "engine is a noun", so the correct suffix should be <-eer>, as an engineer is a person who deals with engines, and "engine" is also a noun.

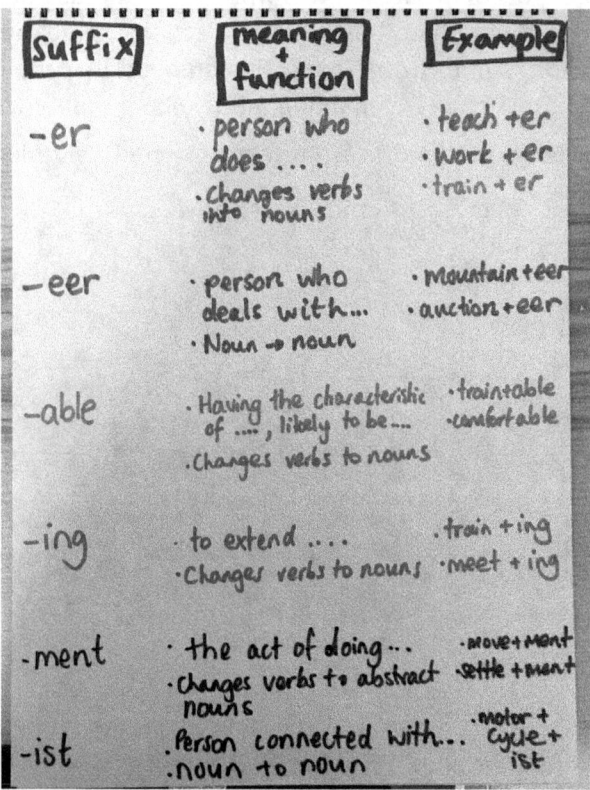

These suffix investigations empowered students in their writing. They began to experiment with creating their own words, demonstrating both creativity and a growing understanding of word structure.

3. Is there a prefix? What meaning does it have? How does it change the base?

Now, let's look at the prefix in "conscience": <con-> means "with" or "together". It modifies the base word <science> to mean "with knowledge" or "shared knowledge" of right and wrong. This prefix helps us understand how "conscience" refers to an internal sense of moral knowledge.

4. What are the morphological relations?

Now, we're going to look into the morphological relations of the word "conscience". "Morphological relations" refers to the connections between words based on their structure, including how they are formed and related to other words. This involves looking at components like base words, prefixes, suffixes and any processes that change the word.

Let's break down "conscience". We know it has the base word <science>, which means "knowledge", and it comes from the Latin word <scientia>, and the prefix <con->, which means "with" or "together", so it changes "science" to mean "with knowledge". The prefix <con-> modifies the base word to create "conscience", which refers to an internal sense of moral knowledge. This is a great example of how morphology works.

Morphological relations also involve understanding how words can be transformed. For example, if we add different prefixes or suffixes, we can create related words. Can you think of a word related to "conscience"?

"Conscientious" is related to "conscience". It describes someone who is diligent and guided by their conscience. Here, the suffix <-ious> turns the noun into an adjective.

You should notice when you are writing "Conscience → Conscientious" on the board that there is so much to explore, particularly regarding the spelling (orthography) and how this morphological component changes the spelling of the base. *Please do not be tempted to skip over this teaching point* as it is so important for your students to understand the truth about English spelling: that it is logical and ordered, and there are reasons for why words are spelled the way they are. Here, etymology is key for us to understand orthographic spelling patterns. This is a great example of an incidental teaching point which links all of the Lenses and shows the need for all four!

Take a look at this word structure analysis. "Conscience" originates from the Latin word <conscientia>, meaning "knowledge within oneself". It's composed of two key elements:

1. The prefix <con->, meaning "with" or "together".
2. The base <science>, meaning "knowledge".

This structure beautifully captures the essence of conscience as an internal awareness or knowledge.

When we transform "conscience" into its adjective form, we get "conscientious". This transformation involves a specific word sum: <con-> + <science> + <-ious>.

The journey from "conscience" to "conscientious" involves several key steps:

1. The <con-> prefix remains unchanged, preserving its meaning of "with" or "together".
2. We keep the base <science>, but notice the <-ti-> spelling—this is vital for maintaining the word's etymological integrity.
3. We append the adjectival suffix <-ious> to form the new word.
4. The final non-syllabic <e> in "science" is dropped when we add <-ious>. This change follows a common English spelling pattern when adding vowel-initial suffixes.

The <-tious> ending in "conscientious" isn't a simple letter swap, can't be ignored and must be explained by you, the teacher! It results from retaining the <-ti-> from the original Latin root <scientia> and adding the suffix <-ous> The retention of <-ti-> is crucial because it preserves the link to the Latin root <scientia>, maintains consistency with related words like "scientific" and "omniscient", and ensures the correct pronunciation, giving us the <sh> sound in /ʃəs/.

A common adjectival suffix in English, particularly with words of Latin or French origin, <-ious> is a variant of <-ous> that often appears after bases ending in <-ion>, such as "spacious" (<space> + <-ious>), "gracious" (<grace> + <-ious>) and ambitious (<ambit> + <-ious>).

To reinforce understanding, consider highlighting these similar transformations:

- <caution> + <-ious> = "cautious", from Latin <cautio>
- <nutrition> + <-ious> = "nutritious", from Latin <nutritio>.

In each case, note how the <-ti-> from the Latin root is retained and <-ous> is added to form the adjective. This consistent spelling convention in English means that this is an orthographic pattern!

5. Is there an inflectional morpheme?

Now, we'll determine if "conscience" has an inflectional morpheme. An inflectional morpheme is a suffix that changes the form of a word to express tense, mood, number or comparison, but not its core meaning. It modifies a word's grammatical properties.

"Conscience" does not contain any inflectional morphemes. It remains the same regardless of tense, number or comparison.

6. Is there a derivational morpheme?

A derivational morpheme is a prefix or suffix that changes the meaning or part of speech of a word. So, does "conscience" have a derivational morpheme?

The prefix <con-> is a derivational morpheme because it changes <science> to mean "with knowledge".

Case study: the mystery of "penal settlement"—a morphological extension in Year 2

After our deep dive into the world of Australian convicts through a captivating non-fiction text, I decided to revisit the intriguing term "penal settlement" with my Year 2 class. Remember this lesson? As any seasoned teacher knows, the magic often happens in these moments of revision and extension.

Picture this: a classroom buzzing with seven-year-olds, their minds still filled with images of distant shores and the echoes of clanking chains from our previous lesson. I wrote "penal settlement" on the board, and suddenly, a forest of eager hands shot up. "We remember that!" they chorused, eyes sparkling with recognition.

But why stop at mere recognition? I thought. *Let's embark on a word adventure!*

"Alright, junior word detectives," I announced, donning an imaginary Sherlock Holmes hat. "We're going to crack the code of these words!"

What followed was nothing short of linguistic magic. We dove into the world of morphology—though to my young learners, it was simply "word building." We dissected "penal" and "settlement" like eager scientists, discovering base words and affixes.

We began by revisiting the word "penal". I explained that "penal" is a morphological base word in modern English, related to "punishment". We remembered that it came from the Latin etymological root <poena>. This distinction between current usage and historical origin intrigued the students and helped them understand why some words seem unusual.

Next, we looked at "settlement". The students quickly identified "settle" as a familiar word. I explained that <-ment> is a suffix that transforms the verb "settle" into a noun. We discussed how adding affixes to base words can change their meaning or grammatical category.

As we dug deeper, we explored more examples of derivational morphology. We discussed "penalty" and how it relates to "penal", noting that both words share the same base but have different suffixes. This helped students see connections between words with similar meanings.

We then examined "settler," identifying <settle> as the base word and <-er> as a derivational suffix that creates an agent noun. An agent noun is a person or thing that performs the action of a verb. In this case, <-er> is added to the verb "settle" to create "settler", meaning "one who settles". This concept of adding <-er> to create a "doer" word was particularly exciting for the students. It's a common pattern in English—we can transform many verbs into nouns describing the person or thing performing the action.

Lastly, we broke down "resettled". We talked about how <re-> is a prefix meaning "again", <settle> is our base word and <-ed> is an inflectional suffix indicating past tense. This example allowed us to discuss how words can have both prefixes and suffixes and introduced the concept of inflectional morphology.

We discovered that affixes can be categorised into two main types. First, there are derivational morphemes; these can change the meaning or grammatical category of a word. We called these "meaning changers" for simplicity. Examples include <-ment> in "settlement" and <-er> in "settler". Second, we identified inflectional morphemes; these modify a word to express grammatical features without changing its core meaning or lexical category. We called these "grammar helpers". Examples include <-ed> in "settled" and <-s> in "settlements".

To reinforce this concept, I asked the class, "What happens when we add <-s> to 'penalty'?" This led to a great discussion about how inflectional morphemes work.

Let me break down why this is such an effective approach:

- **It provides a concrete example.** By using "penalty"—a word the students have just learned and can relate to—you're building on familiar ground. This makes the abstract concept of inflectional morphemes more tangible.
- **It demonstrates visible change.** Adding <-s> to "penalty" creates a visible and easily understandable change (penalty → penalties). This allows students to literally see the morpheme at work and provides an opportunity to identify the orthographic pattern: Here, the pattern of changing <-y> to <-ies> applies to words ending in a consonant plus <-y>, such as baby (→ babies), city (→ cities) and fly (→ flies).

Before you go thinking that this orthographic pattern is only relevant for younger students, have a look at this upper primary word study (and take note of the bottom-right corner):

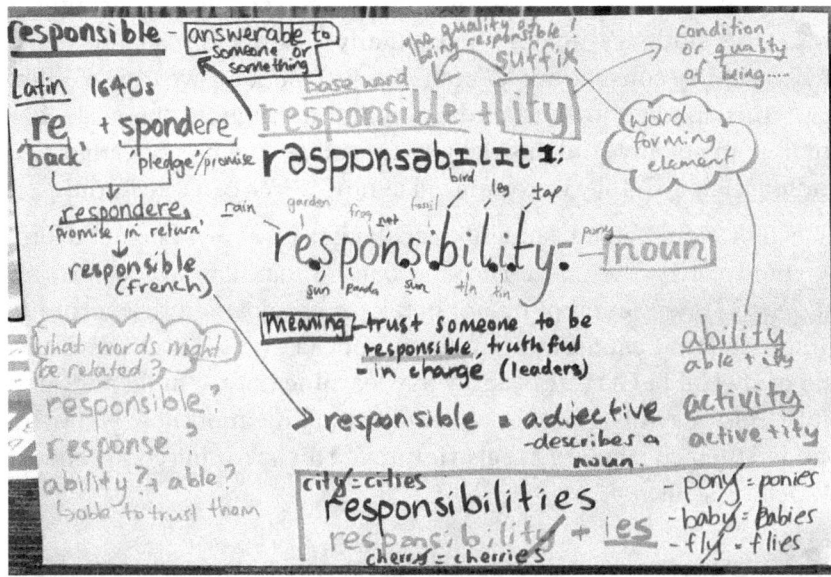

- **There is minimal meaning shift.** Unlike derivational morphemes that significantly change meaning, the <-s> here only indicates plurality. This helps students grasp that inflectional morphemes modify grammatical features without altering the core meaning.
- **It shows a predictable pattern.** The <-s> suffix follows a common pattern in English for forming plurals. This predictability helps reinforce the pattern-based nature of inflectional morphology.
- **It contrasts with earlier examples.** If you've previously discussed derivational morphemes (like <-ty> in "penalty"), this provides a clear contrast. Students can see how <-ty> changes the word dramatically, while <-s> only adjusts its grammatical function.
- **It introduces phonological awareness.** The pronunciation change from "penal" (/piːn.əl/) to "penalties" (/pen.əl.tiːz/) subtly introduces the concept that morphemes can affect pronunciation.
- **It illustrates grammatical function.** This example beautifully illustrates how inflectional morphemes work with syntax. You can demonstrate how "penalties" fits into sentences differently than "penalty".

- **It provides a springboard for discussion.** This simple addition opens up discussions about other inflectional morphemes such as past tense <-ed>, possessive <-'s> and comparative <-er>.

The students were fascinated by how morphemes could significantly alter words. One student's analogy particularly resonated: "So, 'penal' and 'penalty' are like cousins, but 'penalties' is just 'penalty' wearing a different outfit!" This sparked joy and understanding throughout the class. It was incredible to see my students delight in finding "meaning changers" and "grammar helpers". They were amazed at how words can transform!

This exploration helped students see language as a systematic puzzle they could solve. They began to approach unfamiliar words with more confidence, often attempting to break them down into morphemes. Another student beautifully summed up our learning: "It's like words are made of special LEGO bricks and we're learning how to build and rebuild them!" This playful approach to understanding morphology not only expanded their vocabulary but also improved their reading comprehension and spelling skills.

Teaching Tip!

The Morpheme Transformers Charts are powerful visual tools designed to help your students understand the dynamic nature of word formation in English.

The first chart illustrates two things:

1. how derivational morphemes, which I call "meaning changers", can transform words by altering their meaning or grammatical category
2. how inflectional morphemes, which I call "grammar helpers", modify a word to express grammatical features without changing its core meaning or lexical category.

The second chart clearly demonstrates the process of word transformation.

To use these charts effectively in your classroom, start by introducing the concept of word building. Encourage your students to create new words by combining base words with different morphemes from the charts. This hands-on approach will help your students actively engage with the material and reinforce their understanding of how words are formed.

Next, guide your students in pattern recognition. Help them identify common prefixes and suffixes, and discuss how these morphemes affect the meaning and structure of words. This activity will develop your students' analytical skills and deepen their understanding of language patterns.

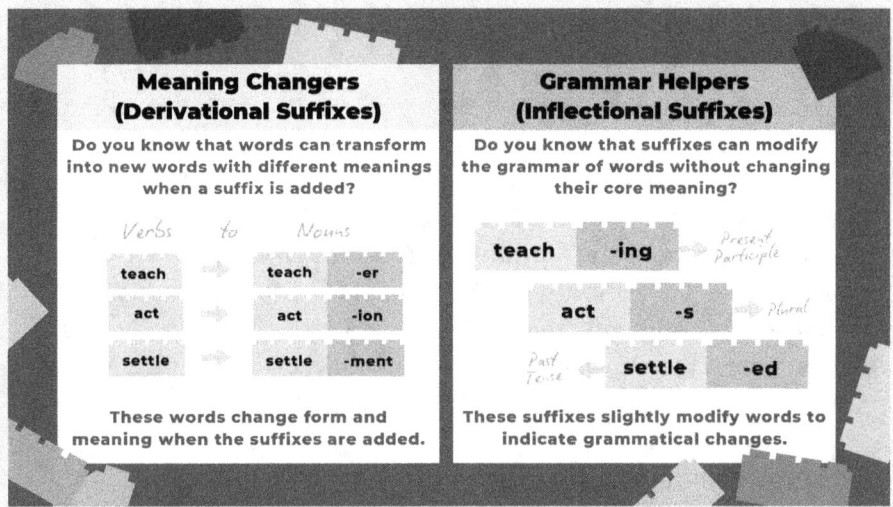

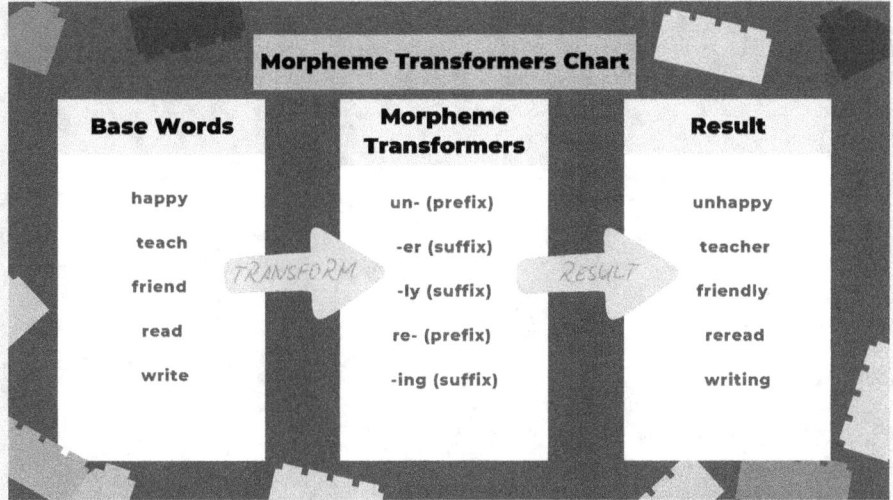

These charts also serve as an excellent tool for vocabulary expansion, so use them to introduce new words and facilitate discussions about how their meanings relate to the base words. This approach helps students make connections between words and enhances their ability to deduce the meanings of unfamiliar terms. Remember, you can download these charts at www.linguisticlenses.com.

Grammar exploration is another valuable application, so be sure to discuss with your students how certain morphemes can change a word's part of speech, such as transforming an adjective into an adverb, helping them understand the flexibility of language and, of course, improving their grammatical awareness.

Lastly, consider incorporating morphological family activities into your lessons. Group words with similar base words or affixes to reinforce connections between words. This activity can help your students recognise relationships between words and strengthens their overall vocabulary skills. By incorporating the Morpheme Transformers Charts into your lessons, you can make the abstract concept of word formation more concrete for your students. They will serve as a springboard for discussions about language, meaning and the building blocks of English orthography!

Contemplate and Consider!

If you're interested in introducing basic morphological analysis in your classroom, here's a step-by-step guide:

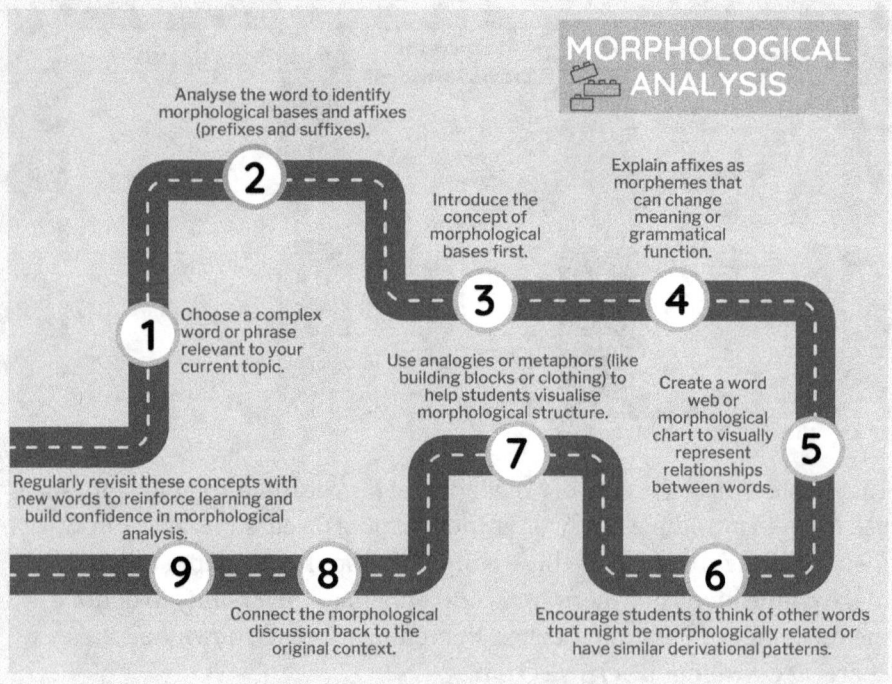

Remember to balance accurate terminology with age-appropriate explanations. At this age, the goal is to spark curiosity about language structure rather than to master complex linguistic concepts. By fostering this early interest in morphology, you lay a strong foundation for future language learning and linguistic study.

Implement and Innovate!

As teachers, it's vital not only to understand pedagogical concepts but also to experience them firsthand. This activity is designed to help you put into practice the morphological concepts you've been learning about.

You'll need these materials:

- Sets of base words and affixes (printed on cards or sticky notes)
- Coloured pens or highlighters
- A timer
- A whiteboard or large piece of paper for group discussions.

1. **Word Construction Workshop (15 minutes):** Form small groups of three or four teachers. Provide each group with a set of base words (e.g. "educate", "assess", "develop") and affixes (e.g. <-ion>, <-ive>, <-ment>, <re->, <un->). Set a timer for 10 minutes and challenge groups to create as many new words as possible. Encourage creativity while maintaining grammatical plausibility. Discuss the pedagogical implications of this activity and how it could be adapted for different year levels.

2. **Semantic Shift Charades (10 minutes):** Write an example word chain on the board, such as "educate → educator → educational". In pairs, have teachers take turns acting out or drawing the meaning shift between these words without using verbal cues. After each round, discuss how this activity could be modified to suit various learning styles and abilities in a classroom setting.

3. **Morpheme Classification Challenge (15 minutes):** Create two "morpheme categories" labelled "Derivational" and "Inflectional", and place them in different parts of the room. Call out words related to education (e.g. "assessed", "reassessment", "developments"). Have teachers move to the appropriate category, explaining their choice. The last person to categorise each word must provide an example sentence using the word in an educational context. Reflect on how this kinaesthetic approach could benefit different types of learners.

4. **Linguistic Rainbow Analysis (15 minutes):** Provide a short professional reading. Challenge teachers to highlight function words in cool colours (such as blue or green) and content words in warm colours (such as red, orange or yellow). After completion, discuss the ratio of function to content words and its implications for teaching vocabulary and reading comprehension.
5. **Etymology Exploration (10 minutes):** Form a circle. Beginning with the Latin root <educare>, play a rapid-fire word association game, with each teacher adding a related word in any language they know. Discuss how understanding word origins can enhance vocabulary instruction across subjects.

Reflection and Application (20 minutes): In small groups, discuss the following questions:

1. Which activity did you find most illuminating from a teacher's perspective? Why?
2. How could you adapt these activities for different subject areas or student proficiency levels?
3. What challenges might students face with these activities, and how could you address them?
4. How do these hands-on experiences with morphology inform your approach to teaching language concepts?
5. Brainstorm other linguistic concepts that could benefit from this experiential learning approach.

By engaging in these activities, you not only reinforce your understanding of morphology but also experience firsthand the cognitive processes your students might undergo. Use these insights to inform your lesson planning and create more engaging, multisensory language learning experiences in your classrooms.

7. Is this a complex word? Is it a base or a stem?

Let's determine if "conscience" is a complex word.

A complex word has more than one morpheme, like prefixes or suffixes, in addition to the base word. So, "conscience" is a complex word because it has the prefix <con-> in addition to the base word <science>.

Now, is "conscience" a base or a stem?

"Conscience" is a stem because it can function independently and includes a prefix.

Implement and Innovate!

This is an opportunity for you and your colleagues to deepen your understanding of morphological structures by collaboratively analysing and constructing words using morphemes, enhancing your ability to teach these concepts effectively when standing at the front of the classroom!

You will need these materials:

- Word cards with bases, prefixes and suffixes
- Handouts for recording findings
- Access to dictionaries or online etymology resources
- Chart paper and pens.

Instructions:

1. **Introduction (10 minutes):** Begin with a brief review of this Key Feature. Discuss the distinction between inflectional and derivational morphemes and their impact on word meaning and grammatical function.
2. **Forming groups (5 minutes):** Organise participants into small, diverse groups, ensuring a mix of teaching experiences and subject areas. Assign roles within each group, such as facilitator, recorder, researcher and presenter, to encourage active participation and accountability.
3. **Word analysis (20 minutes):** Distribute a set of word cards to each group. Collaboratively construct new words by combining the cards using arrows or equal signs to create word sums. Within groups, encourage open dialogue and exchange of ideas to identify the base and any prefixes or suffixes, and determine whether the morphemes are inflectional or derivational. Discuss how these morphemes influence the word's meaning and grammatical role, ensuring a supportive environment where all voices are heard.
4. **Research and inquiry (20 minutes):** Select one newly formed word per group. Use dictionaries or online resources to research the etymology and semantic evolution of the word. Record findings on the handout, noting any changes or consistencies in the word's meaning over time. Encourage collaboration by having group members share insights and challenge each other's assumptions, promoting critical thinking.
5. **Group presentation (10 minutes):** Each group presents their findings to the larger group, explaining the morphological structure and history of their chosen word. Facilitate a discussion on strategies for teaching

these concepts to students, encouraging groups to share diverse perspectives and approaches.
6. **Reflection and feedback (10 minutes):** Individually, write a short reflection on how this activity has enhanced your understanding of morphology and how you can apply these insights in your teaching practice. Groups can also provide feedback on the dynamics of their collaboration, discussing what worked well and areas for improvement.

Can you and your colleagues:
- accurately identify and categorise morphemes?
- understand the impact of morphemes on meaning and grammatical function?
- conduct research into word etymology and semantics?
- connect morphological knowledge to your teaching practice?

8. Is this a function word or a content word?

Let's determine whether "conscience" is a function or content word.

A function word is used to express grammatical relationships; examples include "and", "but" and "in." A content word carries meaning; nouns, verbs, adjectives and adverbs are content words. "Conscience" is a content word because it conveys a specific concept: moral knowledge. Content words are crucial for understanding the main ideas in sentences.

9. Is there a homophone?

Now, let's explore whether "conscience" has a homophone.

When teaching about homophones, it's important to clarify the distinction between true homophones and near-homophones. True homophones are words that sound exactly the same but have different meanings and spellings, such as "bear" and "bare". However, your students may confuse words like "conscience" and "conscious", which are actually near-homophones. While these words sound similar, they have slightly different pronunciations: "conscience" (/kɒnʃəns/) has an additional /n/ sound that "conscious" (/kɒnʃəs/) doesn't have. Understanding this subtle difference will help your students improve their pronunciation and spelling. The IPA is incredibly useful for illustrating these distinctions—you'll wonder how you ever taught without it!

10. Is this a homograph or a homonym?

Let's determine if "conscience" is a homograph or homonym.

A homograph is a word that is spelled the same as another word but has a different meaning and pronunciation. A homonym is a word that is both a homophone and a homograph. "Conscience" is neither a homograph nor a homonym, because it has a unique spelling and meaning.

11. Write this word in a sentence.

Now, let's use "conscience" in a sentence. How about this: "His conscience told him to apologise for his mistake." This sentence shows how "conscience" guides moral decisions.

Case study: exploring "conspiratorial"—a morphological journey for gifted Year 6 readers

Visualise a Year 6 classroom where a group of highly able students are engrossed in the novel *Chinese Cinderella*. They come across this intriguing passage: "The eight of us held a council and carefully made our plans. We felt very grown up and conspiratorial." The word "conspiratorial" catches their attention, presenting a perfect opportunity to dive deep into vocabulary exploration.

The classroom buzzes with energy, set up for collaborative learning. Small groups of students sit together, ready to embark on a linguistic adventure. Our objectives? We're not just looking to define a word—we're aiming to enhance vocabulary acquisition through in-depth word study, develop morphological awareness, apply Linguistic Lenses metalanguage (particularly that of the Morphology Lens), connect new vocabulary with known concepts and explore the fascinating interplay between morphology, orthography and etymology.

The Morphology Lens was at the heart of my approach in this lesson. Why this strategy? It's a powerful tool that helps students deconstruct and understand complex words by analysing their meaningful parts. As I say to my students, "It's like giving you a linguistic magnifying glass!"

Throughout the lesson, I peppered our discussion with guiding questions: "What are the meaningful parts of this word?" I'd ask, or "Can you think of any related words?" These open-ended queries acted as stepping stones, guiding students through their exploration without giving away the answers. To anchor our investigation visually, I wrote "conspiratorial" on the board in big, clear letters. This simple act gave students a constant reference point, something tangible to return to as we delved deeper into the word's structure.

While our main focus was morphology, we couldn't ignore pronunciation. We used the IPA as a guide. The students' eyes lit up when they identified six vowel symbols, realising the word had six syllables. It was a small detour into phonology that helped cement the connection between the written word and its spoken form.

The lesson unfolded like a linguistic story, with students taking the lead in uncovering the word's secrets. You should have seen their faces when they first recognised <con-> and <spire> as meaningful parts of the word. As we dug deeper, the students' appreciation for the complexity of "conspiratorial" grew. They identified multiple affixes, their morphological awareness expanding before my eyes. One student even hypothesised that <-torial> might be a suffix, showing their ability to look for patterns in word structure. Imagine the pride in their voice as they shared this insight, sparking a lively discussion about suffixes and their functions.

The real magic happened when we created the word sum. Together, we constructed it on the board:

<con-> + <spire> + <-ate> + <-or> + <-ial>

You could almost see the lightbulbs going off as students visualised how each part contributed to the whole word. We turned our attention to each affix, discussing its function and finding examples in other words:

- We connected the prefix <con-> to words like "connect", "construct" and "contribute", noting its meaning of "with" or "together".
- The bound base <spire> we linked to words such as "inspire", "aspire" and "perspire", relating to the idea of "breathing" or "spirit".
- We discovered the link of <-ate> to words like "considerate" and "activate", noting that it often forms adjectives.
- Students recognised <-or> as a suffix that creates nouns.
- To confirm <-ial> as a suffix, we explored words like "residential", "memorial" and "territorial".

But here's where it got really interesting: we observed how adding vowel suffixes affected the spelling of the base word. The students were fascinated to see how the <e> in "conspire" was crossed out when we added <-atorial>. It was a perfect demonstration of the interplay between morphology and orthography, deepening their understanding of spelling conventions.

To round out our investigation, we delved into etymology. Armed with their devices, students looked up the word "conspiratorial" in the Online Etymology Dictionary (etymonline.com). They discovered its Latin root <conspirare> meaning "to agree, unite, plot", comprised of <con-> meaning "with" and <spirare> meaning "to breathe".

This exploration led us to etymologically related words like "aspire", "expire", "inspiration", "spirit" and "perspire". The students were amazed to see the <spire> element in these seemingly unrelated words, broadening their understanding of language connections.

This exercise helped students appreciate the complex web of language evolution, showing how words with similar meanings can have diverse linguistic roots, and how understanding etymology can deepen their grasp of vocabulary.

Looking back, the multilayered approach to exploring "conspiratorial" was incredibly effective. Students didn't just learn a definition—they engaged deeply with the word, understanding its structure, meaning and origins. Yes, we faced challenges. Some students were initially overwhelmed by the word's complexity, but breaking it down into manageable parts turned this challenge into a strength of the lesson. It was remarkable to see how their understanding evolved, from initial confusion to a rich appreciation of the word's elements and connections.

This lesson exemplified why it's crucial to challenge students. The depth of learning went far beyond learning a new word, developing critical thinking skills applicable to future word encounters. The investigative nature of the lesson appealed to their curiosity and desire for complex problem-solving. By linking morphology, orthography and etymology, I provided a holistic view of language that satisfied their often interdisciplinary interests. Perhaps most importantly, the guided discovery approach empowered them to take ownership of their learning—a crucial skill for learners.

I hope this case study serves as a reminder that even seemingly simple elements of language can open doors to complex and engaging investigations, providing rich opportunities to challenge and inspire our learners.

Contemplate and Consider!

After exploring our case study on "conspiratorial," consider: in the words "conspiratorial", "conspire" and "conspiracy", is <spire> a bound base, a free base or a stem?

Take a moment to reflect on this. What's your initial thought? Write it below:

_____

_____

_____

Now, let's break it down together.

In these words, <spire> is a bound base. Here's why this understanding is crucial for your teaching.

A bound base carries the core meaning of a word but cannot stand alone in modern English. It needs affixes to form a complete word. This concept is key to understanding how complex words are built.

Look at how these words are constructed:

- <con-> + <spire>
- <con-> + <spire> + <-acy>
- <con-> + <spire> + <-ate> + <-or> + <-ial>

Notice how <spire> is always accompanied by other elements? This is a hallmark of a bound base.

The root <spire> comes from Latin <spirare> meaning "to breathe". While it's the meaning core, it doesn't exist as a standalone word with this meaning in English. Sharing this etymology with students can spark their interest in word origins.

This bound base appears in many words, such as "inspire", "expire", "perspire" and "respire". Recognising this helps students connect seemingly unrelated words, expanding their vocabulary exponentially.

Unlike <spire>, a free base can stand alone—for example, <write> in "rewrite". Understanding this difference helps students distinguish between different types of bases.

We add inflectional endings to stems, such as <-s>, <-ed> and <-ing>, but <spire> goes further, forming the core of words with various prefixes and derivational suffixes.

By recognising <spire> as a bound base, you equip your students with a powerful tool for word analysis. This knowledge allows them to:
- decode unfamiliar words more effectively
- make connections between related words
- understand how complex words are built
- appreciate the layered nature of English vocabulary.

As you plan your vocabulary instruction, consider how you might incorporate this level of morphological analysis. How could exploring bound bases like <spire> enrich your students' understanding of word structure and meaning? How might it change your approach to teaching new vocabulary?

Implement and Innovate!

This activity exploring the <spire> word family is designed to support your understanding of word formation and how precise morphological analysis can reveal the intricate structure of words in English. Look at the following table:

Word	Structure	Definition	Example sentence
spire	<spire>	To breathe	N/A (bound base, not used alone)
conspire	<con-> + <spire>	To plot or scheme together secretly	The two rivals decided to conspire against their common enemy.
conspiracy	<con-> + <spire> + <-acy>	A secret plan by a group to do something harmful or illegal	The government uncovered a conspiracy to overthrow the elected officials.
conspirator	<con-> + <spire> + <-ate> + <-or>	A person who takes part in a conspiracy	The conspirator was caught trying to smuggle sensitive documents out of the building.

Word	Structure	Definition	Example sentence
conspiratorial	<con-> + <spire> + <-ate> + <-or> + <-ial>	Relating to or suggestive of a conspiracy	His conspiratorial whispers made everyone in the room feel uneasy.
inspire	<in-> + <spire>	To fill someone with the urge or ability to do or feel something	The teacher's passion for literature helped inspire a love of reading in her students.
inspiration	<in-> + <spire> + <-ate> + <-ion>	The process of being mentally stimulated to do something	The artist found inspiration for her latest work in the bustling city streets.
inspirational	<in-> + <spire> + <-ate> + <-ion> + <-al>	Providing encouragement or motivation	The coach's inspirational speech motivated the team to victory.
expire	<ex-> + <spire>	To come to an end or cease to be valid	Remember to use the milk before it expires next week.
expiration	<ex-> + <spire> + <-ate> + <-ion>	The act of coming to an end or ceasing to be valid	The expiration of the contract left both parties free to negotiate new terms.
respire	<re-> + <spire>	To breathe	Plants respire through their leaves, taking in carbon dioxide and releasing oxygen.
respiration	<re-> + <spire> + <-ate> + <-ion>	The action of breathing	The doctor carefully monitored the patient's respiration during the procedure.
respiratory	<re-> + <spire> + <-ate> + <-ory>	Relating to breathing or the organs of breathing	The respiratory system includes the lungs and airways.

Word	Structure	Definition	Example sentence
perspire	<per–> + <spire>	To produce and emit sweat through the pores of the skin	Athletes often perspire heavily during intense workouts.
perspiration	<per–> + <spire> + <–ate> + <–ion>	The process of sweating or the sweat produced	The runner wiped the perspiration from his brow after the marathon.

Your task is to use Neil Ramsden's Mini Matrix-Maker (neilramsden.co.uk/spelling/matrix/) and create a detailed word matrix specifically for the bound base <spire>. This is a very effective tool you could use with your own students.

Answer Key

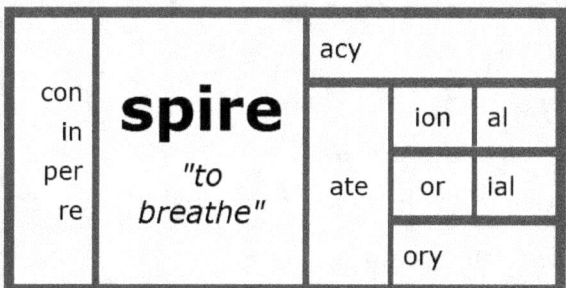

Teaching Tip!

Let's explore how the bound base <spire> is hiding inside "expire" and "expiration"!

First, let's break these words apart: "expire" = <ex–> + <spire> and "expiration" = <ex–> + <spire> + <–ate> + <–ion>. Next, let's look at each morpheme:

- <ex–> is a prefix meaning "out" or "from"
- <spire> is our bound base, meaning "to breathe"
- <–ate> is a suffix that forms verbs
- <–ion> is a suffix that turns verbs into nouns.

When something expires, it's like it "breathes out" its last breath. Its time is up!

"Expiration" is the noun form, describing the act of expiring or the moment when something expires. Notice that the <e> at the end of "spire" is dropped before adding <-ate>.

You might wonder why we don't see "exspire" or "exspiration". This is because of a common orthographic pattern or spelling convention: when <ex-> is added to a word beginning with <s>, we drop the <s>.

The cool part is that once you know <spire> means "to breathe", you gain insight into many other words:

- "Inspire" (<in-> + <spire>) means to "breathe in" ideas or motivation.
- "Respire" (<re-> + <spire>) means to breathe again and again—what we do all day!
- "Perspire" (<per-> + <spire>) means to breathe through, which is what happens when we sweat.

By recognising <spire> in these words, you can help your students comprehend the meaning of new words they encounter that have <spire> in them.

12. List synonyms and antonyms

Finally, let's list some synonyms and antonyms for "conscience":

- Synonyms: morality; scruples
- Antonyms: immorality; unconsciousness

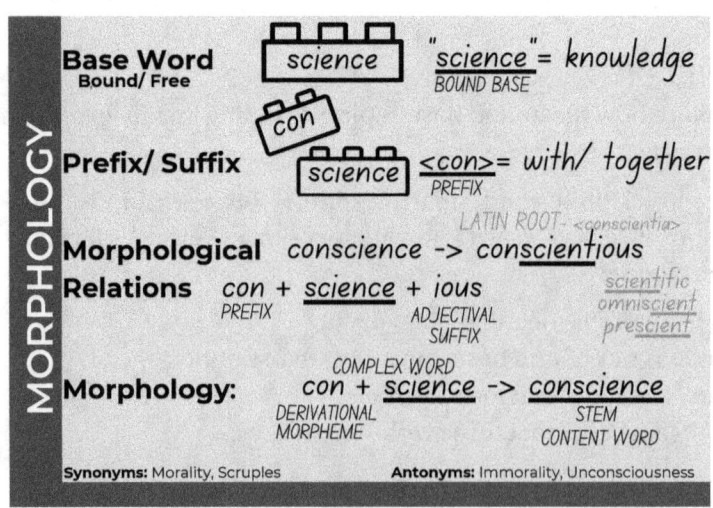

Contemplate and Consider!

Here's a short quiz designed to test your understanding of the morphological concepts discussed throughout this chapter relating to the word "conscience".

Part 1—Multiple Choice:

1. What is the morphological base word of "conscience"?
   A) <con>
   B) <science>
   C) <conscious>
   D) <morality>

2. Is the base word bound or free?
   A) Bound
   B) Free
   C) Compound
   D) Neither

3. Does "conscience" have a prefix? If so, what is it?
   A) No prefix
   B) <con->
   C) <sci->
   D) <en->

4. The word "conscious" is a _____ of "conscience"?
   A) Homophone
   B) Homonym
   C) Homograph
   D) Near-homophone

5. Is "conscience" a function or content word?
   A) Function
   B) Content
   C) Both
   D) Neither

Part 2—Short Answer:

1. Define a homograph and explain why "conscience" is not a homograph.
2. Write a sentence using the word "conscience" that demonstrates its meaning.

3. List two synonyms and two antonyms for "conscience".
4. Explain why "conscience" is considered a complex word.
5. What does the prefix in "conscience" mean and how does it modify the base word?

Answer Key

Part 1—Multiple Choice:

1. B) <science>
2. A) Bound
3. B) <con->
4. D) Near-homophone
5. B) Content

Part 2—Short Answer:

1. A homograph is a word that shares the same spelling as another word but has a different meaning and possibly different pronunciation. "Conscience" is not a homograph because there are no other words with the same spelling that have a different meaning or pronunciation.
2. After cheating on the test, John's conscience bothered him so much that he confessed to his teacher.
3. Some examples of synonyms might include moral sense, inner voice. Some examples of antonyms might include amorality, unscrupulousness.
4. "Conscience" is considered a complex word because it consists of more than one morpheme. It has a bound base <science> and a prefix <con-> <tautology>.
5. The prefix <con-> in this context means "with" or "together". When combined with the base <science>, meaning "knowledge", it forms "conscience", which literally means "with knowledge". This combination creates the concept of an inner sense of right and wrong, or moral knowledge that guides one's behaviour.

Tracking and Monitoring Student Progress in Morphology

Understanding how to effectively track and monitor your students' progress is important to ensure that they develop a robust understanding of the morphological terminology specific to The Morphology Lens. This section provides strategies that you can use to assess and enhance your students' morphological knowledge.

1. **Formative assessments:**
   - Regular quizzes can help assess students' understanding of key morphological concepts such as prefixes, suffixes and base words. These can be multiple-choice, fill-in-the-blank or short-answer formats.
   - Assign projects where students create mini matrices that visually represent the relationships between words and their components.
   - During class activities, observe students as they engage in word analysis tasks, noting their ability to identify and manipulate morphemes.
2. **Summative assessments:** Have your students compile a portfolio of their word study throughout the term, or throughout the novel study you are completing. This could include the LLGOs, student handouts and Post-it notes from their novels on their learning process.
3. **Systematic data collection:**
   - Use digital platforms like Google Forms or Kahoot for quizzes, which can automatically collect and organise data on student performance.
   - Using The Morphology Lens Rubric (overleaf), track individual and class-wide progress, noting areas of strength and those needing improvement:

The Morphology Lens Rubric

Key Feature	Glimpser	Observer	Analyst
Word Morphology	Identifies basic affixes (e.g. <un->, <-ed>, <-ing>) in common words	Distinguishes between free and bound morphemes; identifies base words and affixes in multisyllabic words	Analyses complex words to determine base, affixes and word-formation processes (e.g. compounding); utilises advanced morphological analysis to comprehend academic vocabulary
Word/Semantic Relationships	Identifies common synonyms and antonyms; recognises basic homophones and homographs	Explains relationships between words in the same morphological family; identifies most homophones and homographs and explains their related meanings	Analyses and applies knowledge of morphological families when spelling; explains etymological influences on spelling (e.g. homophones)
Word Class, Grammatical Form and Function	Identifies basic word classes (noun, verb, adjective, adverb) in simple sentences	Explains how words can change class through derivational processes (e.g. happy → happiness); identifies grammatical function of words in complex sentences	Analyses how inflectional and derivational morphemes affect grammatical function and meaning; explains semantic implications of word class changes

Constructive feedback

Provide feedback soon after assessments to ensure it is relevant and actionable. Focus on specific areas of improvement and strengths. For example, "You correctly identified the prefix <un-> as meaning "not", but let's work on recognising the suffix <-able>". Hold one-on-one or small group conferences to discuss feedback and set goals for improvement.

From Contemplation to Classroom Innovation

As we draw our exploration of the Morphology Lens to a close, I want you to reflect on this transformative journey through the world of morphemes. This chapter has delved deep into the heart of language structure, examining word morphology, semantic relationships and the dynamic interplay between word class, grammatical form and function.

Throughout this book, I've incorporated case studies from my own classroom to bring these morphological concepts to life so that you can have the confidence to try them in yours. These real-world examples illustrate how the study of morphemes can be seamlessly integrated into various subjects and across a wide range of year levels. From dissecting scientific terminology to historical texts, the applications of morphological analysis have proven both versatile and impactful.

I am hoping that your journey through this chapter has also been enriched by the reflective activities, which I designed to spark collegial discussions within your schools. These collaborative exercises have the power to foster a vibrant learning community among teaching teams, encouraging the exchange of ideas, challenges and successes in implementing the Morphology Lens. Through shared experiences and collective problem-solving, you will be able to discover innovative ways to make morphology accessible and engaging for all. This is why I have included a range of examples, even from the beginning of schooling!

As we conclude this chapter, I invite you to engage in two final activities designed to consolidate your learning and inspire your future teaching practice.

Contemplate and Consider!

Gather in small groups of three or four colleagues. Begin by reviewing key sections of this chapter, focusing on essential morphological concepts such as base words, affixes and morphological relationships. Using a whiteboard or a large piece of paper, collaboratively create a concept map that visually represents the interconnections between these morphological terms and ideas.

Once your concept map is complete, present it to the larger group, explaining your insights and the connections you've drawn. As you share, consider how these morphological concepts enhance our understanding of language and how they can be integrated into your teaching strategies. Discuss potential challenges in teaching morphology, and brainstorm creative solutions.

Through this collaborative exercise, you'll gain a clearer grasp of morphological concepts and their interrelations, develop strategies for incorporating morphology into your lessons and engage in critical reflection on the chapter's content. This activity aims to foster a deeper comprehension of the material and inspire innovative approaches to language instruction.

Implement and Innovate!

Form small groups of three or four teachers. Each group will select or be assigned a specific teaching scenario. Here are some examples:

1. **Prefix Power in Science (Year 5):** As part of a unit on the solar system, design a lesson that helps students understand prefixes such as <astro->, <geo->, <helio-> and <exo-> and apply them to scientific vocabulary.

2. **Suffix Stories in Literature (Year 8):** While analysing character development in a novel, create a lesson that encourages students to use suffixes that change adjectives into nouns (e.g. <-ness>, <-ity> and <-ion>) to describe character traits and their evolution throughout the story.

3. **Root Word Detectives in History (Year 7):** Investigate Latin and Greek roots while studying ancient civilisations by developing a lesson

that helps students decode common roots like <civ-> ("citizen"), <dem-> ("people"), <arch-> ("rule") and <polis-> ("city") using their knowledge of etymological roots.

4. **Compound Word Creativity in Art (Year 6):** Design a lesson that combines artistic creation with compound word formation by exploring compound words related to art (e.g. "watercolour", "sketchbook" and "paintbrush"), perhaps having students create visual representations of compound words.

As you craft your lesson, focus on creative approaches that will engage students and make morphology accessible and exciting.

Once your lesson plan is complete, exchange it with another group for peer review. Provide and receive constructive feedback, paying particular attention to clarity, student engagement and overall effectiveness. During this process, consider how morphological concepts can be woven into your existing lessons, brainstorm innovative strategies to captivate students' interest in word structure and reflect on how peer feedback can enhance your lesson design and delivery.

By the end of this activity, you'll have a refined, peer-reviewed lesson plan ready to implement in your classroom, along with fresh ideas for incorporating morphology into your teaching practice.

CHAPTER 6

Your Guide to the Etymology Lens

"Morphology frames and etymology explains many components of written words."
~ Sue Scibetta Hegland

By the end of this chapter, you'll have gained the following skills and insights:

1. **Unlocking word origins:** Discover how to effectively harness the power of the online etymology dictionary etymonline.com and learn how to trace the roots and origins of the words you teach.
2. **Distinguishing roots from relatives:** Gain clarity on the differences between etymological roots and morphological relatives. Understand why it's important to make these distinctions and how they can enhance your students' understanding of language.
3. **Engaging with eponyms and cognates:** Recognise how eponyms and cognates can significantly enhance your students' recall by leveraging familiarity and connections to known concepts or languages.
4. **The importance of etymology in all classrooms:** Delve into why etymology is a vital component of multilinguistic word study, appreciating its role as an independent Linguistic Lens that offers unique insight into words.

Introducing the Etymology Lens

Welcome to the Etymology Lens, designed to transform the way you and your students perceive language. This section of the book invites you to embark on a journey through the world of etymology. By exploring words through the Etymology Lens, you will not only enrich your students' vocabulary but also foster a profound appreciation for the interconnectedness of languages and the historical narratives they carry.

The purpose of the Etymology Lens is to peel back the layers of language, revealing the stories embedded within words. Consider the word "school", which traces its roots back to the Greek <skholē>, originally meaning "leisure" or "philosophical discussion". This journey from ancient Greece to modern classrooms illustrates how words evolve, carrying with them echoes of past cultures and ideas. Similarly, the term "boycott", named after Charles Boycott, exemplifies how historical events can give rise to new expressions. By uncovering these connections, your students will gain insight into the dynamic nature of language and its role in shaping human experience.

A critical aspect of this exploration is distinguishing between etymological roots and morphological bases. While etymological roots trace a word's historical and crosslinguistic journey, morphological bases focus on word formation within a family. Understanding this distinction empowers students to grasp the complexities of word origins and development, promoting critical thinking and a deeper appreciation for language. For example, recognising that "biology" combines the Greek <bios> (life) and <logos> (study) enriches students' comprehension of scientific terminology.

Research underscores the significance of etymology in literacy development, highlighting the benefits of etymological knowledge in enhancing vocabulary, comprehension skills, spelling and critical thinking (Adoniou, 2014; Scibetta Hegland, 2018; Daffern, 2017; Bowers & Kirby, 2010; Crystal, 2004). So, as we delve into the Etymology Lens, I invite you and your students to embrace this linguistic adventure. Together, let us travel back in time to uncover the rich tapestry of words, exploring the stories they tell and the connections they forge across cultures and eras. This journey promises to be as enlightening as it is engaging, opening new vistas of understanding and appreciation in the ever-evolving world of language.

At last, we unveil our final Linguistic Lens—the Etymology Lens, the magnifying glass that reveals the hidden roots and origins of words. This essential tool is brimming with Key Features designed to help you and your students delve into the fascinating history of language. My thoughtfully crafted Guiding Questions promise to make your exploration of etymology as thrilling and rewarding as a journey through a linguistic time machine.

On the front of the Etymology Lens, we see that <etym-> means "reason" and <-ology> means "the study of". So, etymology is quite literally "the study of reason". Did you know that etymology can explain some of the most notorious spelling difficulties? There are just so many reasons why our words are spelled the way they are!

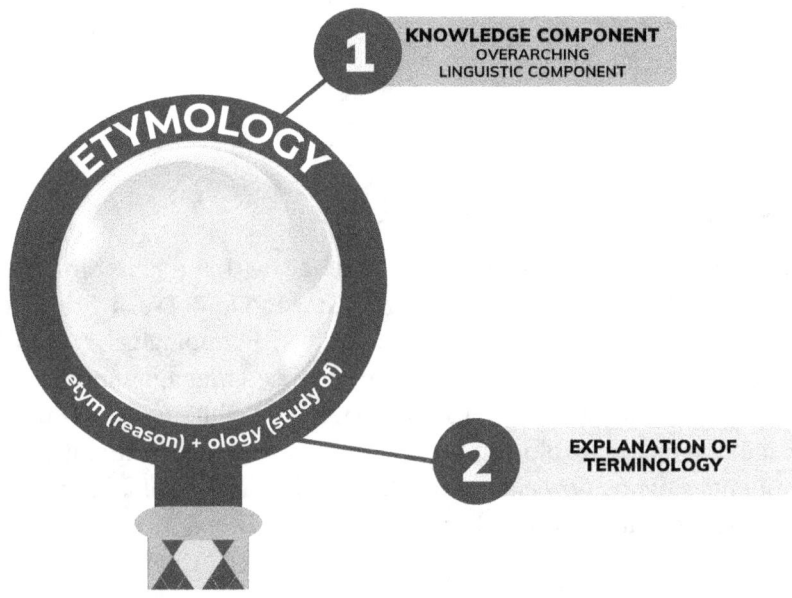

The back of the Etymology Lens displays its **Key Features**, which have been transformed into a set of **Guiding Questions** that will facilitate classroom discussions and support your word structure analysis.

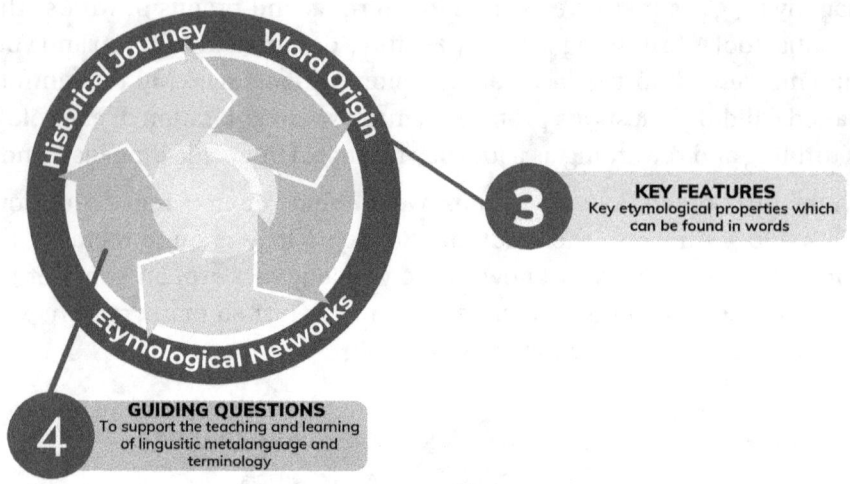

Key Features of the Etymology Lens

Let's step into the enchanting forest of language, with the Etymology Lens revealing three Key Features of our linguistic woodland: Word Origin, the ancient trees showcasing primordial meanings; Etymological Networks, the hidden mycelial connections between diverse language families; and Historical Journey, the growth rings of each word tree telling tales of cultural and social change. By exploring this rich ecosystem, you can cultivate in your students a deep appreciation for the dynamic nature of language and its fascinating journey through time.

Take a closer look:

1. **Word Origin:** Imagine words as ancient trees in a vast linguistic forest. Tracing a word to its origin is like examining the roots of these trees. Just as roots anchor a tree and provide essential nutrients, word origins form the foundation of language, nourishing our understanding with core meanings. By exploring these linguistic roots with students, you unearth the rich soil from which modern usage has grown, allowing them to see how the seeds of ancient languages have blossomed into the diverse vocabulary we use today.

2. **Etymological Networks:** Envision these as the vast underground networks connecting different species of trees in our linguistic forest. Just as mycorrhizal fungi form intricate webs linking diverse tree species, allowing nutrients and information to flow between seemingly unrelated trees, etymological networks link multiple languages, revealing shared meanings across different language families. While morphological base words are like the unique branches and leaves of individual trees, visible within a single species, etymological root forms represent the unseen connections beneath the forest floor, showcasing the historical ties and shared linguistic heritage across the entire woodland of human communication.

3. **Historical Journey:** In our linguistic forest, each word is like a living tree that has grown and adapted over centuries. Just as a tree's rings tell the story of its life—periods of drought, abundant rainfall, forest fires—a word's history reveals its journey through time. The trunk represents the word's core meaning, while the branches showcase how it has expanded or shifted in usage. Cultural, historical and social factors act like the changing seasons and environmental conditions, shaping the word's growth. Some branches may wither and fall away as certain meanings become obsolete, while new shoots emerge to represent fresh interpretations or applications. The tree's bark might change texture or colour, mirroring alterations in spelling or pronunciation. By studying this linguistic dendrochronology, students can observe how words, like trees, are not static entities but dynamic, living parts of our language ecosystem.

Components of Word Origin: The Teachers' Toolkit

Exploring the origins of words offers a captivating glimpse into the evolution of the English language, shaped by influences from Anglo-Saxon, Norman French, Latin and Greek, among others. Each language has left its mark, contributing unique spelling and linguistic conventions that tie a word's history to its current spelling and pronunciation.

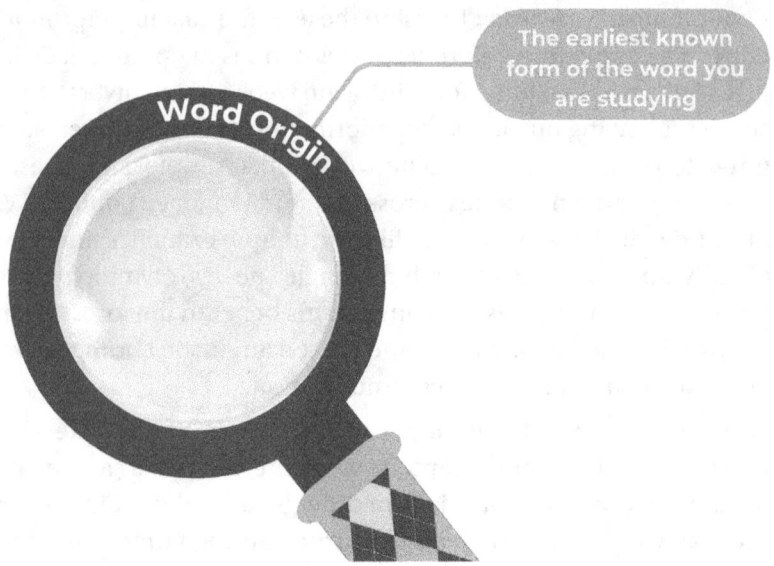

Focusing on word origin involves tracing back to the earliest known form of the word you are studying and identifying its root meanings. Consider the word "transport", which originates from the Latin root <transportare>, meaning "to carry across". This connection highlights how language evolves through borrowing and adaptation.

Components of Etymological Networks: The Teachers' Toolkit

Etymological networks form the foundation for etymological families of words which share common themes and meanings.

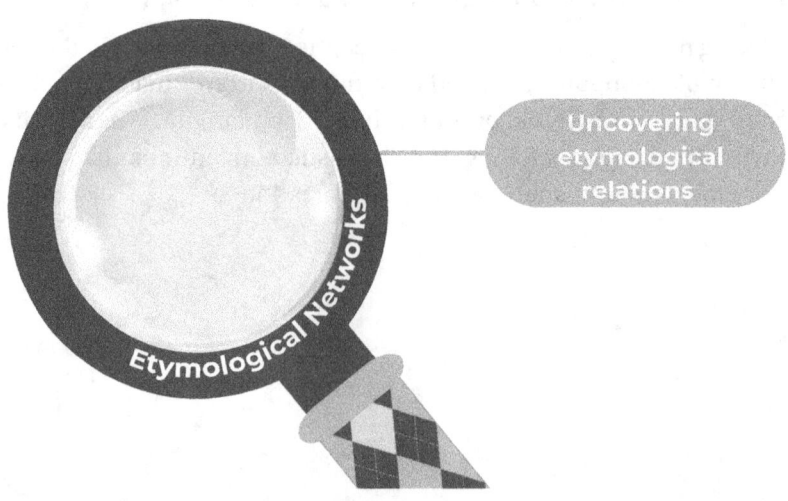

Etymological root words serve as fascinating gateways into the history and development of language, offering you an engaging way to explore word origins with your students. For instance, the Latin root <scrib>, meaning "write", connects words such as "inscribe", "describe" and "manuscript", each reflecting an aspect of writing. Similarly, the root <aud>, meaning "hear", links words like "audience", "auditory" and "audible", all related to hearing. Understanding these connections not only enriches vocabulary but will also provide your students with a deeper appreciation of language's interconnectedness.

It's important to distinguish these etymological roots from morphological base words, which are the simplest forms of words within a language to which prefixes and suffixes are added, like <act> in "react" or "action". While etymological roots delve into the historical connections of words across languages, morphological bases focus on word formation within a language. In the Linguistic Lenses framework, the term "root" is distinct from "base" and "stem" as it specifically refers to a word's origin, much like its representation in a dictionary.

Components of Historical Journey: The Teachers' Toolkit

Understanding the history of a word is like embarking on a journey through time.

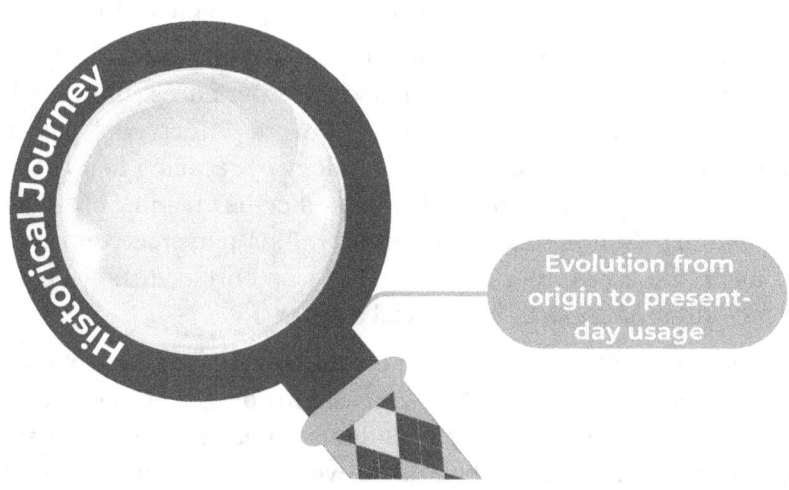

Embarking upon the historical journey of a word reveals its evolution from origin to present-day usage, encompassing changes in meaning, pronunciation and spelling influenced by cultural, social and historical factors. For instance, the word "colonel" traces back to the French <coronel>, providing an example of how English has borrowed and adapted words from other languages. Such cognates highlight shared linguistic roots, supporting students to recognise familiar patterns. Additionally, eponyms—words derived from names—offer intriguing insights into language evolution. Consider "sandwich", named after the Earl of Sandwich, or "diesel", after Rudolf Diesel. These words connect language to historical figures and innovations, demonstrating how new concepts become embedded in our vocabulary.

Exploring "Conscience" Through the Etymology Lens

Now, we're going to dive even deeper into our exploration of the word "conscience" using the LLGO. We've already examined this word through the Phonology, Orthography and Morphology Lenses; now, it's time to uncover its historical roots using the Etymology Lens.

To kick things off, I like to project the LLGO onto the interactive screen at the front of the classroom. This visual aid serves as our roadmap for the lesson's journey. With a bit of theatrical flair, I place the Etymology Lens magnet next to the Etymology Lens section, signalling to students that we're about to embark on a historical exploration of the word "conscience".

In my classroom, I've noticed that students become more engaged when they can link etymology to their personal experiences, bringing history to life. For example, while exploring the word "iridescent", one student connected it to her love for Greek mythology by recalling that Iris was the goddess of the rainbow, allowing her to predict the meaning of "iridescent" as something shimmering like a rainbow. This personal connection not only made the lesson more relatable but also enriched the whole class's understanding of the word's historical context.

By using the LLGO and focusing on etymology, we empower our students to see words as dynamic entities with rich histories. Let's embark on this journey together, encouraging our students to become linguistic detectives uncovering the rich histories behind the words they encounter daily. Here's to inspiring and impactful teaching!

Commencing a Word Odyssey: The five Guiding Questions of the Etymology Lens

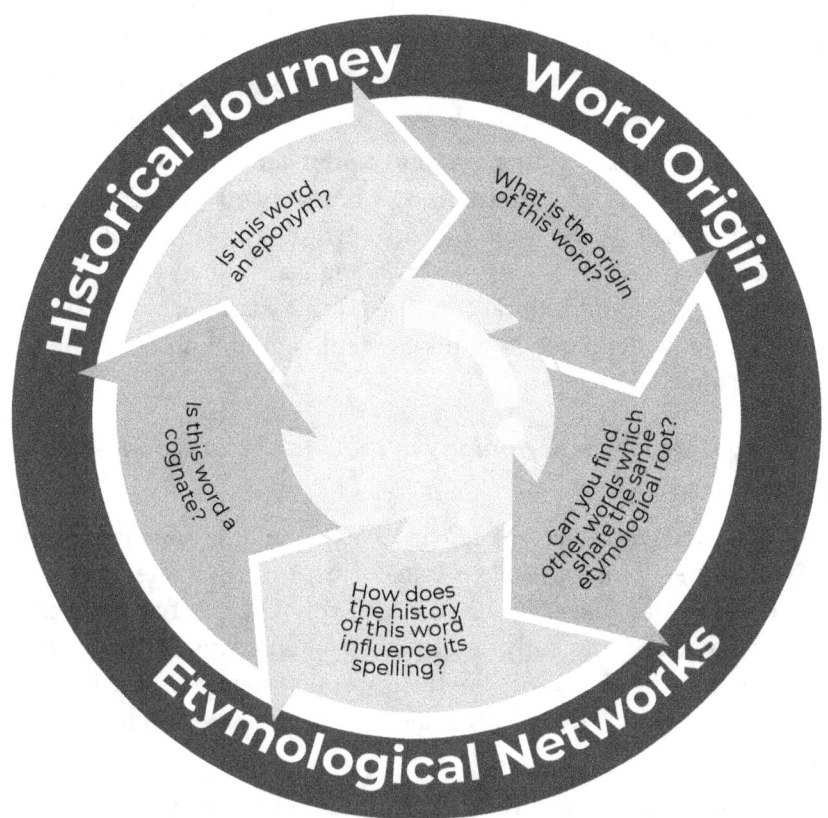

By working through these five questions, you can take students on a fun-filled journey into the world of English spelling through the Lens of etymology, where every word is like a mystery waiting to be solved.

1. What is the origin of this word?

We're going to continue our exploration of the word "conscience". To understand it better, let's start by looking at its origin. One great resource for this is the Online Etymology Dictionary (etymonline.com). Let's see what it tells us about "conscience".

According to this resource, "conscience" comes from the Latin word <conscientia>, which means "knowledge within oneself" or "joint knowledge". It's derived from <con-> meaning "with" or "together", and <scire> meaning "to know".

This tells us something about the word's original meaning: it has to do with knowing something inside or with others. Originally, <conscientia> referred to an internal awareness or shared knowledge, especially in a moral or ethical sense. As the word evolved into Middle English around the 13th century, it became "conscience", maintaining its connection to moral awareness.

This historical context influences our understanding of "conscience" today: "conscience" is that internal sense of right and wrong guiding our actions and decisions. By exploring its etymology using tools like the Online Etymology Dictionary, we see how language reflects and shapes our understanding of complex moral concepts. Understanding its origins helps us appreciate how deeply rooted this concept is in human behaviour and ethical decision-making.

Case study: the role of etymology in the Year 1 classroom—a case study on "pizza"

In the dynamic environment of a Year 1 classroom, the seemingly simple task of teaching spelling can quickly transform into an enlightening journey into the depths of language. This case study explores how etymology can be effectively integrated into early literacy instruction, using the word "pizza" as a focal point. By delving into the history and structure of words, we can equip students with a richer understanding of spelling beyond the basic 'sound it out' approach.

One day, Sarah, an inquisitive Year 1 student, came to class with an intriguing observation. "Mrs Cullen," she exclaimed, "did you know that the word 'pizza' has the sounds /t/ and /s/ and the two <z> letters aren't a digraph or a blend?" Her insight sparked a realisation—how many students are taught to spell "pizza" merely by sounding it out without understanding its complex structure?

While phonological strategies are beneficial in the early years, they are one part of the comprehensive spelling toolkit students need. Overreliance on sounding out often leads to spelling errors and can mislead students more often than not (Adoniou, 2017). With "pizza", it became evident that its spelling was influenced by its history and meaning, prompting an exploration to uncover why it is spelled the way it is.

To address Sarah's question, we embarked on an investigation, using IPA tiles to visualise the word's phonetics: /piːtsə/.

Together, we traced the word's history using the Online Etymology Dictionary:

1. In 1935, "pizza" appeared in the Oxford English Dictionary, borrowed from Italian, where it meant "cake, tart, pie".
2. In 1907, the word <pinza> was documented in the *Vocabolario Etimologico della Lingua Italiana*, meaning "clamp."
3. It is derived from the Latin <pinsere>, meaning "to pound, stamp".

By connecting these historical meanings to the act of pounding dough, students gained a deeper understanding of the word's etymology.

Further exploration revealed links to Medieval Greek <pitta> (meaning "cake, pie") and Old High German <bizzo> or <pizzo> (meaning "bite, morsel"). This led to a discussion on voiced and unvoiced phonemes.

By feeling the vibrations of the /b/ sound and comparing it to the unvoiced /p/, students grasped why historical spellings varied. This exercise also demonstrated how the IPA preserves a word's historical pronunciation, emphasising the value of etymology.

Etymology should not be reserved for advanced learners—understanding word origins should be foundational in spelling education for all ages (Adoniou, 2017). By engaging students with the history and structure of words, we enhance their spelling skills and linguistic awareness.

Addressing Sarah's second observation, we clarified that "pizza" contains no digraph or blend. The <z> graphemes represent individual phonemes /t/ and /s/ and the syllable break between vowels indicates no blend. The <z> graphemes in "pizza" are pronounced /t/ /s/ because that's the sound the <zz> digraph represents in Italian, the language we borrowed the word from. Moreover, the Old High Germanic <bizzo>/<pizzo> shows how the spelling also preserves parts of the word's history. This analysis dispels the myth that all words can be spelled by sounding them out.

This case study illustrates how a student's curiosity about "pizza" inspired a lesson rich in linguistic exploration. It underscores the importance of teaching etymology as an integral part of spelling. By moving beyond phonological approaches, we can provide students with the tools to navigate the complexities of the English language, fostering a deeper appreciation and understanding of words.

2. Can you find other words which share the same etymological root?

Now that we've explored the origin of "conscience", let's take it a step further. Can you find other words that share the same etymological root as "conscience"? Remember, we're looking at the Latin origin <conscientia>, which comes from <con-> meaning "with" and <scire> meaning "to know".

First, let's look at "conscious". "Conscious" refers to an awareness or knowledge of oneself and one's environment, much like "conscience". Now, what about "science"? Science is the systematic study of the structure and behaviour of the physical and natural world through observation and experiment. It comes directly from <scire>, meaning "to know", representing the pursuit of knowledge and understanding.

Lastly, let's look at "omniscient". "Omniscient" combines <omni>, meaning "all", with <scire>, emphasising total knowledge or awareness. It's often used to describe someone's all-encompassing knowledge.

By examining these words, we can see how they connect back to the concept of knowledge and awareness, all sharing the root <scire>. This helps us understand the richness of language and its connections.

As a teacher, you have the opportunity to ignite curiosity and deepen understanding by exploring etymological root words with your students. The thrill of students discovering that seemingly unrelated words share a common ancestry is palpable—trust me! These etymological roots form the backbone of etymological word families that carry shared meanings and themes across time.

Contemplate and Consider!

The purpose of this activity is to help you and your colleagues deepen your understanding of etymological roots and apply this knowledge in your own classroom setting:

1. Choose a set of words that share a common etymological root. For instance, explore the Latin root <scrib>, meaning "write", and the root <aud>, meaning "hear". Use the Online Etymology Dictionary to research the origins and meanings of these words.
2. In teams, use large poster paper to collaboratively construct a visual representation of the words. Include columns for the word, its definition, its etymological root and how it relates to the concept of writing or hearing.
3. Form small groups to discuss the words you've researched. Share insights on how understanding these roots can enhance vocabulary teaching.

By exploring these connections yourself, you will be better equipped to show your students how words with shared roots often relate to similar concepts or actions, reflecting their common origins.

Answer Key

Word exploration ideas for the Latin root <scrib>:

- **Scribe:** A person who copies out documents, especially a person employed to do this before printing was invented. From Latin <scriba>, meaning "public writer, clerk, secretary". Directly related to the act of writing.
- **Describe:** To give a detailed account in words (of someone or something). From Latin <describere>, meaning "to write down, copy;

sketch, represent". Involves writing or speaking about something in detail.
- **Inscribe:** To write or carve (words or symbols) on something, especially as a formal or permanent record. From Latin <inscribere>, meaning "to write in or on". Involves writing on a surface, often permanently.
- **Manuscript:** An author's handwritten or typed text that has not yet been published. From Latin <manu scriptus>, meaning "written by hand". Directly related to handwritten documents.
- **Prescription:** An instruction written by a medical practitioner that authorises a patient to be issued with a medicine or treatment. From Latin <praescribere>, meaning "to write before, order, direct". Involves writing instructions for medication.

Word exploration ideas for the Latin root <aud>:

- **Audible:** Able to be heard. From Latin <audibilis>, meaning "that can be heard". Directly related to the ability to hear something
- **Audience:** The assembled spectators or listeners at a public event. From Latin <audientia>, meaning "a hearing, listening". Refers to people who listen to or watch a performance.
- **Auditorium:** A large building or hall used for public gatherings, especially for speeches or concerts. From Latin <auditorium>, meaning "lecture room". A place where people gather to hear performances or speeches.
- **Audit:** An official inspection of an organisation's accounts. From Latin <auditus>, meaning "a hearing". Originally referred to the hearing of accounts, now means to examine them.
- **Obedient:** Complying or willing to comply with orders or requests. From Latin <oboedientem>, meaning "listening to, obeying". Implies listening to and following instructions.

Teaching Tip!

Understanding the distinction between etymological roots and morphological bases is important:

- Etymological roots trace back to ancient languages, offering historical insights into word development. For instance, <geo> (Greek for "earth") appears in "geography" and "geology."

- Morphological base words are the simplest forms of words within a language, to which prefixes or suffixes are added. Consider "act", which becomes "react", "action" and "active".

While etymological roots delve into the historical and linguistic origins across languages, morphological bases focus on word families.

Case study: family picnics with immediate family versus extended family gatherings

Imagine a classroom buzzing with excitement as students explore the word "commotion". During a recent classroom observation, I witnessed a teacher transforming a simple vocabulary lesson into an interactive exploration of language. By weaving together morphological and etymological insights, the teacher provided students with a rich understanding of words, making the lesson both memorable and impactful.

Morphological families are words connected by shared roots and affixes—like how your immediate family is connected by shared lineage. In this lesson, the teacher used the analogy of a family picnic to make these connections clear and engaging.

She started by explaining how a base word is the simplest form of a word, to which prefixes and suffixes can be added. For example, "motion" is a base word that can be expanded into "commotion", "emotion" and "promotion".

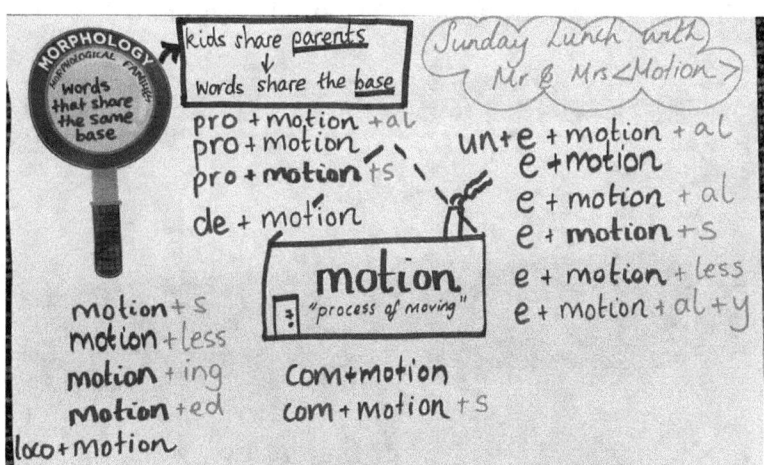

The teacher then laid out a picnic blanket labelled "Mr and Mrs Motion", serving as a visual anchor for the lesson.

"If Mr and Mrs Motion were having a picnic," she said, "who would they invite? "

A student replied, "Everyone with the base word 'motion', like their children! They are Mr and Mrs Motion; their children would all have the same surname".

The students brainstormed words like "emotion", "emotional" and "motioning". Using Neil Ramsden's Word Searcher tool (neilramsden.co.uk/spelling/searcher/) on the interactive whiteboard, the class explored related words, creating word sums and arranging them on the picnic blanket. The students then gathered around the picnic blanket, reinforcing the idea of an immediate family of words.

Etymological connections are like an extended family, tracing words back to their historical roots. Using the Online Etymology Dictionary, the teacher showed how the root word of "motion" is <movere>, which is Latin for "to move". Several English words share this etymological root, reflecting the concept of movement or change. She highlighted some examples:

- **Move:** Directly derived from <movere> and meaning "to change position or place"
- **Motion:** The process of moving or being moved
- **Motivate:** To provide someone with a reason to act or move
- **Mobile:** Capable of moving or being moved freely or easily.

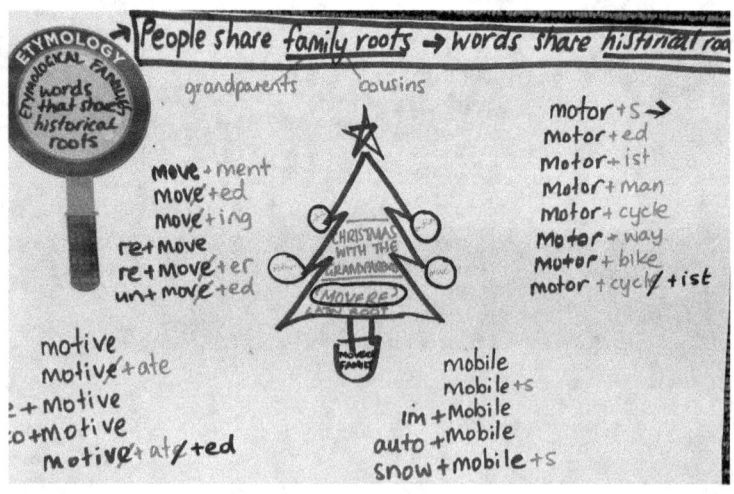

These words highlight the theme of movement inherent in their Latin origin and are essentially "cousins", with the Latin grandparents being Mr and Mrs Movere.

"What does 'mobile' mean?" she asked the class.

A student answered, "To move".

"Is it related to motion?"

"Yes, through etymology!"

"What does that mean?"

"By its history or origin—Latin, Greek or French roots."

"Would the 'mobile' morphological family be invited to the 'motion' family picnic?"

"No, but they might join the Christmas gathering with the grandparents!"

This festive analogy helped students visualise and appreciate the historical journey of words, making the lesson both educational and festive.

The teacher's creative approach brought language to life through activities like the "family picnic" and the "Christmas lunch". She even added baubles for each cousin's surname to the Christmas tree.

These engaging scenarios made abstract concepts tangible and relatable, fostering a deeper understanding of language dynamics. Moreover, this case study highlights the importance of tailoring instruction to various learning styles. By incorporating tactile, auditory and visual methods, you can ensure that all students grasp morphological and etymological concepts effectively. Interactive and multisensory learning not only enhances engagement but also boosts retention.

Teaching Tip!

Diagrams, charts and visuals that illustrate word relationships are powerful tools for reinforcing key concepts and aiding comprehension.

Implement and Innovate!

This exercise is designed to help you reflect on what you've learned and explore innovative ways to incorporate etymology into your teaching practice.

1. **Implement:** Choose a set of common etymological roots relevant to your subject area. Research and compile a list of words sharing these roots, considering how they connect to your curriculum.
2. **Innovate:** Reflect on how these roots and their associated words can be integrated into your lessons. Develop a mini lesson or activity that encourages your students to explore these connections, such as creating word family trees or conducting a root word scavenger hunt.
3. **Reflect and share:** After implementing your mini lesson, take time to reflect on its impact. How did students respond? What insights did they gain? Consider sharing your experience and any innovative approaches you discovered with your colleagues, perhaps during a team meeting or professional development session.

Case study: delving into the roots of "implicating" with Year 6 students

In the vibrant setting of a Year 6 classroom, the exploration of etymology offers a thrilling opportunity to deepen students' understanding of language. This case study examines how a simple question, "Can you find other words that share the same etymological root?" transformed a vocabulary lesson on the word "implicating" into a rich, interconnected linguistic journey.

During a novel study of *Chinese Cinderella*, my students encountered the word "implicating" and were poised to skip over it, a common habit I have observed among older readers who often read silently to themselves. That's why I am a big advocate for novel studies in the older years. This tendency highlights the importance of teachers probing and asking questions about comprehension, ensuring that students truly grasp the material rather than glossing over unfamiliar terms. Recognising this challenge, I decided to turn this moment into an opportunity for deeper exploration and understanding.

Through collaborative research and discussion, we uncovered that "implicating" stems from the Latin root <plicare> meaning "to fold". This discovery served as the key to unlocking a network of related words, each offering a unique perspective on the concept of folding:

- **Explicit:** Emerging from <explicare> meaning "to unfold", suggesting clarity and openness.
- **Exploit:** Linked to <exploiter> involving the unfolding of resources or opportunities.
- **Application:** From <applicare> meaning "to fold toward" or "to apply", indicating purpose or intent.
- **Accomplice:** Someone "folded" into an endeavour with another.
- **Duplicate:** To fold or replicate an original.
- **Multiply:** Increasing by folding or layering multiple times.
- **Complicate:** Folding together to create complexity or intricacy.

By examining these connections, I could see my students gaining insights into how etymology can reveal hidden relationships between words that appear unrelated at first glance.

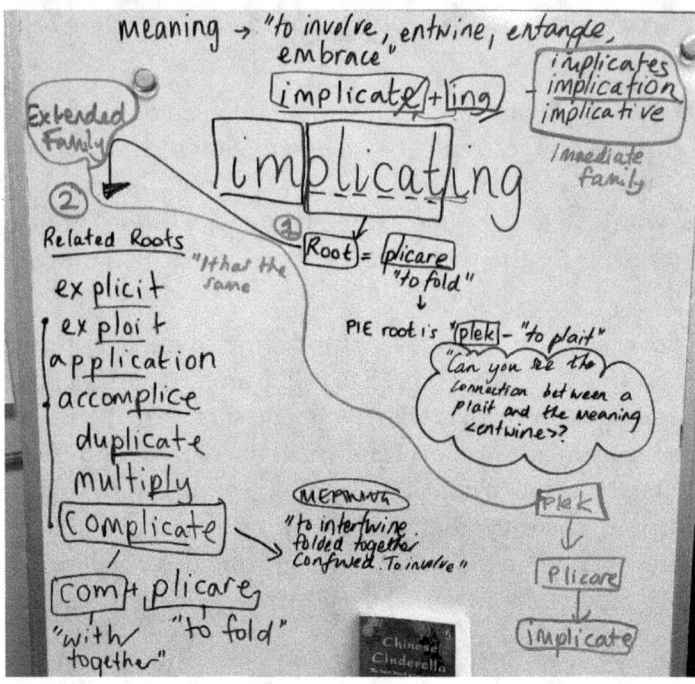

The lesson also involved distinguishing between words sharing etymological roots and those with purely morphological connections. Words like "implicates", "implication" and "implicative" are morphologically related to "implicating", with affixes added to change the meaning of the word:

- "Implicates" refers to the act or process of involving or suggesting.
- "Implication" is the effect or outcome of implicating.
- "Implicative" describes something that carries or suggests implications.

This case study demonstrates the value of etymology, offering practical insights, so be sure to do the following in your own classroom:

- Equip students with etymological dictionaries and digital tools to support independent research.
- Help students draw links between words, enhancing vocabulary retention and understanding.
- Teach the difference between root and morphological relationships to deepen linguistic comprehension.

Studying a single word through the Etymology Lens often opens the door to exploring other linguistic perspectives, such as morphology or phonology. As you and your students uncover the historical roots of a word, you will naturally encounter its morphological structure, leading to a deeper understanding of how words are formed and related. This interconnectedness between Linguistic Lenses allows your students to make connections across different aspects of language, enriching their comprehension and appreciation of its complexity.

3. How does the history of this word influence its spelling?

Here's a thought-provoking question for you: how does the history of the word "conscience" influence its spelling? Think about the origins of words and how understanding them can help us remember their spelling.

As we've discussed, "conscience" comes from the Latin word <conscientia>, which means "knowledge within oneself" or "moral sense". We can trace it back further to two parts: <com-> and <scire>. This Latin prefix <com-> underwent a process of assimilation, which is when one sound becomes more similar to a neighbouring sound for ease of pronunciation—here, when <com-> was attached to <scire>, the <m> changed to <n> before the /s/ sound. This assimilation makes the word flow more smoothly when spoken. Try saying "comscience" versus "conscience"—you'll notice the latter is much easier to pronounce!

The <sci> in "conscience" reflects the root <scire>. It's a reminder of its connection to knowledge. The word came into English through Old French as "conscience" which kept the Latin spelling. The French influence helped preserve that structure. Understanding these roots can help us remember the spelling. Remember, every word has a story, and understanding it can make spelling and meaning much clearer.

Teaching Tip!

Here are some ideas on how you can teach assimilation in language:

1. **Start with familiar examples.** Begin with words students already know, like "impossible" (<in-> + <possible>) or "irregular" (<in-> + <regular>). This helps them recognise the concept in their existing vocabulary.
2. **Use visual aids.** Create charts or diagrams showing how prefixes change. For example:
    - <in-> → <im-> before p, b, m
    - <in-> → <il-> before l
    - <in-> → <ir-> before r

3. **Incorporate the Phonology Lens.** Have students practice pronouncing words before and after assimilation to hear the difference, like "<in-> + <possible>" vs "impossible".
4. **Group similar patterns.** Organise words with similar assimilation patterns together. This helps students recognise and remember the patterns more easily. Use this visual to support your students' learning:

ASSIMILATION

The process where one sound becomes more similar to a neighbouring sound to facilitate pronunciation.

Prefix	Examples
in-	illegal (in + legal), immature (in + mature), irregular (in + regular), impossible (in + possible)
ad-	accuse (ad + cuse), affect (ad + fect), aggravate (ad + gravate), announce (ad + nounce)
sub-	succeed (sub + ceed), suffice (sub + fice), suppress (sub + press), support (sub + port)
ob-	occur (ob + cur), offend (ob + fend), oppose (ob + pose)
com-	collaborate (com + laborate), correct (com + rect), collide (com + lide), correspond (com + respond)
syn-	syllable (syn + lable), symmetry (syn + metry)
dis-	diffuse (dis + fuse), differ (dis + fer)

5. **Use word-building activities.** Create exercises where students combine prefixes with root words, focusing on how the prefix changes due to assimilation.
6. **Highlight etymology.** Explain the Latin or Greek origins of prefixes and how assimilation developed over time. This historical context can deepen understanding.

Case study: an etymological journey into the logic of "known"

As teachers, we often encounter spelling errors that reveal deeper insights into our students' understanding of language. This case study explores how an etymological approach can transform a simple spelling correction into a rich learning experience.

Picture this: A bright-eyed Year 3 student with diagnosed literacy learning difficulties hands in her writing. As you scan her work, a sentence catches your eye: "Bats have been nowean to live for about 30 years."

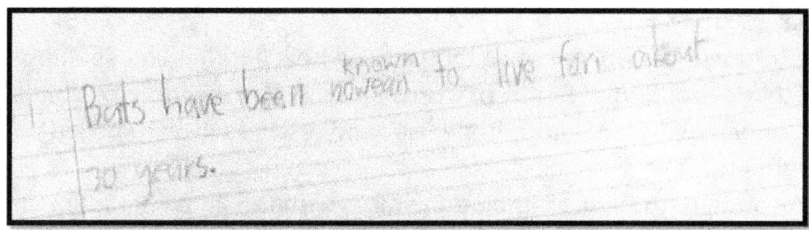

At first glance, it's clear the student has used "known" in the correct context, demonstrating a solid grasp of its meaning, but the spelling presents an interesting teaching point. This isn't a simple error—it's a window into the complex world of English orthography.

As you analyse the error, several questions arise:

1. Does the student understand the difference between the base word "know" and its homophone "no"?
2. Is she aware of the connection between "know" and "known"?
3. What led her to choose the grapheme <n> to represent the initial sound?

This is where the Etymological Lens becomes invaluable. Many homophones in English have distinct spellings due to their historical origins. In this case, the <kn> in "know" and "known" traces back to Old English, when both the <k> and <n> were pronounced. Over time, the pronunciation evolved, but the spelling preserved this linguistic history. Interestingly, the student intuitively used the <n> from the Germanic spelling to represent the /n/ phoneme. In this example, the student has correctly used the letter <n> to represent the /n/ sound, showing their grasp of basic phoneme–grapheme relationships. However, to improve their spelling accuracy, they need to draw upon their etymological knowledge. This orthographic pattern appears in several English word pairs, such as "knight" and "night", where the words have identical pronunciations but different meanings and origins. The digraph serves as a visual distinction, preserved by history; so, by teaching our students about these etymological patterns and the underlying structure of words, we can equip them with problem-solving strategies for spelling. This approach helps them choose the appropriate grapheme when faced with words that sound the same but have different spellings and meanings.

Armed with this etymological insight, you can transform this spelling correction into a fascinating mini lesson:

1. Acknowledge the student's correct usage and explain the spelling discrepancy.
2. Introduce the concept of etymology and how it influences spelling.
3. Explore the "know" family of words and their connection to "knight".
4. Compare with the homophone "no" and discuss why it's spelled differently.
5. Encourage students to find other words with the <kn> digraph (e.g. "knit", "knot" and "knead").

By explicitly unpacking the spelling error through this Etymological Lens, you provide targeted, feedback-driven instruction that goes beyond simple correction—you invite students to become language detectives, uncovering the logic behind English spelling. Take a look at this in action:

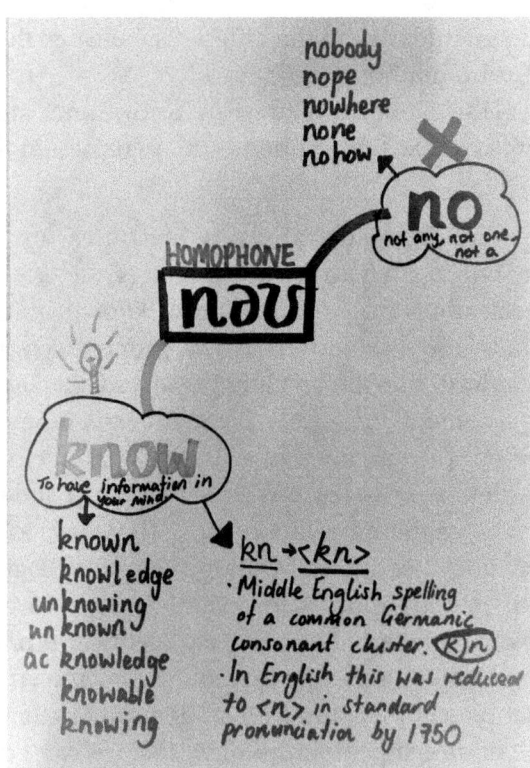

Teaching Tip!

Here are the practical takeaways from this case study:

- Use etymological explanations to address spelling errors, especially with homophones.
- Introduce accurate linguistic terminology (e.g. "digraph" instead of "silent letter") to build a robust vocabulary for discussing language.
- Encourage students to explore word histories and make connections between related words.
- Create engaging activities that allow students to apply their etymological knowledge, such as word family trees or etymology-based spelling bees.

4. Is this word a cognate?

Cognates are words in different languages that share similar meanings, spellings and pronunciations due to their common linguistic origins. They are valuable for your students to understand, offering a bridge between languages that can greatly enhance vocabulary learning and comprehension. They can be particularly handy when teaching novels set in other countries or cultures, helping students navigate unfamiliar vocabulary with ease.

For students of all ages, cognates serve as linguistic gateways that connect their existing language knowledge to new concepts. For instance, English speakers can intuitively understand French cognates like "information" (French: "information"), "nation" (French: "nation") and "animal" (French: "animal"), empowering them to grasp content more efficiently. In secondary schools, the relevance of cognates becomes even more pronounced in content-specific areas. In science, terms like "photosynthesis" (French: <photosynthèse>) and "atom" (Spanish: <átomo>) are instantly relatable. Mathematics students will find "geometry" (French: <géométrie>) and "algebra" (Spanish: <álgebra>) easier to tackle, while history learners can connect with "revolution" (French: <révolution>; Spanish: <revolución>) and "democracy" (French: <démocratie>; Spanish: <democracia>). These examples demonstrate how cognates can reveal complex vocabulary. Incorporating cognates into your teaching across the curriculum can also boost your students' confidence by reducing the cognitive load associated with learning new vocabulary.

"Conscience" is a cognate. It shares its roots with words like the French <conscience> and the Spanish <conciencia>. They all come from the Latin <conscientia>.

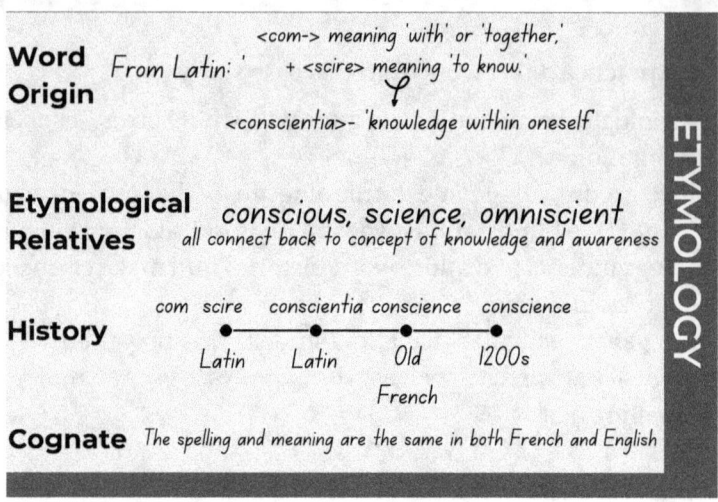

Case study: discovering the power of cognates—bridging languages and cultures

This case study highlights how delving into the etymology and pronunciation of words can enrich students' understanding, using the novel *Chinese Cinderella* by Adeline Yen Mah as a focal point.

While studying *Chinese Cinderella* with my Year 6 class, we encountered, "Chagrined but defiant, big brother…". Students were puzzled by the pronunciation of "chagrined", debating between /ʃ/ and /tʃ/ for the sound. Recognising this as a teachable moment, I introduced the IPA to clarify pronunciation. By recording the IPA symbols, students deciphered the word "chagrin" as /ʃægrɪn/. This exercise not only resolved their pronunciation dilemma but also opened doors to deeper comprehension.

To fully appreciate the vocabulary in *Chinese Cinderella*, understanding its historical context is crucial. The book recounts Adeline Yen Mah's early schooling in Tianjin, China, at a French-run boarding school. This setting reflects the broader historical interactions between China and Western countries, particularly during the late Qing dynasty and the Republican era. After the Opium Wars, several Chinese ports, including Tianjin, became treaty ports open to foreign influence. Here, Western missionary and educational activities flourished, leaving a linguistic legacy evident in the novel's vocabulary.

As we read further, students identified several French cognates within the text, such as "chauffeur" and "chateaux". Recognising these words as French, they understood that etymology influences orthography. This realisation extended to other words like "omelette" and "brunette", where students noticed the French-originated spelling pattern, identical in both English and French.

Teaching cognates not only enriches vocabulary but also deepens reading comprehension. By exploring the origins of these words, students can gain insights into cultural exchanges and historical events that shape our language, transforming a vocabulary lesson from rote memorisation into an exploration of history and linguistics.

Teaching Tip!

- **Use the IPA for pronunciation.** This tool explains pronunciation and empowers students to tackle unfamiliar words confidently.
- **Explore historical contexts.** Understanding the context in which words are used enhances comprehension and appreciation.
- **Identify and discuss cognates and their origins.** This builds connections between languages and deepens vocabulary knowledge.
- **Engage in interactive learning.** Use Post-it notes for students to record new vocabulary and insights. These notes can be kept in their books for easy reference, reinforcing learning.

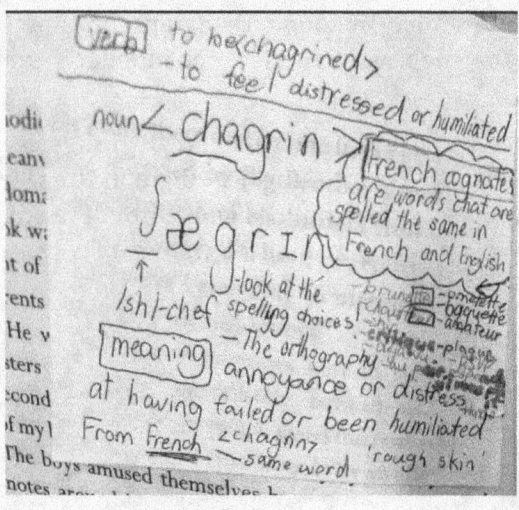

Case study: exploring language and cognates in the classroom

During a Year 4 novel study lesson on *Nim's Island* by Wendy Orr, we found ourselves on an unexpected exploration of language intricacies and etymology, sparking curiosity and engagement.

The classroom was abuzz with anticipation as the book was projected onto the TV screen, allowing students to follow along and observe my annotations of our classroom conversation in real time. This novel approach not only enhanced the learning experience but also fostered an interactive environment where students felt encouraged to participate.

During the reading session, we encountered the word "knife". To deepen understanding, I prompted the class for synonyms. Hands shot up with enthusiasm, suggesting words like "sword", "dagger", "blade", "razor" and "machete". It was the mention of "machete" that steered the lesson in an unexpected yet enriching direction.

The word "machete" opened a door to discussing cognates. We placed "machete" at the centre of our word web on the board and focused on the /ʃ/ sound represented by the <ch> digraph. We uncovered that the word "machete" can be considered a cognate of, and originates from, the Spanish word <machete>, which is a diminutive form of <macho> meaning "sledgehammer" or "axe". The term was adopted into English from Spanish, retaining its spelling and meaning. This realisation demonstrated how languages borrow words from one another, often preserving their original form and meaning, similar to the French cognates discussed in the case study of "chagrined".

The /ʃ/ sound represented by the <ch> digraph prompted us to gather a collection of words such as "charades", "chandelier", "machine", "chalet" and "champagne".

Our exploration revealed another layer of linguistic intrigue. We noted that "chalet" and "ballet" shared the same <et> digraph. This observation led to a hypothesis that these words might originate from French. The realisation sparked an animated discussion about the nature of cognates and their role in word study.

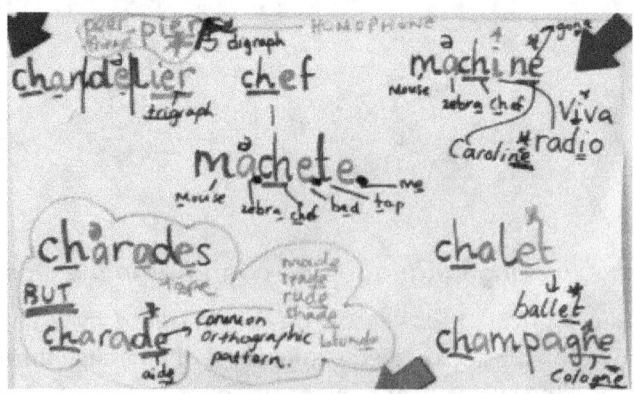

Understanding cognates became a pivotal point in our lesson. Cognates, being words that share a similar meaning and form across languages, offer students a bridge to learning new vocabulary. Recognising these connections can significantly enhance your students' reading comprehension.

Teaching Tip!

Incorporating cognates into language lessons can be revealing. Here are some practical takeaways from my experience:

- **Use real-life examples.** Engage students by drawing connections between their native language and the language being studied, or from words they are actually interacting with. This not only aids in retention but also makes learning relatable.
- **Create interactive activities.** Encourage students to create their own word webs exploring cognates. This hands-on approach fosters deeper understanding.
- **Foster curiosity.** Encourage students to ask questions about word origins and patterns, promoting an inquisitive mindset that extends beyond the classroom.

By transforming a simple reading session into an exploration of synonyms and cognates, my students' passion for linguistic discovery was ignited.

5. Is this word an eponym?

Let's discuss whether "conscience" is an eponym.

Eponyms are words derived from the names of people. "Conscience" is not an eponym. It doesn't originate from a person's name.

Case study: when parents become pronunciation police—a "Cartesian" comedy

As teachers, we often encounter the challenge of teaching words that carry different meanings across subjects. For instance, explaining a "plane" in mathematics versus in history can be perplexing. With over 70% of academic words being polysemous (having more than one meaning; Johnson et al., 1983), the complexity of vocabulary acquisition and the need for instructional strategies that address multiple word meanings is critical for our students. This case study explores strategies for teaching subject-specific vocabulary and the importance of Linguistic Lenses in enhancing comprehension.

Recently, a concerned parent emailed me about one of my teachers mispronouncing "Cartesian plane" in a mathematics class. The parent advised the child to inform the teacher, who still insisted there were two acceptable pronunciations. This incident highlights the challenges teachers face when navigating complex vocabulary.

Mistakes are opportunities for growth in the classroom, both for students and teachers. A powerful example of this is illustrated in Ron Berger's "Austin's Butterfly" project from 2016, which demonstrates the power of specific, constructive feedback in student learning. In this project, a student named Austin was guided through multiple drafts of a scientific drawing of a butterfly, improving dramatically with each iteration based on feedback.

This approach to learning—embracing mistakes and using them as stepping stones for improvement—applies not only to students but to teachers as well. As this concerned parent aptly noted, "teachers can make mistakes; they are human". This acknowledgment highlights the importance of creating a classroom environment where errors are seen as part of the learning process for everyone involved.

The question then arises: how do teachers articulate and explain sophisticated vocabulary, especially when they might not always have all the answers? This challenge presents an opportunity for teachers to model lifelong learning by demonstrating how to research, verify information and admit when they're unsure.

In this situation, I encouraged my teacher to consider the interconnected roles of our Linguistic Lenses, with each element crucial for understanding and teaching complex words like "Cartesian":

1. The **Etymology Lens** reveals that "Cartesian" pertains to the works of French philosopher René Descartes. Understanding its origin provides context and depth.
2. The **Morphology Lens** breaks down "Cartesian" into <Cartes> and <-ian>, indicating it's an adjective meaning "pertaining to or from (Des)cartes". This analysis aids comprehension but not pronunciation.
3. The **Phonology Lens:** guides us to the IPA, where we learn to pronounce "Cartesian" as /kɑːtiːziːən/, identifying four vowel sounds, four syllables and eight phonemes. This is vital for correct pronunciation.
4. The **Orthography Lens** allows us to recognise patterns in English, such as that words ending in <-ion> or <-ian> often stress the penultimate syllable. This insight helps pronounce "Cartesian" correctly. Exploring

similar words like "Caucasian" or "Amazonian" can extend this vocabulary knowledge.

Sharing this approach with the teacher and encouraging her to include word study analysis in her mathematics classroom was the way forward here!

Eponyms, words derived from names, are particularly important in scientific and mathematical vocabulary. Further examples include the following:

- **Fahrenheit:** named after Daniel Gabriel Fahrenheit, who invented the mercury thermometer.
- **Watt:** this unit of power honours James Watt, known for steam engine improvements.
- **Alzheimer's Disease:** Named for Alois Alzheimer, who identified its characteristic brain changes.

By applying the four Linguistic Lenses to vocabulary encountered in any subject, you can confidently navigate complex vocabulary, empowering your students (and teachers) to grasp the intricacies of language across disciplines.

Tracking and Monitoring Student Progress in Etymology

It is important to track and monitor your students' progress in etymology and etymological understanding, so the following strategies, assessment tools and activities focus on the Key Features and Components you have explored throughout this chapter.

Here are some practical strategies to try:

- **Etymology Journals:** Encourage your students to maintain personal etymology journals. Assign weekly entries where students explore the etymology of new words they encounter. Ask your students to include word origin, historical journey through time, related words or cognates, and current usage and any semantic changes. Review the journals regularly, assessing depth of research and understanding.
- **Etymology Family Trees:** Students create visual representations of etymological families. (Remember the family picnic!) They should include root words, derivatives and cognates across languages. Evaluate their accuracy, comprehensiveness and presentation.
- **Etymological Timeline Projects:** Students choose a word and trace its history through different time periods and languages, developing their understanding of word evolution over time. They should create a visual timeline showing changes in meaning, spelling and usage. Assess their research skills, historical accuracy and presentation clarity.

- **Cognate Comparison Charts:** Students create charts comparing cognates across multiple languages to enhance their understanding of linguistic connections between languages, including pronunciation, meaning and notable differences. Evaluate their charts for accuracy, language diversity and analytical skills.
- **Eponym Exploration Presentations:** Allocate students to research and present on specific eponyms to deepen their understanding of words derived from names. Encourage them to consider content words from a range of subject areas. They should include the origin story, current usage and any related terms. Assess their presentation skills, research depth and audience engagement.

Here are some assessment tools to try:

1. **Etymology Quizzes:** Use multiple-choice, short-answer and matching questions fortnightly or monthly to explore word origins, etymological root identification, cognate recognition and eponym identification.
2. **Etymology Analyses:** Once per term or semester, ask your students to prepare short written or creative responses analysing the etymology of specific words or phrases. Evaluate them based on research depth, historical accuracy, analytical skill and writing clarity; these could be used to inform reports.
3. **Digital Etymology Portfolios:** Ask students to collect their etymological work online, including etymology journal highlights, family tree or etymological relatives projects, timeline projects, and quizzes and written responses. Holistically assess their progress over time.

Rooted in time: navigating the etymological forest using the Etymology Lens Rubric

Students can peer review each other's work or you can use the Etymology Lens Rubric to assess your students' etymological skills. Do this monthly or as needed for major projects.

The Etymology Lens Rubric

Key Features	Glimpser	Observer	Analyst
Word Origin	Identifies language of origin for common words	Traces words to earlier forms in other languages	Explains historical and linguistic changes leading to current word forms
Etymological Networks	Recognises basic etymological roots; uses resources to look up origins	Identifies multiple words sharing roots; discusses etymology's influence on spelling and meaning	Explains root influence across parts of speech; synthesises information to explain semantic and orthographic changes
Historical Journey	Understands historical effects on words	Provides examples of historical influence on words; identifies eponyms and obvious cognates	Explains complex etymological changes due to history; explains common eponyms; recognises less obvious cognates

Teaching Tip!

Remember to use the progression from Glimpser to Observer to Analyst! This approach to tracking and monitoring your students' etymological understanding will no doubt provide you with clear data and examples for evaluation, reporting and specific feedback.

From Contemplation to Classroom Innovation

As we conclude, let's engage in two final activities aimed at empowering you to confidently implement what you've learned in your own classroom.

Contemplate and Consider!

Take a moment to reflect on your understanding and application of the Etymology Lens. Consider the following questions:

1. How has your perspective on teaching vocabulary and language structure evolved through this exploration of etymology?
1. What challenges do you anticipate in implementing the Etymology Lens, and how might you overcome them?
2. Which etymological concepts or activities do you feel will resonate most with your students and why?
3. How can you incorporate etymology into your existing curriculum to enhance student learning?
4. What resources or support might you need to effectively implement this approach in your classroom?

Implement and Innovate!

Now, let's put your insights into action. Develop an innovative strategy for teaching etymology in your classroom:

1. Choose a topic or unit from your current curriculum.
1. Identify five to ten key words from this unit that have interesting etymologies.
2. Design a lesson plan that incorporates these words, their etymologies and related linguistic concepts.
3. Create an engaging activity or game that helps students explore these words' histories and connections.
4. Outline how you will assess students' understanding of both the curriculum content and the etymological concepts.
5. Share your plan with a colleague and invite feedback.

As we close this chapter, remember that the Etymology Lens is not just a teaching tool but a gateway to a world of linguistic discovery. Each word you explore with your students is an opportunity to uncover the stories of human history, culture and thought embedded within our language. I hope that your classrooms resonate with the excitement of etymological exploration, and may each lesson bring new insights and joys to the art of vocabulary study.

CHAPTER 7

The Summit–Bringing It All Together

"Students can come to see language as a valuable resource to be explored deeply. My experience has shown that once students gain this perspective, they are more likely to have something to say when they write and will produce pieces of writing worth editing and reading."
~ *Doreen Scott-Dunne*

By the end of this chapter, you will understand and be able to implement the following:

1. **Linguistic Lenses integration:** Synthesise the four Linguistic Lenses (Phonology, Orthography, Morphology and Etymology) to create a comprehensive approach to word study and vocabulary instruction.
2. **Multiple exposure strategies:** Evaluate the effectiveness of multiple exposures in vocabulary acquisition and implement strategies like the Vocabulary Vortex, Linguistic Lenses Language Layer Scaffolds (LLS) and Linguistic Lenses Jigsaw in your classroom.
3. **Gradual release of responsibility:** Design lessons using the gradual release of responsibility model ("I do, We do, You do") to enhance student engagement and foster independent learning in word study.
4. **Collaborative learning techniques:** Integrate collaborative learning strategies, like the jigsaw puzzles, to deepen students' grasp of linguistic concepts and promote peer learning.

5. **Structured literacy block development:** Develop a structured literacy block that incorporates various Linguistic Lenses and scaffolding techniques to support diverse learner needs and learning styles.

As we near the end of our journey through Linguistic Lenses, I can't help but reflect on the transformative power this approach has had, not only in my own classroom but also in the classrooms of the teachers I've had the privilege to mentor and observe. We've explored each Lens individually, but now it's time to bring them all together and see the combined impact they can have on student understanding.

Remember the experiences I shared from my own classroom that really drove home the importance of this multifaceted linguistic approach to literacy instruction?

While exploring the word "iridescent" one day, a usually quiet student eagerly made her own connection: "Mrs Cullen," she exclaimed, "isn't that related to Iris, the Goddess of the Rainbow?" In that moment, I saw the Etymology Lens light up in her eyes, and suddenly, the whole class was engaged in a lively discussion about mythology and its connection to modern language.

Another time, we were discussing "cerebral palsy", a term we encountered in a novel we were studying. One of my more confident students corrected her peer on the pronunciation. This led to an exploration of how words can have different pronunciations, but if we're unsure of how to decode a word (how to translate graphemes into phonemes when reading), the IPA provides us with a consistent and correct guide for articulation. We also found ourselves reflecting on the importance of morphemes in medical terminology and even touched on the evolution of language in professional fields.

These moments reminded me why we do what we do. Each of our students learns differently and has unique interests. Our job, as their teacher, is to find that "hook" or "anchor" that makes word learning meaningful for every single one of them. By integrating these Lenses, we're not just teaching words—we're opening doors to curiosity, critical thinking and a deeper understanding of language itself.

Now, you might be wondering, *This sounds great, but how does it fit with our current phonics instruction?* It's an important question and one I've thought about deeply. Phonics has been a cornerstone of literacy instruction for years, and for good reason—it provides the foundation for decoding and encoding skills. However, recent research has shown the need for a more comprehensive approach to fully address our students' broader literacy needs. While phonics instruction is essential, it's most effective when combined with other strategies to develop vocabulary, comprehension skills and the ability to analyse and interpret complex texts (Gamse, 2008; Machin et al., 2016). These are all components of advanced literacy.

This is where Linguistic Lenses come into play. Rather than replacing phonics, they build upon and enhance it. By intertwining phonology, orthography, morphology and etymology, we create a powerful synergy that enhances both reading comprehension and spelling proficiency. These Lenses identify the key features and specific metalanguage related to each linguistic component, addressing the call for more comprehensive "key ingredients" of linguistic knowledge to inform literacy instruction (Colenbrander et al., 2024). I've seen it in action in my classroom and I've watched the impact this has on my school's reading, writing and spelling results, not to mention both teacher and student confidence. This linguistically-informed approach doesn't diminish the importance of phonics; instead, it amplifies its effectiveness by providing a broader context for understanding language.

Imagine your students analysing words not just through one Lens but four. Picture them making connections, asking questions and engaging with the truth about our language. It's not just about memorising spellings anymore; it's about understanding the "why" and "how" of English orthography.

Now, I know what some of you might be thinking: *I'm not sure I have the linguistic knowledge to implement this effectively.* Trust me, I felt the same way at first. In fact, research highlights that many of us teachers lack sufficient linguistic knowledge, which can impact the quality of our literacy instruction (Daffern et al., 2024). But here's the thing: we're all on this journey together. Throughout this book, I've aimed to provide clear explanations and practical strategies that you can implement in your classroom right away. It's not about becoming a linguistics expert overnight—it's about being open to new approaches, revisiting and rereading these chapters, and being willing to have a go and learn alongside our students. This book is your guide and toolbox.

Remember, every journey begins with a single step. Maybe tomorrow, you'll introduce one new Lens into your word study. Perhaps next week, you'll try combining two. Before you know it, you'll be weaving all four

Lenses together, creating a tapestry of language understanding that will impact your students for life.

Teaching Tip!

The Linguistic Lenses approach combines phonology, orthography, morphology and etymology for a comprehensive understanding of language. This approach addresses the limitations of phonics-only instruction, enhancing reading comprehension, spelling proficiency and overall literacy skills.

Integrating all four Lenses creates multiple entry points for student engagement and understanding. Implementation can be gradual—start with one Lens and build up to using all four together.

Contemplate and Consider!

How might you incorporate one aspect of the Linguistic Lenses approach into your next lesson? What impact do you think it could have on your students' engagement and understanding?

Case study: a multi-lens "expedition" to vocabulary instruction

In a Year 5 selective (gifted) classroom, the novel *The Mapmaker's Race* by Eirlys Hunter, typically read by students aged 11 to 13, had captivated the imagination of the young readers with its thrilling tale of young cartographers on an adventurous journey. At the heart of this narrative lay the word "expedition", a term crucial to understanding the plot's essence. However, the class teacher found herself grappling with how to fully convey the depth and significance of this word to her students. As the Literacy Leader, I was called in to conduct a demonstration lesson. The teacher's struggle was not uncommon—many find themselves challenged when faced with explaining complex vocabulary that goes beyond simple definitions. This case study details how I approached this challenge, turning a potentially daunting task into an engaging, multifaceted exploration of language.

Upon entering the classroom, I could sense both the teacher's apprehension and the students' curiosity. I began by explaining that we were about to embark on our own expedition—a journey into the heart of a word. This framing immediately piqued the students' interest.

I introduced the concept of the four Linguistic Lenses: Phonology, Orthography, Morphology and Etymology. To make these abstract terms more accessible, I compared them to different types of magnifying glasses, each revealing unique aspects of our word "expedition". This analogy helped set the stage for our in-depth exploration.

We started our journey with the **Phonology Lens**, focusing on the sounds within "expedition". I asked students to close their eyes and listen carefully as I pronounced the word slowly. Then, I invited them to say it with me, paying attention to how their mouths moved as they formed each sound.

"Let's zoom in on that interesting /k/ and /s/ sound," I suggested. "What do you notice about it?" This prompt led to a lively discussion about the grapheme <x> as a diphone. To illustrate this concept further, I wrote several words on the board: "excited"; "excellent"; "box"; "taxi"; "exam"; "exist". I then asked students to come up and circle the <x> in each word, pronouncing them aloud. This hands-on activity helped them discover how the same letter could represent different sound combinations.

"Now, let's clap out the syllables in 'expedition,'" I instructed. As we clapped four times, I explained, "Each syllable typically has a vowel sound. Can you identify the vowels?" This exercise led to a fascinating discussion about schwa sounds, with students realising that different letters (<e> and <o> in this case) can represent the same sound.

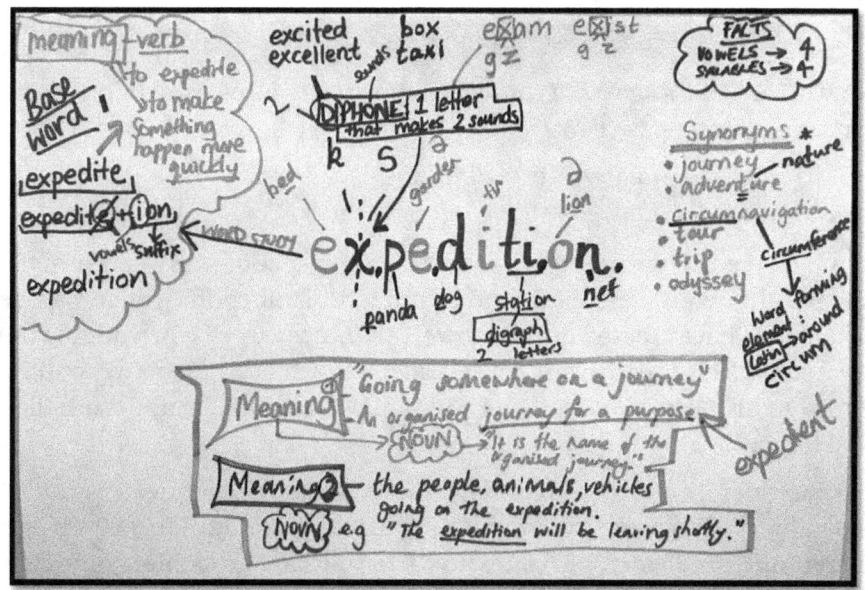

Throughout this phonological exploration, I encouraged students to make connections to other words they knew, fostering an environment of active discovery rather than passive learning.

Transitioning to the **Orthography Lens**, I drew students' attention to the spelling of "expedition". "Let's look closely at these letters. Do you see any letter combinations that might represent a single sound?" I prompted.

As students identified the <ti> digraph, I explained how this spelling pattern often appears in words with Latin roots. To reinforce this concept, we brainstormed other words with the same pattern, such as nation, motion and action. This activity not only enhanced their understanding of "expedition" but also provided them with a valuable spelling strategy for similar words.

Moving to the **Morphology Lens**, I began by asking, "What words come to mind when you think of an expedition?" As students called out synonyms like "journey", "adventure" and "trip", I wrote them on the board.

When a student mentioned "circumnavigation", I seized the opportunity to discuss prefixes. "That's a fantastic word! What do you think <circum-> might mean?" This led to a brief but enlightening tangent about circular journeys and related words like "circumference".

Returning to "expedition", I challenged the class to identify its base word. After some discussion, we agreed on "expedite", meaning "quickly". I then introduced the concept of word sums, demonstrating on the board:

<expedite> + <-ion> = "expedition"

"Now," I said, "let's see if we can build some relatives of 'expedition' using this base." Together, we constructed:

<expedite> + <-ious> → <expeditious>
<expedite> + <-ious> + <-ly> → <expeditiously>

As we worked, I encouraged students to think about how each suffix changed the word's meaning and grammatical function. Notice on the poster how I have crossed out the vowel on the base word when adding the vowel suffix. This exercise not only clarified the relationship between these words but also provided students with a powerful tool for understanding word formation.

For our final Lens, the **Etymology Lens**, I shared a brief history of "expedition". "This word comes from Latin," I explained. "The <ex-> part means "out" and <ped-> relates to "foot". So, an expedition originally meant something like 'setting out on foot.'"

This revelation led to an exciting brainstorming session. Students eagerly suggested words that might be related:

- pedometer ("A foot measurer!" one student exclaimed)
- millipede ("A thousand feet!" another chimed in)
- pedal
- pedicure.

To extend this further, I introduced the Greek root <pod->, related to <ped->. We discovered connections to words like "tripod", "podium" and even "cephalopod", much to the students' delight. Throughout this etymological exploration, I encouraged students to think about how understanding a word's origins can provide clues to its meaning and connections to other words.

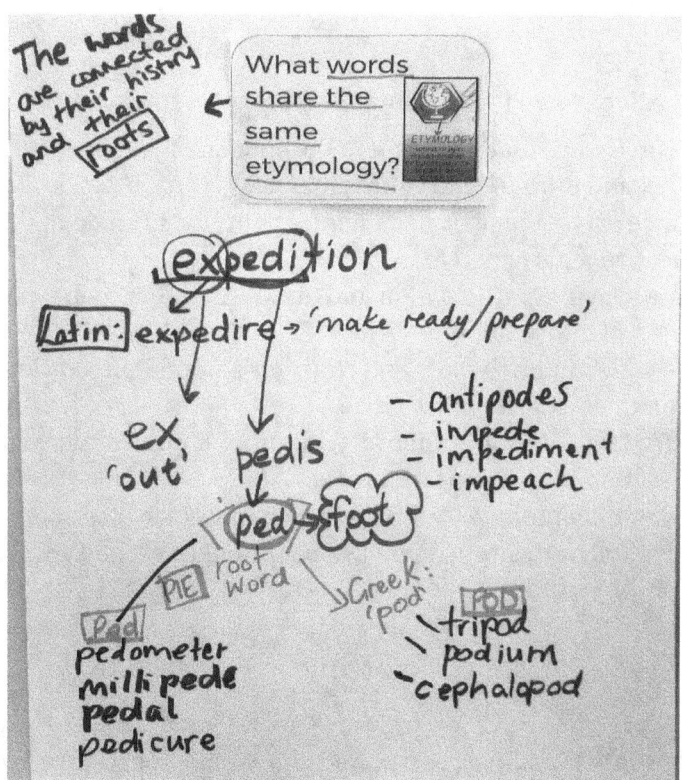

As our lesson ended, the excitement in the room was palpable. Students who had initially been intimidated by the word "expedition" were now eagerly sharing their new insights and discoveries. I turned to the class teacher, who had been observing the lesson with growing enthusiasm. "What you've just witnessed," I explained, "is how a single word can open up a world of language learning. Instead of memorising definitions, we've engaged in active exploration, making connections and discoveries that will stick with these students far longer than any list of vocabulary words."

To the students, I said, "You've not just learned about one word today—you've embarked on an expedition through language itself, discovering tools and strategies that you can use to understand any new word you encounter." This approach to vocabulary instruction goes beyond mere comprehension—it fosters a genuine curiosity about language. By guiding students through these multiple Lenses, we equip them with the skills to become independent word detectives, capable of unravelling the mysteries of language on their own.

> **Teaching Tip!**
>
> For teachers looking to implement this approach, remember this process:
> 1. Start with a word that's relevant in the context of your teaching and learning, and intriguing to your students.
> 2. Introduce each Linguistic Lens sequentially, using analogies to make abstract concepts concrete.
> 3. Encourage active participation and discovery rather than passive reception of information.
> 4. Make connections to words and concepts students already know to build on their existing knowledge.
> 5. Allow for tangents and student-led inquiries—these often lead to the most memorable learning moments.
> 6. Record or document the learning in a word web, in classroom conversation or in any way you feel confident or excited about.

Throughout this book, we've explored the word "conscience" using our Linguistic Lenses. This journey has shown us how to look at words from different angles, making language learning an exciting adventure. When we enable our students to examine words from different perspectives, we deepen their comprehension and strengthen our memory. By connecting words to their origins and related morphological and etymological relatives, and illuminate how they are structured, we create a rich network of associations in students' minds. This approach helps students not only remember words better but also understand how to apply them more effectively in their own writing.

Remember when we first encountered "conscience" at the base of our linguistic mountain? As we applied each Lens, it was as if we were scaling the slopes of linguistic understanding, gaining new perspectives with every step. The "conscience" explorations and snippets served as our climbing gear, providing practical tools to navigate the sometimes-challenging terrain of the English spelling system.

As you look at this completed LLGO for "conscience," I hope you see more than just a word study—it's a map of the territory we've explored together, a reflection of the journey we've taken and a glimpse of the exciting adventures into the English spelling system that await you and your students.

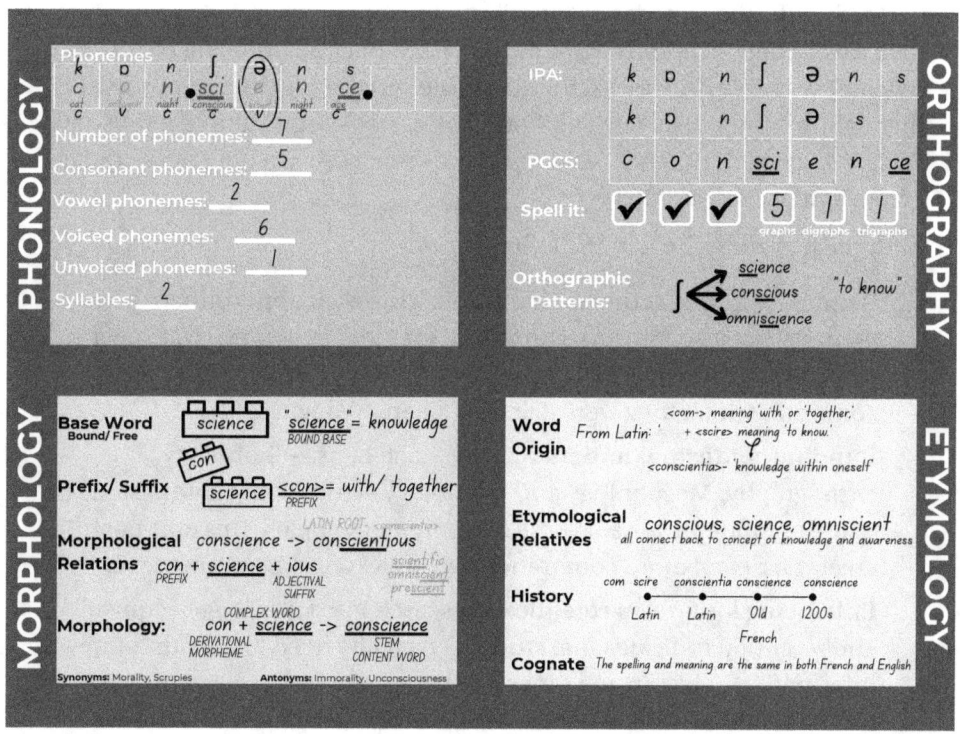

The Importance of Multiple Exposures

Imagine you're learning to play a new instrument. Would you expect to master a complex piece after playing it just once? Of course not! The same principle applies to our students' learning journey.

As teachers, we're constantly on the lookout for that magic key to unlock our students' potential. That key exists and has been hiding in plain sight all along. Enter the world of multiple exposures—a powerful learning strategy for spelling and vocabulary instruction supported by research in cognitive psychology. But what exactly are multiple exposures and how can they transform your classroom?

The Victorian Government Department of Education and Training's High Impact Teaching Strategies (HITS) framework (2022) emphasises the role of multiple exposures, where students have time to practice what they have learnt through repeated exposure, with timely feedback providing opportunities for immediate correction and improvement. This aligns perfectly with the concept of "distributed practice", where each encounter with a word or concept strengthens neural connections, making recall more efficient and robust. Research into visible learning further supports this, highlighting the effectiveness of strategies involving multiple exposures, such as spaced practice and retrieval practice, in boosting student achievement (Hattie, 2009).

Multiple exposures help in the following ways:

- **Reinforcing connections:** Multiple exposures not only enhance item memory but also improve contextual memory over time. This means that students not only remember specific facts but also the broader context in which they were learned (Chen & Yang, 2020).
- **Building contextual understanding:** Each Lens—Phonology, Orthography, Morphology and Etymology—adds a new dimension, allowing students to see words from different angles. This approach creates a richer, more comprehensive understanding of language.
- **Enhancing long-term retention:** Research into knowledge acquisition and retention indicates that students typically need to encounter new information at least three times in a meaningful way to ensure long-term retention (Nuthall, 2000). This principle highlights the limitations of traditional spelling methods that rely heavily on rote memorisation.

The effectiveness of traditional spelling methods can be limited:

- **Short-term focus:** Students often memorise words just for the test without truly internalising the spelling patterns or conventions being studied.
- **Lack of context:** Words learned in isolation often do not transfer well to real-world writing situations.
- **Limited engagement:** The repetitive nature of the task does not stimulate deeper cognitive processes or interest in language.
- **Favours certain learning styles:** Students with strong memorisation skills may perform well, while others struggle, regardless of their overall literacy abilities.

To enhance spelling instruction and retention, you could consider the following approaches:

- **Incorporating spaced repetition:** Revisit words over extended periods rather than expecting your students to cram before a test.
- **Providing varied contexts:** Use target words in different sentences through dictation, or activities to reinforce understanding and application.
- **Focusing on spelling patterns and conventions:** Teach the underlying structure of language through the Lenses rather than individual words in isolation. The LLGO is great for this!
- **Applying words in authentic writing tasks:** Encourage the use of target words in meaningful contexts to improve retention and practical application.

Enhancing Vocabulary Retention Through Multiple Exposures: Linguistic Lenses Language Layer Scaffolds

Word study, spelling or vocabulary instruction is not a one-time event but a process that requires multiple exposures and revisitations. Research consistently shows that students need to encounter new words in various contexts and analyse them from different angles to achieve deep, lasting understanding. This set of Linguistic Lenses Language Layer Scaffolds (LLSs) are specifically designed to facilitate multiple exposures and reinforce vocabulary learning over time. These LLSs—blank templates that students can fill out to review their word study—are particularly effective tools for revision and revisiting vocabulary. Their strength lies in promoting comprehensive word analysis, encouraging your students to examine words from various linguistic angles with each revisit. This comprehensive approach includes the following focus points:

1. **Phoneme–grapheme and Orthographic focus:** Explore phonemes and investigate orthographic patterns.
2. **Morphology focus:** Analyse word structure, including base words, affixes and word relationships.
3. **Etymology focus:** Investigate word origins, related words and historical influences on spelling.

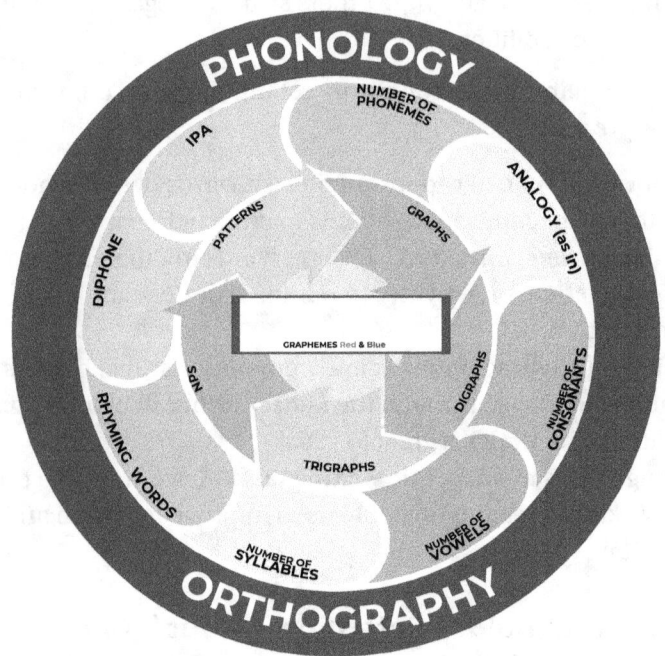

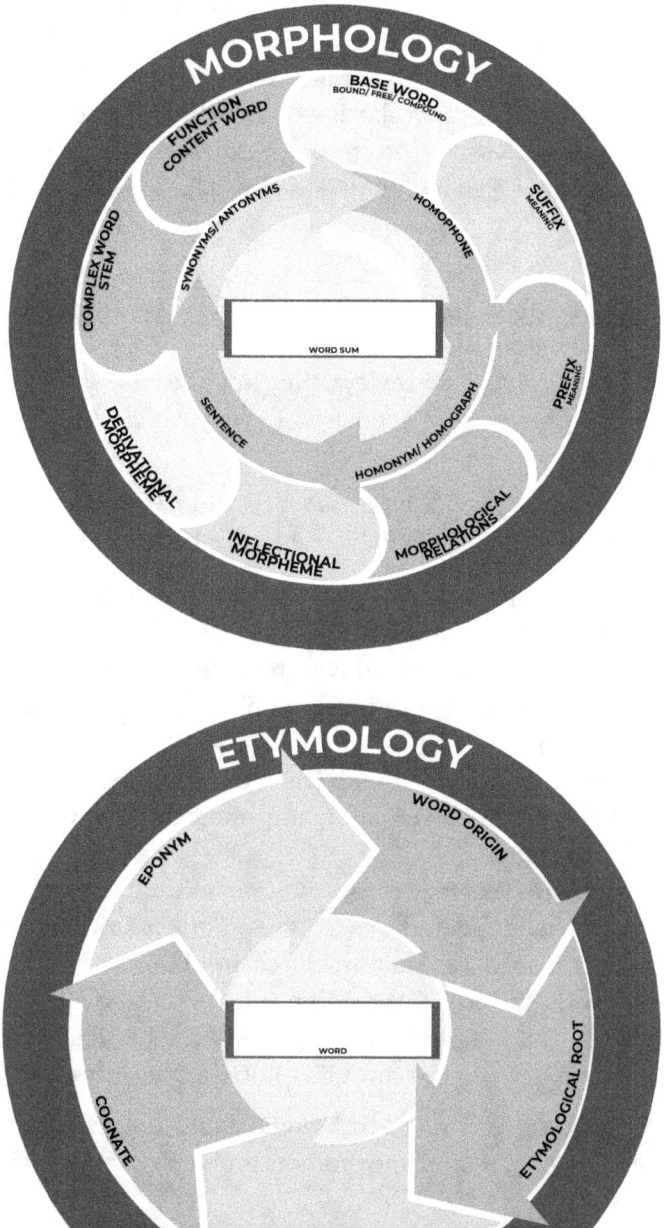

The Summit—Bringing It All Together

These scaffolds facilitate layered learning, allowing students to focus on different aspects of the word during each exposure. This gradual approach builds a comprehensive understanding over time, reinforcing previous knowledge while adding new layers of insight. Moreover, they foster metacognitive awareness by prompting students to revisit words and notice new aspects with each interaction. This process enhances students' consciousness of their own learning journey, helping them recognise how their understanding evolves and deepens.

Each scaffold's flexible application is another key advantage, as they can be seamlessly integrated into various stages of the learning process. From initial exposure to final review, they adapt to the student's growing understanding, providing a consistent yet evolving framework for vocabulary study.

Here's one way to implement the LLSs for revision and multiple exposures (noting that these scaffolds would be used *after* the LLGO lessons):

1. **Initial exposure:** Introduce the word and complete the parts of the scaffolds that students can manage with their current knowledge.
2. **Second exposure (one to two days later):** Revisit the word, adding information to new sections of the scaffolds and reinforcing previous learning.
3. **Third exposure (one week later):** Delve deeper into linguistic aspects such as IPA representation, morphological relationships and etymological origins.
4. **Fourth exposure (two to three weeks later):** Complete any remaining sections and challenge students to make connections between different linguistic features across the scaffolds.
5. **Final review (at the end of the unit or term):** Use the fully completed scaffolds as comprehensive review tools, discussing how understanding has evolved through multiple exposures.

These scaffolds are grounded in well-established cognitive science principles, enhancing their effectiveness as tools for vocabulary acquisition and retention:

- **The spacing effect:** Information is better retained when learning is distributed rather than concentrated in a single session, as per the multiple exposures of the scaffolds (Cepeda at al., 2006).
- **Elaborative rehearsal:** The scaffolds' design engages students with words on multiple linguistic levels. This deep processing aligns with

research showing that information is better remembered when it's thoroughly analysed and connected to existing knowledge (Craik & Lockhart, 1972).
- **Dual-coding theory:** Presenting information in both visual and verbal forms enhances learning and recall (Paivio, 1971).
- **Active recall:** Each time your students revisit the scaffolds, they engage in active recall, strengthening memory pathways (Karpicke & Roediger, 2008). This process also fosters metacognition as students reflect on their understanding of the word's various linguistic aspects.
- **Chunking:** The human mind can process approximately three to five pieces of information simultaneously, a concept known as chunking (Cowan, 2001). This supports this scaffolds' structure, which breaks down words into smaller components like phonemes, morphemes and etymological roots, making complex information more manageable and easier to process, just like we've witnessed with the strategy of using IPA in the classroom.

> **Teaching Tip!**
> Integrate these scaffolds into your long-term vocabulary or spelling instruction plans, using them as frameworks for structured, repeated encounters with target words. By doing so, you can significantly enhance your students' vocabulary depth and breadth, leading to improved overall language proficiency.

Now, step into my classroom to see the word "iridescent" come alive through the four Linguistic Lenses. The following examples show the explicit teaching (image #1) and my students' recordings (image #2), then experience the magic as they revisit "iridescent" using the LLS (image #3), deepening their understanding and weaving a rich tapestry of knowledge.

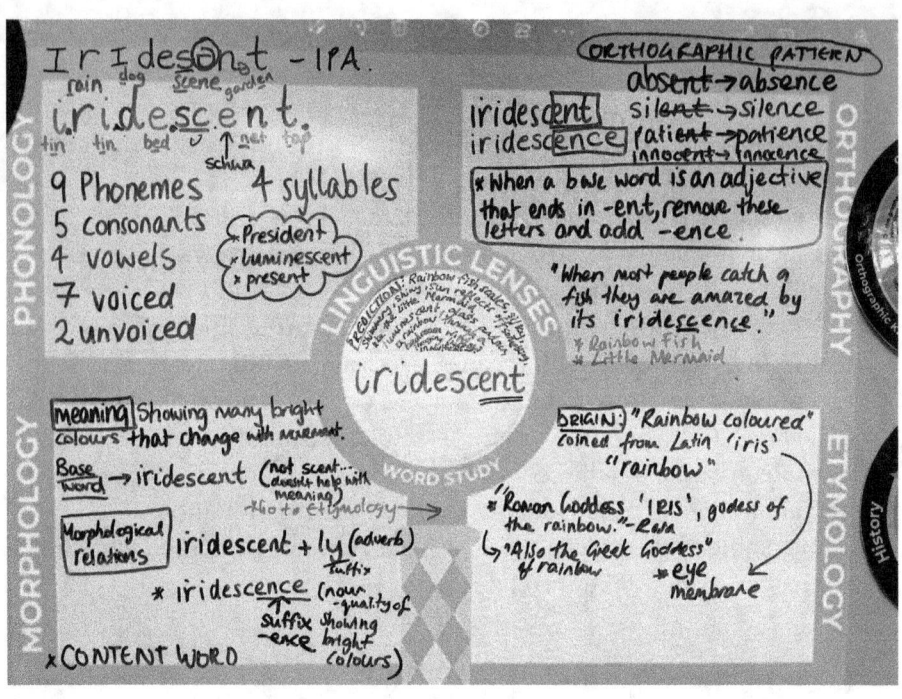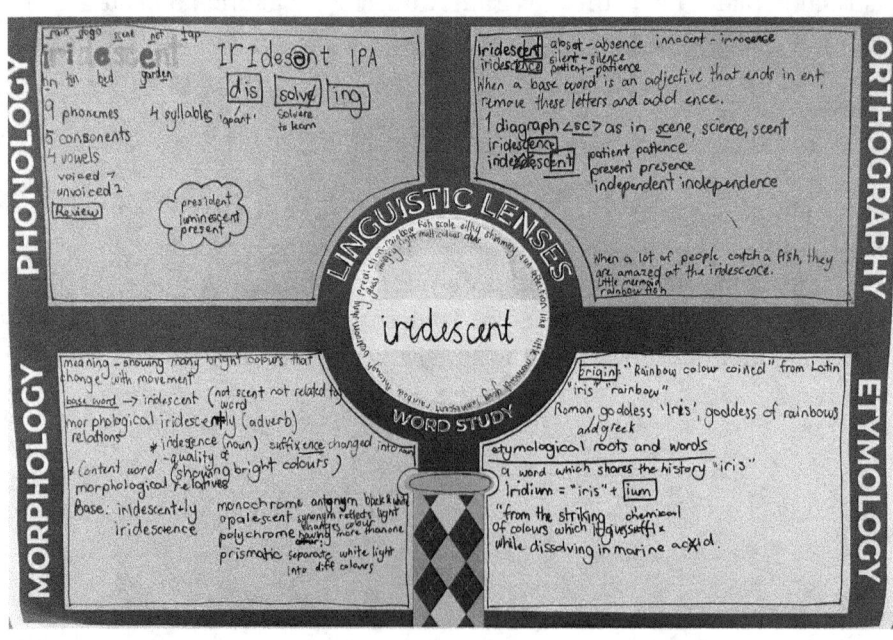

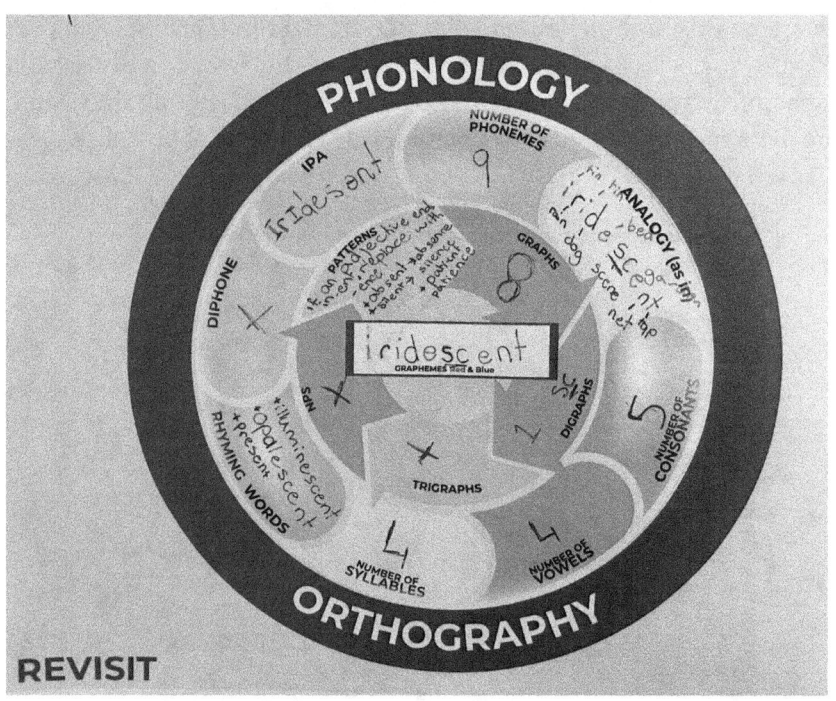

Spiralling Through Words: Revisiting and Enriching Word Study Learning with the Vocabulary Vortex

In my classroom, I created what I call the Vocabulary Vortex—an engaging visual tool that supports my students with the process of returning to and deepening their understanding of words over time. The Vocabulary Vortex acts as a scaffold for my students' thinking, supporting an ongoing, iterative learning process that aligns well with effective vocabulary learning and retention strategies.

The Vocabulary Vortex is a flexible, spiral-shaped diagram designed to deepen students' understanding of words and their various linguistic components. It places a target word at the centre and spirals outward, encompassing multiple layers of word knowledge. This flexible approach empowers students with creative freedom in their word analysis. They can choose their preferred method and location for recording their explorations. In my classroom, the whiteboard tables were a particular hit! Students eagerly used these surfaces to sketch out their Vocabulary Vortexes, allowing for easy modifications and collaborative work. This hands-on, customisable approach not only made the learning process more engaging but also catered to different learning styles. Whether it was on whiteboards, in notebooks or through digital tools, giving students the autonomy to decide how and where to conduct their word analysis fostered a sense of ownership over their learning and made vocabulary study a more dynamic and interactive experience. Have a look at how the students unpacked the word "future" by creating their own Vocabulary Vortex:

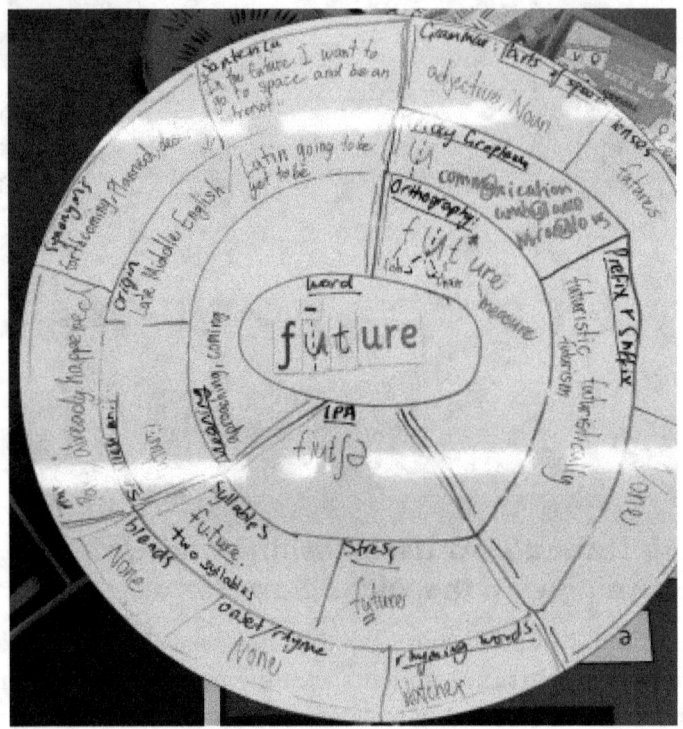

What also makes this approach particularly effective is its adaptability—students can choose which parts of the Linguistic Lens terminology they wish to explore through the Vortex based on their previous learning and the explicit teaching of the word through the LLGO. Remember, this is because some words are like party animals, sparking great discussions where the real learning happens, while other words are more like wallflowers, not needing as much attention, and that's okay too. The Vocabulary Vortex is designed to accommodate this variability, allowing for in-depth exploration where it's most beneficial.

The exciting lightbulb moments often happen during our collaborative phase. I've created a Vocabulary Vortex Puzzle—it's basically a gigantic Vocabulary Vortex that I've cut up into word parts. Watching the students work together to fit the pieces back into place is both entertaining and enlightening. It's amazing how quickly they can do it now—we usually complete it in the first 10 minutes of the lesson. Talk about an effective warm-up!

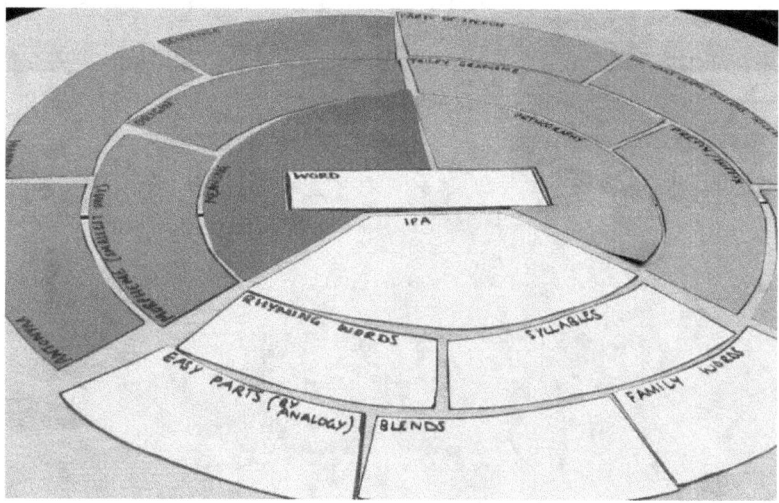

However, it's the independent practice that really cements their learning. Giving students the chance to create their own Vocabulary Vortex allows them to process and internalise the linguistic aspects of words at their own pace. I've been blown away by the creativity and depth of understanding I've seen in their work.

Since implementing these visual and structured approaches, I've noticed a significant uptick in student engagement. It's as if they've realised that words aren't just static things on a page but living, breathing entities with histories and relationships. It's truly transformed the way we approach vocabulary in the classroom.

Linguistic Lenses Jigsaw: The jigsaw strategy

Another effective tool is the Linguistic Lenses Jigsaw, which uses the jigsaw strategy, offering an engaging and effective approach to revisiting and reinforcing previously learnt vocabulary. This collaborative method, grounded in cooperative learning principles (Aronson & Patnoe, 2011), will encourage your students to deepen their understanding of words by examining them through multiple Linguistic Lenses. To implement this strategy, begin by selecting four to six vocabulary words that you and your students previously encountered on the LLGO (think morphological or etymological relations!).

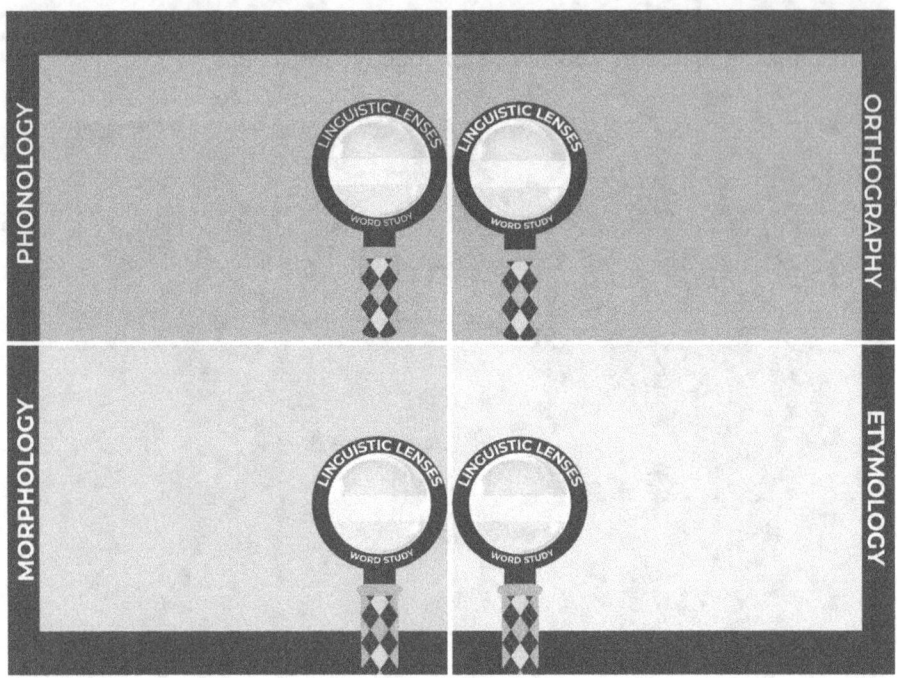

Ask your students to prepare one of the four jigsaw pieces—representing the Phonology, Orthography, Morphology and Etymology Lenses—for each word. Divide your class into four "expert" groups, each assigned to one of the Linguistic Lenses, and provide them with the corresponding jigsaw piece and Linguistic Lens to guide their analysis.

Distribute one jigsaw piece for each word to every expert group, instructing students to analyse their assigned words through their specific Linguistic Lens. After the initial analysis, reorganise students into new groups, ensuring each new group has a representative from each of the four Linguistic Lenses. In these mixed groups, have students share their expert knowledge about each word and work collaboratively to complete a comprehensive analysis of each word, filling in each jigsaw piece. Conclude the activity with a whole-class discussion where groups share their completed jigsaw pieces, encouraging students to compare analyses and discuss any new insights they've gained about the words.

This approach aligns with research on effective vocabulary instruction, which emphasises the importance of multiple exposures and deep processing for word learning (Beck, McKeown & Kucan, 2013). By revisiting words through different linguistic perspectives, students engage in elaborative rehearsal, a process that enhances long-term retention (Craik & Lockhart, 1972). Moreover, the collaborative nature of the jigsaw strategy supports peer learning and promotes active engagement, factors that have been shown to positively impact vocabulary learning (Nation, 2001).

The following examples from my own classroom shine a light on the success I have had with the "I do, we do, you do" model, also known as the "gradual release of responsibility" model (Fisher & Frey, 2013), especially when unpacking complex words just like we have been doing throughout this book with "conscience" using the LLGO. Implementing this model is like a well-choreographed dance of learning. It starts with the teacher taking the lead, then inviting your students to join in, and finally stepping back to watch them shine on their own. Let's break it down:

1. **"I do"—setting the stage:** Picture yourself at the front of the class, introducing a new complex word using the LLGO and guiding your students through each Lens. Here, you're modelling a comprehensive approach to word analysis. This aligns perfectly with the explicit teaching strategy highlighted in the HITS framework (Victorian Department of Education and Training, 2022). By making your thought process visible, you're tapping into a strategy that has shown to significantly impact student achievement (Hattie, 2009).
2. **"We do"—collaborative exploration:** The following lesson, you could invite your students to join you in analysing the word through the LLSs, or by using the giant Vocabulary Vortex Puzzle or the Linguistic Lenses Jigsaw. As you work together to populate any of these, use Linguistic Lenses to guide your exploration of each linguistic layer. This collaborative phase incorporates guided practice and immediate feedback, both key elements of the HITS framework. It's a chance for students to practice the strategies under your guidance, building their confidence and deepening their understanding.
3. **"You do"—independent discovery:** Finally, watch as your students take the lead, creating their own Vocabulary Vortexes and applying the LLSs independently. This phase aligns with the HITS principle of multiple exposures and fosters metacognitive skills as students reflect on their learning process. The beauty of this approach lies in its flexibility: students can choose to sketch their Vortexes on whiteboard tables, jot them down in notebooks or create digital versions. Here, they are engaging in differentiated learning—another key HITS strategy. This flexibility caters to different learning styles, aligning

with the theory of multiple intelligences (Gardner, 1983), and fosters a sense of ownership over the learning process. This autonomy supports self-directed learning, which has been shown to enhance motivation and learning outcomes (Knowles, 1975).

Below is an example of how you could incorporate these learning strategies into a structured four-day cycle, promoting deep word knowledge through a gradual release of responsibility model.

Day 1: "I do"—Phonology and Orthography focus	Day 2: "I do"—Morphology and Etymology focus	Day 3: "We do"—Collaborative analysis	Day 4: "You do"—Independent application
Context: Introduce a word from current student learning (e.g. a novel, or new subject-specific vocabulary). **Activity:** Linguistic Lens Graphic Organiser **Focus:** Explicit teaching using Phonology and Orthography Lenses **Teacher's role:** Model the analysis process, thinking aloud to demonstrate how to examine the word's sound structure and spelling patterns.	**Word choice:** Use the key word from Day 1. **Activity:** Linguistic Lens Graphic Organiser **Focus:** Explicit teaching using Morphology and Etymology Lenses **Teacher's role:** Demonstrate how to break down the word's structure and explore its origin.	**Activity 1: Vocabulary Vortex Puzzle** Distribute puzzle pieces to students at the start of the lesson. Students complete their piece with a peer and create a whole-class Vortex **Activity 2: Linguistic Lenses Jigsaw** Students work in small groups to complete and assemble the complete jigsaw. Encourage discussion and knowledge-sharing.	**Activity 1: Vocabulary Vortex Creation** Students create their own Vocabulary Vortexes by sketching on whiteboard tables, jotting in notebooks or creating digital versions. **Activity 2: LLSs** Students complete the LLS independently. Can be used as an in-class activity or for homework.

Teaching Tip!
- Ensure word selection is always contextualised within current learning.
- Gradually release responsibility from teacher-led to student-led activities.
- Encourage peer collaboration and discussion throughout the process.
- Provide support as needed but allow students to take ownership of their learning.
- Use the created Vocabulary Vortexes, Puzzle, Jigsaw and LLS as assessment tools to gauge understanding.

Contemplate and Consider!

Reflect on the impact of using concept maps to scaffold student thinking. How might these visual frameworks, when labelled with linguistic elements, support your students' understanding and retention of new vocabulary? Consider how the visual representation of relationships and connections between words could deepen their grasp of linguistic concepts.

Consider the effectiveness of the "I do, we do, you do" model in your classroom:

- **"I do":** How can you make your demonstrations more impactful when introducing new vocabulary or linguistic concepts?
- **"We do":** What collaborative activities could you implement to reinforce newly learned vocabulary?
- **"You do":** How might you structure independent practice to ensure students are confidently applying their new knowledge?

Implement and Innovate!

Try the Linguistic Lenses LLS and Vocabulary Vortex by diving into the world of "photosynthesis" with your fellow teachers during year-level collaborative planning sessions or staff meetings.

Here's an exciting way to explore this word from multiple linguistic angles:

1. **Phoneme focus:** Kick off by breaking down "photosynthesis" using the phoneme–grapheme scaffold. Challenge each other to identify the phonemes and graphemes, turning it into a friendly competition.
2. **Morpheme magic:** Next, unravel the word's structure. Discover the power of <photo–> and <–synthesis> as you brainstorm related words. Who can come up with the most creative connections?
3. **Etymology expedition:** Embark on a journey through time and language. Trace the Greek roots of "photosynthesis" and uncover its cognates in other languages. Share interesting facts or stories about its origin.
4. **Synthesis showdown:** Bring it all together! Create mini presentations combining insights from all three analyses.
5. **Reflection roundtable:** Conclude with a discussion on how this multilayered approach deepens understanding. Share ideas on adapting this method for different year levels and/or subject areas.

By engaging with "photosynthesis" through these varied scaffolds, you'll not only enhance your own understanding but also develop exciting new strategies for vocabulary instruction alongside your teaching teams!

CHAPTER 8

The Briefing–Preparing for Your Linguistic Journey

"As the debate gets more public, we get into solutions that don't work ... We are unfortunately moving away from the notion that we need to develop expertise in our teachers and school leaders ... if I'm given trillions, I'd rather spend the money on developing teacher expertise."

~ Dr John Hattie

By the end of this chapter, your school leadership, colleagues and teaching teams will be confident with the following:

1. **Metalinguistic foundations:** Explain the concept of metalinguistics and its importance in boosting literacy outcomes.
2. **Assessment of teacher knowledge:** Describe the key components of the Linguistic Lenses Metalinguistic Knowledge Assessment (MKA) and its role in evaluating teacher understanding.
3. **Classroom observation techniques:** Understand the purpose and structure of the Linguistic Lenses Metalinguistic Observation Protocol (MOP) and its application in classroom observations.
4. **Effective feedback practices:** Demonstrate knowledge of effective strategies for providing constructive feedback and fostering reflective conversations post-observation.
5. **Professional development planning:** Develop an action plan for ongoing professional growth in metalinguistic instruction.

6. **Collaborative learning culture:** Recognise the importance of continuous learning and collaboration in enhancing metalinguistic teaching practices.

It's time to equip you with the tools necessary for your ongoing exploration into Linguistic Lenses. This chapter serves as your pre-trip briefing, setting out key concepts, clarifying expectations and guiding you through what lies ahead.

Throughout this journey, I've had the privilege of being your guide, sharing insights and discoveries as we've navigated the intricate landscape of English orthography together. From our first steps into the world of Linguistic Lenses to this final chapter, we've experienced a rich and diverse journey through language. We've attended the linguistic concert, where the symphony of phonology resonated with the intricate melodies of speech sounds. We've wandered through the linguistic city, marvelling at the architectural wonders of orthography that form the skyline of written language. We've played with the linguistic LEGO, creating elaborate structures of meaning through the versatile blocks of morphology. And finally, we've explored the linguistic woodland, tracing the ancient and winding paths of etymology through the forest of word origins. Each of these adventures has contributed to our deeper understanding of the fascinating world of language.

As your guide, I've imagined the growth in understanding and confidence you've experienced, picturing your moments of revelation about the power of language. Your potential questions, insights and enthusiasm have shaped this journey, making it as rewarding for me to write as I hope it has been for you to read. Now, as we prepare for the next phase of your linguistic adventure, I'm excited to equip you with the final tools you'll need to continue your exploration long after you turn the last page of this book.

Remember, while this may be our last chapter together, it's just the beginning of your ongoing journey with Linguistic Lenses. The path ahead is filled with opportunities for discovery, growth and the joy of sharing your knowledge with others. As you step forward, know that the spirit of our shared journey through these pages will continue to guide and inspire you.

Now, let's dive into the crucial aspects of your linguistic adventure that lie ahead:

- The Power of Metalinguistics in Boosting Literacy Outcomes
- The Linguistic Lenses Metalinguistic Knowledge Assessment (MKA)
- The Linguistic Lenses Metalinguistic Observation Protocol (MOP).

These tools and concepts will serve as your compass, map and provisions for the exciting journey that awaits you, not only helping you gauge your own understanding but also fostering collaborative growth within your teaching community. Let's begin this final leg of our exploration together as you prepare to confidently continue your linguistic adventure long after you close this guide.

The Power of Metalinguistics in Boosting Literacy Outcomes

Metalinguistics is the ability to reflect on and consciously consider both oral and written language and its usage. It goes beyond mere communication, focusing on the underlying structures of language and allowing for the evaluation of language as a process or system (Newman, 2024). This ability to treat language as an object accessible to reflection is crucial for advanced literacy skills. Recent research has highlighted the importance of metalinguistic awareness in education and its significant impact on literacy outcomes, defining it as the active focus of attention on the explicit properties of language (Bialystok, 2001). This awareness is part of general cognition and is related to overall cognitive development in children.

Explicit teaching of metalinguistic knowledge has been shown to have beneficial effects on students' literacy outcomes. It involves using metalanguage that operates at various levels—from the whole text to individual words—emphasising the functional role of language at each level. Of particular value is classroom talk that supports thinking about writerly choice, termed "metalinguistic talk" (Newman, 2024). Metalinguistic talk can support learners' capacity to better craft and control their writing. It can occur in various forms, such as whole-class discussions about mentor texts or peer-to-peer reflections on writing. This type of talk is dialogic because it prompts exploration and reasoning about language use (Newman, 2024).

However, research indicates a concerning trend of teachers often possessing insufficient knowledge in this critical area despite having a positive attitude towards it. This gap can hinder effective literacy instruction, particularly for struggling readers. Research has found that illiterate adults, despite their cognitive maturity, often have levels of metalinguistic awareness similar to those of preschool children (Kurvers et al., 2006). This underscores the importance of developing metalinguistic awareness through formal schooling. Interestingly, bilingualism or multilingualism from birth appears to enhance metalinguistic ability at an early age (Bialystok, 2001; Jessner, 2014). While monolingual children eventually catch up in terms of metalinguistic development, this early advantage highlights the potential benefits of exposure to multiple languages.

Discover Your Language IQ: The Metalinguistic Knowledge Assessment

This comprehensive Metalinguistic Knowledge Assessment (MKA) is designed to evaluate your understanding of key linguistic concepts that are important for effective literacy instruction. As teachers, your grasp of these fundamental elements plays a vital role in shaping your students' language development and literacy skills.

The assessment covers the four main areas of linguistic knowledge: phonology, orthography, morphology and etymology. Each area includes both theoretical questions and practical applications, allowing you to showcase not only your knowledge but also your ability to apply these concepts in a classroom setting.

The MKA is important for several reasons:

1. **Baseline knowledge:** It provides a clear picture of teachers' current understanding of linguistic concepts, helping to identify areas of strength and areas for improvement.
2. **Targeted professional development:** Based on the assessment results, schools can design more effective professional development programs tailored to teachers' specific needs.
3. **Improved instruction:** Teachers with a strong grasp of metalinguistic concepts are better equipped to provide explicit, effective instruction in literacy skills.
4. **Student outcomes:** Ultimately, improved teacher knowledge in this area can lead to better student outcomes in literacy and language learning.

Remember, this assessment is not just a test—it's an opportunity for professional growth. It will help you identify areas of strength and potential improvement in your linguistic knowledge, ultimately enhancing your teaching practice. Take your time, reflect on each question, and don't hesitate to provide detailed explanations and examples in your answers. Your insights and practical approaches are valuable components of this assessment.

Teaching Tip!

To maximise the impact of the MKA, consider implementing it both before and after professional development. Administer the assessment at the beginning of the school year to establish a baseline of your teachers' linguistic knowledge. Use the results to tailor your professional development programs to address specific areas of need. Then, re-administer the assessment at the end of the school year or after completing targeted professional development sessions. This approach will allow you to:

- measure the effectiveness of your professional development initiatives
- track individual teacher growth in linguistic knowledge
- identify persistent knowledge gaps that may require additional support
- celebrate improvements and recognise teachers' efforts in enhancing their skills.

By spacing the assessments throughout the year, you create opportunities for continuous learning and reflection. This strategy not only supports your teachers' journey to deeper linguistic knowledge but also helps you refine your professional development approach for maximum impact on student learning outcomes. I would even suggest asking teachers to complete it before reading this book! This proactive approach allows you to gauge the teachers' initial understanding and track your progress as you delve into the material, making the learning journey more targeted and effective.

Phonological Knowledge	
Prompt	Answer (please provide examples)
What is a phoneme?	
What is phonics?	
What is the difference?	phoneme awareness
	phonological sensitivity
	phonetics
What is a consonant phoneme?	
What is a vowel phoneme?	
How many vowels are there in English?	
How many consonants are there in English?	
What is a diphthong?	
What is a diphone?	
What is the schwa?	
What is a homophone?	
Practical Application of Phonological Knowledge	
How many syllables are there in these words?	environment
	bread
	measure
	emu
	opposite
	ability
Circle the blends in the following words.	squared string trays
	shirt sleuth through

254 Using Linguistic Lenses to Journey into Words

Circle the vowels in the following words (keep graphemes together).	beach saw	hypertension house	biscuit aerodynamic
Circle the consonants in the following words.	letter gate	plaque yawn	sneeze tongue
Underline the digraph/s in the following words	scene	erosion	station
Circle the words with a diphone.	emu	amusing	about
Mark the syllables in the following words with a dot.	dolphin Wednesday		school Hallelujah
In which words is the letter underlined a voiced phoneme?	dis__g__ust __h__and		dis__c__uss __b__all
In which words is the letter underlined an unvoiced phoneme?	trea__s__ure __p__anda		__s__un __b__arometer
Write your name in IPA			

Orthographic Knowledge

Prompt	Answer (please provide examples)
What is a grapheme?	
What is a graph?	
What is a digraph?	
What is a trigraph?	
What is a quadgraph?	
What is a blend?	
What is the relationship between phoneme–grapheme correspondence and grapheme–phoneme correspondence	

Explain the alphabetic principle.	

Practical Application of Orthographic Knowledge		
Underline the digraphs in the following words.	shark ladder	twin sleeve
Which words have a digraph and a blend?	straw snail	dolphin bridge
Write two compound words.		
Write two words with traditional "silent letters".		
How would you teach these words now?		

Morphological Knowledge	
Prompt	**Answer (please provide examples)**
What is a morpheme?	
What is a free base?	
What is a bound base?	
What is a stem?	
Give an example of a complex word and explain why it is so.	
Explain the difference between derivational and inflectional morphemes.	

Practical Application of Morphological Knowledge	
Write the number of morphemes in the following words. Include word sums.	swimming
	unprecedented
	handballer

How many words can you make using the base word <sign>?	sign
Separate these words into prefix, base word or suffix as appropriate	million
	hemisphere
	triangle
	misdirection
	conviction
	bicycle

Etymological Knowledge

Prompt	Answer (please provide examples)
What does etymology mean?	
What is a cognate? Give an example.	
What is an eponym? Give an example.	

Practical Application of Etymological Knowledge

Which words would be best studied through the Etymology Lens? Why?	Magician
	Pizza
	Bicycle
	Perimeter
	Wednesday
	Superman

The Power of Lesson Observations: The Metalinguistic Observation Protocol

Just as we've explored linguistic landscapes together, it's important for colleagues to observe and learn from each other in the classroom. Building on the concept of Quality Teaching Rounds developed by researchers at the University of Newcastle, Australia, I've created the Linguistic Lenses Metalinguistic Observation Protocol (MOP). This framework provides a specialised approach for teachers to observe, analyse and discuss each other's linguistic teaching practices. The MOP takes the structured, collaborative nature of Quality Teaching Rounds and applies it specifically to the area of literacy instruction. It allows teachers to focus on how linguistic concepts are taught and integrated into various subjects, providing a unique lens through which to view and improve teaching practices.

By using this framework, you and your colleagues can:

1. observe how linguistic concepts are woven into lessons across different subject areas
2. analyse the effectiveness of various strategies for teaching phonology, orthography, morphology and etymology
3. discuss and reflect on the implementation of Linguistic Lenses in real classroom settings
4. share innovative approaches to making linguistic concepts accessible and engaging for students.

This structured approach to peer observation not only enhances individual teaching practices but also fosters a community of teachers and school leaders committed to linguistic awareness and effective language instruction.

The MOP centres on teachers' understanding and application of metalinguistics, incorporating the four Linguistic Lenses. It assesses the use of metalanguage by teachers in their classrooms. Newman (2024) emphasises that implementing and managing metalinguistic talk is challenging because it demands both linguistic and pedagogical expertise. The MOP helps address this challenge by providing a structured approach to observing and analysing metalinguistic instruction.

Here are the key features of the MOP:

1. **Focus on metalinguistic talk:** The MOP specifically looks at how teachers engage students in discussions about language use and structure.
2. **Integration of Linguistic Lenses:** It incorporates all four Linguistic Lenses, providing a comprehensive view of metalinguistic instruction.
3. **Observation of teacher strategies:** It includes sections to document specific strategies teachers use to promote metalinguistic awareness, such as questioning techniques or use of mentor texts.
4. **Student engagement:** It includes sections to note how students respond to and engage with metalinguistic concepts.
5. **Flexibility:** It is designed to be used across different year levels and subject areas, recognising that metalinguistic instruction can occur in various contexts.

Metalinguistic Observation Protocol (MOP)		
Observer Name		
Teacher Name		
Year Level		
Subject		Date
The Phonology Lens		
phonemes		syllables
segmenting/blending		consonants/vowels
voiced/unvoiced		phoneme manipulation
onset/rime		rhyming words
the schwa		non-phonographic spelling
diphones		the IPA
Observations	• • •	

Tools and strategies used	• • •
Student comments and classroom dialogue	• • •

The Orthography Lens	
the IPA	graphs
letter names	digraphs
orthographic patterns	trigraphs
grapheme–phoneme correspondence	quadgraphs
phoneme–grapheme correspondence	orthographic markers

Observations	• • •
Tools and strategies used	• • •
Student comments and classroom dialogue	• • •

The Morphology Lens	
base words	morphological relations
compound words	complex words
bound/free bases	synonyms/antonyms
prefixes/suffixes	homographs
inflectional/derivational morphemes	homophones/homonyms
stems	meaning/sentence

Observations	• • •
Tools and strategies used	• • •
Student comments and classroom dialogue	• • •

The Etymology Lens	
word origins	eponyms
word histories	cognates
etymological roots	

Observations	• • •
Tools and strategies used	• • •
Student comments and classroom dialogue	• • •
Overall observations, suggestions for improvement and notable linguistic integration strategies	

When providing post-observation feedback, trust in your ability to be prompt, precise and practical. Your words have the potential to inspire and motivate, so focus on areas where your colleagues can make meaningful improvements aligned with your shared goals. Remember, you're not just giving feedback—you're part of a collaborative cycle of modelling, co-planning, implementation and review (Newman, 2024). This process isn't about criticism—it's about supporting each other's professional learning and agency.

As you engage in reflective dialogues with your colleagues, approach these conversations with confidence. You're equals in this process, each bringing unique perspectives and experiences. This is your opportunity to learn from each other, embracing the complexity of classroom dynamics across different contexts. Additionally, when creating action plans with your colleagues, draw on your own classroom experiences. Each step you suggest should have clear objectives and accountability measures. This isn't about prescribing a one-size-fits-all solution—it's about collaboratively refining pedagogical principles and strategies learnt in this book to promote metalinguistic talk in your classrooms.

Remember, you have the knowledge and skills to guide this process effectively. Your insights are valuable, and your supportive approach can significantly enhance the teaching practice of your colleagues. Embrace this opportunity to grow together, learn from each other and collectively elevate the quality of education in your school.

Conclusion

Embracing Your Linguistic Journey

As you prepare to embark on your journey with Linguistic Lenses, remember that the MKA and the MOP are not endpoints but rather tools to guide your continuous growth and collaboration. By regularly assessing your knowledge, observing and being observed, and engaging in meaningful discussions with colleagues, you'll not only enhance your own practice but contribute to a vibrant knowledge-sharing community of educators. This collaborative approach can lead to you and your fellow teachers implementing and advancing pedagogical initiatives with understanding and agency.

Your adventure with Linguistic Lenses is just beginning. Embrace the journey of discovery, collaborate with your peers, and watch as your students' understanding of our English language flourishes along a sustainable learning trajectory under your guided exploration through these powerful Lenses. As you continue to develop your metalinguistic knowledge and instructional strategies, you'll become better equipped to support your students' literacy development and language learning across all subject areas. Remember, the development of metalinguistic awareness is a crucial component of literacy instruction. By focusing on this area, you're not just teaching language—you're empowering your students with the tools to think about, analyse and manipulate language in ways that will benefit them across all areas of their academic and personal lives.

Your journey with Linguistic Lenses is a testament to your commitment to excellence in education. As you apply these tools and strategies in your classroom, you're not just improving your own practice—you're contributing to the broader field of education and helping to shape the future of literacy instruction. Embrace this journey with enthusiasm and openness, and watch as both you and your students grow in your understanding and appreciation of the rich, complex world of English orthography.

As you journey forth with these Linguistic Lenses, may each word you encounter be a stepping stone to greater understanding.

Safe travels, my fellow linguistic explorer!

References

Adoniou, M. (2014). What should teachers know about spelling? *Literacy, 48*(3), 144–154.

Adoniou, M. (2022). *Spelling it out: How words work and how to teach them* (Rev. ed.). Cambridge University Press.

Australian Institute for Teaching and School Leadership (AITSL). (2014). Australian Charter for the Professional Learning of Teachers and School Leaders. https://www.aitsl.edu.au/tools-resources/resource/australian-charter-for-the-professional-learning-of-teachers-and-school-leaders

Anderson, L., Whiting, A., & Venable, G. (2019). Learning to be literate: An orthographic journey with young students. In *The alphabetic principle and beyond …surveying the landscape* (pp. 102–126). PETAA.

Apel, K. (2011). What is orthographic knowledge? *Language, Speech, and Hearing Services in Schools, 42*(4), 592–603.

Aronson, E., & Patnoe, S. (2011). *Cooperation in the classroom: The jigsaw method* (3rd ed.). Pinter & Martin Ltd.

Australian Curriculum, Assessment and Reporting Authority (ACARA). (2020). Measurement framework for schooling in Australia 2020. https://www.acara.edu.au/reporting/measurement-framework-for-schooling-in-australia

Australian Education Research Organisation. (2022). Writing development: What does a decade of NAPLAN data reveal? https://www.edresearch.edu.au/sites/default/files/2022-10/writing-development-report-aa.pdf

Australian Government. (2021). Next steps: Report of the quality initial teacher education review. https://www.education.gov.au/quality-initial-teacher-education-review/resources/next-steps-report-quality-initial-teacher-education-review

Beck, I. L., McKeown, M. G., & Kucan, L. (2013). *Bringing words to life: Robust vocabulary instruction* (2nd ed.). Guilford Press.

Bowers, P. N., & Kirby, J. R. (2010). Effects of morphological instruction on vocabulary acquisition. *Reading and Writing, 23*(5), 515–537. https://doi.org/10.1007/s11145-009-9172-z

Bowers, P. N., Kirby, J. R., & Deacon, S. H. (2010). The effects of morphological instruction on literacy skills: A systematic review of the literature. *Review of Educational Research, 80*(2), 144–179.

Carreiras, M., Armstrong, B. C., Perea, M., & Frost, R. (2014). The what, when, where, and how of visual word recognition. *Trends in Cognitive Sciences, 18*(2), 90–98. https://doi.org/10.1016/j.tics.2013.11.005

Cepeda, N. J., Pashler, H., Vul, E., Wixted, J. T., & Rohrer, D. (2006). Distributed practice in verbal recall tasks: A review and quantitative synthesis. *Psychological Bulletin, 132*(3), 354–380.

Chamberlain, M. C., & Medina, E. J. (2020). A case of being the same?: Australia and New Zealand's reading in focus. *The Australian Journal of Education, 64*(3), 243–263. https://doi.org/10.1177/0004944120953235

Chen, H., & Yang, J. (2020). Multiple exposures enhance both item memory and contextual memory over time. *Frontiers in Psychology, 11*, 1–13. https://doi.org/10.3389/fpsyg.2020.00004

Cowan, N. (2001). The Magical Number 4 in short-term memory: a Reconsideration of Mental Storage Capacity. *Behavioral and Brain Sciences, 24*(1), 87–114. https://doi.org/10.1017/s0140525x01003922

Craik, F. I. M., & Lockhart, R. S. (1972). Levels of processing: A framework for memory research. *Journal of Verbal Learning and Verbal Behavior, 11*(6), 671–684.

Crystal, D. (2013). *Spell it out: The singular story of English spelling*. Profile Books.

Cullen, K., & Townsin, L. (2024). Inside the teachers' toolbox: How experienced primary school teachers are equipped to teach vocabulary and word knowledge. *Journal of Pedagogical Research, 8*(3), 279–300. https://doi.org/10.33902/JPR.202428465

Daffern, T. (2017). Linguistic skills involved in learning to spell: An Australian study. *Language and Education, 31*(4), 307–329. https://doi.org/10.1080/09500782.2017.1296855

Daffern, T. (2021). In conversation with Dr Tessa Daffern – teaching spelling [Interview]. In *NSW Department of Education Literacy and Numeracy*. https://education.nsw.gov.au/teaching-and-learning/curriculum/literacy-and-numeracy/professional-learning/podcasts/transcript-tess-daffern

Daffern, T., Hogg, K., Callaway, N., Wild, H., & Kelly, S. (2024). Supporting schools to implement an evidence-based and effective approach to teaching spelling. *Learning Difficulties Australia, 56*(3), 31–38.

Dehaene, S. (2009). *Reading in the brain: The new science of how we read*. Penguin.

Department of Education and Training. (2022). High impact teaching strategies (HITS). Victorian Government.

Ehri, L. C. (2014). Orthographic mapping in the acquisition of sight word reading, spelling memory, and vocabulary learning. *Scientific Studies of Reading, 18*(1), 5–21.

Fisher, D., & Frey, N. (2013). *Better learning through structured teaching: A framework for the gradual release of responsibility*. ASCD.

Gardner, H. (1983). *Frames of mind: The theory of multiple intelligences*. Basic Books.

Goodwin, A. P., & Ahn, S. (2010). A meta-analysis of morphological interventions: Effects on literacy achievement of children with literacy difficulties. *Annals of Dyslexia, 60*(2), 183–208.

Graves, M. F. (2006). *The vocabulary book: Learning & instruction*. Teachers College Press.

Graves, M. F., & Prenn, M. C. (1986). Costs and Benefits of Various Methods of Teaching Vocabulary. *Journal of Reading, 29*(7), 596–602.

Hattie, J. (2009). *Visible Learning: A synthesis of over 800 meta-analyses relating to achievement*. Routledge.

Hattie, J. (2016, July 21). Dr. John Hattie: Assessment should measure teachers' impact (R. Riddell, Interviewer) [Interview]. In *K-12 Dive*. https://www.k12dive.com/news/dr-john-hattie-assessment-should-measure-teachers-impact/422969/

Horst, J. S. (2013). Context and repetition in word learning. *Frontiers in Psychology, 4*(149). https://doi.org/10.3389/fpsyg.2013.00149

Johnson, D. D., Moe, A. J., & Baumann, J. F. (1983). *The Ginn word book for teachers: A basic lexicon*. Ginn.

Karpicke, J. D., & Roediger, H. L. (2008). The critical importance of retrieval for learning. *Science, 319*(5865), 966–968.

Kilpatrick, D. A. (2016). *Equipped for reading success: A comprehensive, step-by-step program for developing phonemic awareness and fluent word recognition*. Casey & Kirsch Publishers.

Knowles, M. S. (1975). *Self-directed learning: A guide for learners and teachers*. Association Press.

Koda, K. (2007). Cross-linguistic variation in L2 morphological awareness. *Language Learning, 57*(s1), 1–31.

Larsen, S. A. (2024). Are Australian students' academic skills declining? Interrogating 25 years of national and international standardised assessment data. *Australian Journal of Social Issues, 00*, 1–32. https://doi.org/10.1002/ajs4.341

McGaw, B., Louden, W., & Wyatt-Smith, C. (2020). NAPLAN review: Final report. State of New South Wales, State of Queensland, State of Victoria, and Australian Capital Territory. https://naplanreview.com.au/

McKeown, M. G., Beck, I. L., Omanson, R. C., & Pople, M. T. (1985). Some Effects of the Nature and Frequency of Vocabulary Instruction on the Knowledge and Use of Words. *Reading Research Quarterly, 20*(5), 522. https://doi.org/10.2307/747940

Miller, G. A. (1956). The magical number seven, plus or minus two: Some limits on our capacity for processing information. *Psychological Review, 63*(2), 81–97.

Mockler, N. (2022). *Constructing teacher identities: How the print media define and represent teachers and their work*. Bloomsbury Publishing.

Moon, B. R., Harris, B. R., & Hays, A. (2019). Can secondary teaching graduates support literacy in the classroom? Evidence from undergraduate assignments. *Australian Journal of Teacher Education, 44*(8), 1–17. https://doi.org/10.14221/ajte.2019v44n8.5

Nagy, W. E., & Scott, J. A. (2000). Vocabulary processes. In M. L. Kamil, P. B. Mosenthal, P. D. Pearson, & R. Barr (Eds.), *Handbook of reading research* (Vol. 3, pp. 269–284). Lawrence Erlbaum Associates.

Nagy, W., & Townsend, D. (2012). Words as tools: Learning academic vocabulary as language acquisition. *Reading Research Quarterly, 47*(1), 91–108. https://doi.org/10.1002/rrq.011

Nation, I. S. P. (2001). *Learning vocabulary in another language*. Cambridge University Press.

National Reading Panel. (2000). Teaching children to read: An evidence-based assessment of the scientific research literature on reading and its implications for reading instruction. National Institute of Child Health and Human Development.

Nuthall, G. A. (2000). The role of memory in the acquisition and retention of knowledge in science and social studies units. *Cognition and Instruction, 18*(1), 83–139.

Paivio, A. (1971). *Imagery and verbal processes*. Holt, Rinehart, and Winston.

Rasinski, T. (2017). *Greek and Latin roots: Keys to building vocabulary*. Shell Education.

Scibetta Hegland, S. (2021). *Beneath the Surface of Words: What English Spelling Reveals and Why It Matters*. Learning About Spelling.

Scott-Dunne, D. (2012). *When Spelling Matters*. Pembroke Publishers Limited.

Seidenberg, M. S. (2017). *Language at the speed of sight: How we read, why so many can't, and what can be done about it*. Basic Books.

Seidenberg, M. S. (2023). Reading in the brain revisited. *Language, Cognition and Neuroscience, 38*(1), 1–23.

Seidenberg, M. S., & McClelland, J. L. (1989). A distributed, developmental model of word recognition and naming. *Psychological Review, 96*(4), 523–568.

Shanahan, T. (2017, August 4). Everything You Wanted to Know about Repeated Reading. *Reading Rockets*. https://www.readingrockets.org/blogs/shanahan-on-literacy/everything-you-wanted-know-about-repeated-reading

Siegel, L. S. (2008). Morphological awareness skills of English language learners and children with dyslexia. *Topics in Language Disorders, 28*(1), 15–27.

Stocker, K. L., Fox, R. A., Swain, N. R., & Leif, E. S. (2023). Between the lines: Integrating the science of reading and the science of behaviour to improve reading outcomes for Australian children. *Behaviour and Social Issues, 33*, 504–531. https://doi.org/10.1007/s42822-023-00149-y

Stone, L. (2021). *Spelling for Life: Uncovering the Simplicity and Science of Spelling* (2nd ed.). Routledge.

The THRASS Institute Australasia & Canada. (2013). *The THRASS phonics word bank*. THRASS Australia PTY LTD. (Original work published 2010)

Thompson, G. (2013). NAPLAN, MySchool, and accountability: Teacher perceptions of the effects of testing. *International Education Journal: Comparative Perspectives, 12*(2), 2. https://openjournals.library.sydney.edu.au/IEJ/article/view/7456

Treiman, R., & Kessler, B. (2004). The role of letter names in the acquisition of literacy. *Advances in Child Development and Behaviour, 32*, 1–33. https://www.sciencedirect.com/science/article/abs/pii/S0065240703310031?via%3Dihub

Tunmer, W. E., & Hoover, W. A. (2019). The cognitive foundations of learning to read: A framework for preventing and remediating reading difficulties. *Australian Journal of Learning Difficulties, 24*(1), 1–19. https://doi.org/10.1080/19404158.2019.1614081

Victorian Department of Education and Training. (2022). High impact teaching strategies (HITS). https://www.education.vic.gov.au/school/teachers/teachingresources/practice/improve/Pages/hits.aspx

Wyse, D., & Bradbury, A. (2022). Reading wars or reading reconciliation? A critical examination of robust research evidence, curriculum policy and teachers' practices for teaching phonics and reading. *Review of Education, 10*(1). https://doi.org/10.1002/rev3.3314

About the Author

Katharyn is an accomplished educational leader, innovator, and curriculum specialist who holds a PhD in Using Linguistic Lenses to Improve Classroom Instruction. Her groundbreaking research presents a Framework for Orthographic Analysis, which promotes a deep understanding of words. She has translated this framework into tangible Linguistic Lenses—this book is your guide! With a First-Class Honours Degree from the University of Sydney, Katharyn has garnered numerous teaching excellence awards and accolades. Her achievements include being Torrens University Australia's Three Minute Thesis (3MT®) Asia-Pacific Finalist 2022 and being included on The Educator Hot List 2020.

As a former Head of Junior School, her creative, high-energy approach and results-oriented vision have significantly improved student engagement and outcomes. She regularly presents at conferences and publishes in peer-reviewed journals, pushing the boundaries of educational innovation.

Katharyn balances her career with family life in Adelaide, South Australia, as a mother of four young children. This unique perspective enriches her understanding of early childhood development, further informing her approach to education and leadership.

www.ingramcontent.com/pod-product-compliance
Lightning Source LLC
Chambersburg PA
CBHW052016070526
44584CB00016B/1779